LANDLORD COLORS

LANDLORD COLORS:
On Art, Economy, and Materiality

LAURA MOTT

Cranbrook Art Museum

CONTENTS

CONTENTS

CONTENTS

DIRECTOR'S FOREWORD

Nearly forty years ago, Roy Slade, my predecessor who was also president of Cranbrook Academy of Art, organized the exhibition *Downtown Detroit: Twenty-One Artists* (1979). It focused on the contemporary art scene that had first emerged in the mid-1960s around Wayne State University in Detroit's Cass Corridor neighborhood (now rebranded as Midtown) and brought together more than sixty works under a shared curatorial theme of assemblage. Featured artists included John Egner, Michael Luchs, Charles McGee, Gordon Newton, Ellen Phelan, and Robert Sestok, among others. The exhibition reads, in retrospect, more as a landmark gathering of artists in one of the first museum surveys of an art scene that had drawn sincere critical interest, both local and national, than the more modestly incomplete sampling of the hundreds of contemporary artists producing work in downtown Detroit as Slade professed. It was a bold decision for Cranbrook to mount such an exhibition, given the racial, economic, and geographic divide that existed (and still does) between the sylvan estates of suburban Bloomfield Hills and urban grit of downtown Detroit. As Slade wrote in his introduction to the show, "To bring the work of Detroit artists to Cranbrook is significant for the Academy, which had been considered by some as aloof and isolated." Although there have been other Detroit-based artists featured at Cranbrook before and since 1979, and certainly more Cranbrook-educated artists compose the city's cultural community today, the confessional nature of that original declaration rings embarrassingly true even four decades later. However, over the past four years, Cranbrook Art Museum has actively sought new engagements, both curatorial and educational, with Detroit artists and citizens in recognition of the fact that the city has always been and remains the most fertile ground for contemporary art in the region. It is also an institutional determination that Cranbrook can no longer exist in its "splendid isolation," apart from the social, cultural, and economic circumstances that helped sow those very divides decades ago.

When Laura Mott, Senior Curator of Contemporary Art and Design, shared with me her curatorial conceit for *Landlord Colors* four years ago, I was drawn immediately to its provocative premise and curious about its curatorial potential. Building on the success of *Nick Cave: Here Hear* (2015), an ambitious museum exhibition and city-wide performance series by Cranbrook alumnus Nick Cave (CAA Fiber '89), Mott's vision for this project was even more expansive, reaching further back in time and around the world. Adopting a more transhistorical, global, and cyclical perspective on art produced during times of economic and social precarity, the project considers the work of *arte povera* in the 1960s through the early 1980s, between the end of Italy's postwar economic miracle and its bullet-riddled period of domestic terrorism, euphemistically called the Years of Lead. It looks to the material restraint and resistance practiced in the work of the *dansaekhwa* artists birthed during South Korea's military rule in the 1970s and 1980s. It tackles the material scarcity and ingenuity of a post-Soviet, US-led embargoed Cuba of the 1990s, as well as the material excess of a divested and de-industrialized Detroit since the rebellion of 1967 to its post-bankruptcy present. Finally, it ponders the artistic scene of contemporary Greece since the financial crisis of 2009 and the refugee crisis since 2015. In this project, heterogeneity and difference reign supreme, but they are not absolute.

There is no dominant aesthetic commonality that unites these art scenes, only an artistic imperative to radically invent by any means necessary. There is no simple economic cause and effect, no base and superstructure model, or empiric formations of capital to explain away the art. One surprising thread that emerges, which seems to connect such disparate works, places, and practices, is a recourse to materiality—a belief in matter and in material transformations—as ubiquitous as rocks, inevitable as rust or irreducible as the human body. Materials can bear witness in a world of abstract financial transactions, ever more immaterial forms of labor, and increasingly incomprehensible webs of social surveillance and manipulation. There seems to be a timeliness to reasserting the importance of materiality, which has been reduced too often to a list of ingredients on an object label, considered secondary to artistic conception, merely a choice to make in outsourced fabrication decisions, or trademarked and branded as proprietary elements of an artist's oeuvre. It is fitting to be an accomplice to materiality in a place such as Cranbrook and a city such as Detroit, where materials and acts of making dominate each landscape and both communities' respective legacies.

A backbone of contemporary Detroit art courses through the show, in which works are not segregated by geography or ordered by a strict chronology. In doing so, Mott avoids the isolated provincialism of the local, while negotiating the complexities of the global. What I identified within her nascent curatorial concept was the need to place art from Detroit into a global and historical dialogue with other makers and scenes. This approach resists the temptation to codify the local, a concern shared by Slade in *Downtown Detroit*: "To say that Detroit art exists apart from other art as a movement or a regional style could be erroneous," he presciently warned. What emerges in *Landlord Colors* are connections and commonalities among the art, artists, and communities that span nearly half a century and connect across thousands of miles. However, the project wisely avoids the leveling effects of a shared and ultimately false universalism in favor of excavating specific episodes of art history, both in the past and in the making, that are shaped by the exigencies of circumstance and conditions of place.

Importantly, *Landlord Colors* extends beyond the galleries of the Cranbrook Art Museum to site-specific projects around Detroit through a series of performances and presentations organized in partnership with Taylor Renee Aldridge, independent curator and founder of ARTS.BLACK, and Ryan Myers-Johnson, founder, curator, and director at Sidewalk Detroit. The global scope of the exhibition and its extensive related public programming make *Landlord Colors* the most ambitious project the Art Museum has undertaken. It has tested the limits of our small but intrepid and resourceful staff and could only ever be possible with the partnership of many others at Cranbrook, in Detroit, and far beyond.

My sincere appreciation goes to Mott for her sustained research and curatorial commitment to steering this ambitious project to a successful conclusion and for her commitment to the artistic community of Detroit. In time, perhaps, this exhibition too will be viewed as another landmark moment for Cranbrook Art Museum and for capturing, at least partially, the vitality of Detroit's resilient artistic scene—a place of unending cultural production. I would like to extend my thanks to some key individuals and organizations without whose support such an endeavor would certainly not be possible: to the Andy Warhol Foundation for the Visual Arts, which generously supported not only the exhibition but also the curatorial research initiative vital to it; to the John S. and James L. Knight Foundation, which was an early believer in Cranbrook Art Museum's sincere desire to support the artistic community in Detroit and which, in turn, has generously supported this and other important projects over the last four years; to the National Endowment for the Arts for its continued support of our ambitious projects; and to the Board of Governors, members of Cranbrook Academy of Art and Art Museum, and the administration and Trustees of the Cranbrook Educational Community, who have supported the Art Museum's renewed growth and vitality.

Finally, I would like to extend my appreciation to the Maxine and Stuart Frankel Foundation, which has generously supported Cranbrook over many years and continues to provide outsized support to the Art Museum to help it make a positive impact in the cultural life of Southeast Michigan and beyond.

—Andrew Blauvelt, Director
Cranbrook Art Museum

ACKNOWLEDGMENTS

Landlord Colors began in earnest four years ago and was inspired by the city of Detroit and its artists, who serve as the creative genesis of this idea. Curators show affection through rigor, so Detroit, I hope my sincere devotion to you is evident in this publication. First and foremost, I would like to extend my fervent gratitude to all the artists in the exhibition for their visionary practices—across different locations, histories, and contexts. The time periods covered in this premise are defined by their difficulty, but you reaffirm my belief in humanity, in the potential for a better world through fortitude, curiosity, and innovation.

I also want to respectfully acknowledge the two early champions of this project. Andrew Blauvelt, Director of Cranbrook Art Museum, has been my primary dialogue partner on this concept since the beginning and has contributed his editorial expertise to this publication. I have the utmost respect for his knowledge, tenacity, and integrity to scholarship; he is truly invaluable. The first external supporter to believe in this project was The Andy Warhol Foundation for the Visual Arts, who granted me a curatorial fellowship to travel to each country for research—an opportunity of a lifetime. The exhibition and publication would not exist without the foundation's support of this idea at its infancy.

I deeply appreciate the insightful writers who have contributed research, original texts, and catalogue entries to this publication: Taylor Renee Aldridge, Andrew Blauvelt, Laurie Chevrot, Abel González Fernández, Rebecca Mazzei, and Ian Gabriel Wilson. I am very fortunate to have Vincenzo de Bellis as an esteemed colleague and thank him for his insightful interview with Michelangelo Pistoletto. To Michelangelo, it is a life-defining honor to have your thoughts contributed to this publication. I also want to extend my thanks to the artists and writers whose previous texts are critical contributions to this publication: Tania Bruguera, Germano Celant, Riccardo Dalisi, Eugenio Valdés Figueroa, Marsha Miro, Park Seo-Bo, and Yorgos Tzirtzilakis.

My co-curators on the *Material Detroit* series—Taylor Renee Aldridge and Ryan Myers-Johnson—are individuals who exemplify everything good about the creative industry. I admire them each tremendously and remain thankful for our collaboration. The ambitious scope of *Material Detroit*'s installations and performances, spread across the city, could only be possible with the cooperation and participation of many artists, individuals, communities, and organizations— some of whom will become collaborators after this book goes to press. I would like to thank: ARTS.BLACK; Olayami Dabls and the MBAD African Bead Museum; Detroit Artists Market; Maria Catarina Duncan; Bill Danaher, Manisha Dostert, Christopher Wells, and the Christ Church Cranbrook Choir; Eliza Howell Park; Everard Findlay; Sinead Finnerty-Pyne; Rachel Frierson and Mark Wallace at the Detroit Riverfront Conservancy; Fringe Society (Ash Arder and Levon Kafafian); GALLERIA CONTINUA; Jennifer Harge; Scott Hocking; Billy Mark; Augusta Morrison; Sidewalk Detroit and SideTrails; Frank Oddo, John Stroh, and Mark Tuttle of Stroh Enterprises; Susana Pilar; Anders Ruhwald; Erika Stowall and Big Red Wall Dance Company; and Sterling Toles.

This exhibition is the result of hundreds of studio visits with artists who greatly informed it, and the checklist is only a small selection of the fascinating practices I encountered. I am also indebted to the following individuals and institutions who provided critical insight on the locations and art movements of the research focus: Armando Andux, Dora Apel at Wayne State University; Maria A. Cabrera Arus at Cuba Material; Cezanne Charles; Ha Chong-Hyun; Ella Cisneros; Maddalena Disch; *documenta 14*; Terence Gower; Scott Hocking; Magazzino Italian Art; the Gwangju Biennial; Joan Kee at The University of Michigan, Ann Arbor; Aylet Ojeda at Museo de Bellas Artes, Havana; Yoandy Rizo; Catharine Rossi at Kingston University, London; Michael Stone-Richards at *Detroit Research*; and Kostis Velonis.

Judy Dyki, Director of Academic Programs and Library at Cranbrook Academy of Art and Art Museum, worked tirelessly contributing her expert prowess as an editor to this publication. Isabella Achenbach, Curatorial Affairs Manager, has been the driving force and sometimes sorceress who brought all the elements together in this book. The depths of my gratitude can be matched only by my deep respect for each of them. I would also like to thank Rachel Harkai for her keen observations as a reader. *Landlord Colors* has been greatly enhanced by work from our Jeanne and Ralph Graham Collections Fellows over the last few years: Steffi Duarte, Shelley Selim, and Ian Gabriel Wilson. I would also like to express my appreciation for the museum's curatorial assistants from Cranbrook Academy of Art and the curatorial interns who have contributed incalculable hours to the tasks surrounding the exhibition and publication over the years: Logan Acton, Elissa Buchalter, Jameson Gower, Francesca Kielb, Erik Magnuson, and Finn Schult. From this group, I would like to give special recognition to Laurie Chevrot and Sarah Thomas, who were integral in seeing this exhibition and publication over the finish line. The library staff of Mary Beth Kreiner and Rachel Pontious are incredible human search engines and were essential to the research process (and graciously let me amass an impressive number of library books in my office for the duration). Speaking of books, Chad Kloepfer has designed some of my favorites on my shelf, and as is evident in what you are holding now, we were so fortunate to have his immense talent for this publication.

My colleagues at Cranbrook Art Museum and the Cranbrook Academy of Art operate at the highest caliber. They are the orchestrators of all the moving parts that must come together with a project of this immense scope, and I am surrounded by a symphony of skill, aptitude, and professionalism. I am ever grateful to Jon Geiger and his crew, especially Wade Tullier, who are masterful at their craft as artists and apply it dexterously to their work as exhibition producers. Corey Gross dominates within the field of registration, and I so appreciate his oversight of the artworks entrusted to us. Kim Larsen is the linchpin in our organization, and I would like to thank her for her daily contributions, large and small. The museum's education department does incredible work within our surrounding community that extends from downtown Detroit to nearby Pontiac; Lindsey Dezman, Sarah Doty, and Kelly Lyons, thank you for your everyday exceptionalism and the lasting impact you make. This extends to our incredible visitor services crew, many of whom are alums of the Academy, who serve as the engaging public face of this project. The communications dream team of Julie Fracker and Bianca Ibarlucea are superheroes among us, and they are at the forefront of Cranbrook's connection to the rest of the world. I also want to acknowledge the temporary extension of this team—Meg Huckaby and Rebecca Taylor at FITZ & CO—for their tremendous efforts made on this project's behalf. Filmmaker and my frequent collaborator Andrew Miller is not technically an employee, but he is always part of my team capturing the heart of these projects. PD Rearick is a gifted and talented photographer and a beloved part

of the Cranbrook family. Vital to our mission and success is
the institutional guidance and adeptness of Michael Stachowiak,
Kelly Lewis-Gump, Autumn Parrott, Alexis Weisbrod, and
Debra Watson. Director Susan Ewing and the entire staff of the
Cranbrook Academy of Art, including the Artists-in-Residence,
are my valued colleagues who challenge and inspire me. To
them and all of the above, I express my sincerest thanks. Lastly,
my presence at Cranbrook and in Detroit is due to Gregory
Wittkopp, and while under his directorship at the museum, I
grew substantially as a curator through his leadership. I cannot
thank him enough for the opportunity and his ongoing support.

Cranbrook Art Museum is part of the larger Cranbrook
Educational Community, deftly overseen by President Dominic
DiMarco. I would like to express my sincere gratitude to
the Board of Trustees for their support of the Cranbrook Art
Museum and the following staff members of this community
who contribute to the unseen but important work that
supports this project: Jean-Claude Azar, Gina Cataldi, Norma
Awesomesauce Evans, Marlene Jenkins, Mary Twaddle,
Rhonda Reed, Rod Sperin, Rita Stedman, Calvin Vincent, and
Julie Yelick-Miller, among many others.

Such an expansive exhibition is indebted to the generous
loans from art museums, private collections, galleries, archives,
estates, and artists' studios. The following individuals were
integral to obtaining the works in the exhibition, and I value
their commitment to seeing this project come to fruition and
offer my enthusiastic thanks:

Alessandra Ammirati, Luisa Ausenda, Lorenzo Fiaschi,
and Charlotte Urgese at GALLERIA CONTINUA, Beijing,
Havana, Les Moulins, San Gimignano; Katia Ayón at the Belkis
Ayón Estate, Havana; Athena Bada and Nadia Geranzouni
at The Breeder, Athens; Kristen Becker and Marianne Boesky
at Marianne Boesky Gallery, New York; Marc Benda and Alice

Higgins at Friedman Benda Gallery; Beryl Bevilacque and Jessica Silverman at Jessica Silverman Gallery, San Francisco; William Boswell; Steven and Lizzie Blatt; Tim Blum, Sam Kahn, and Patty Nam at Blum & Poe, Los Angeles; Gayle and Andrew Camden; Kate Chertavian at Kate Chertavian Fine Art, Cambridge; Bokyung Choi, Christine Chung, Charles Kim, and Bo Young at Kukje Gallery, Seoul; Anthony Curis, JJ Curis, Tara Akitt, Alessandra Ferrara, and Sara Nickleson at Library Street Collective, Detroit; Jeanne Chvosta, Howard Rachofsky, and Meg Smith at THE WAREHOUSE, Dallas; Olayami Dabls; Vincenzo de Bellis, Siri Engberg, Joe King, and John Lyon at the Walker Art Center, Minneapolis; Simone de Sousa at Simone de Sousa Gallery, Detroit; Alistair Economakis; Dora Economou; Marty Eisenberg; Maxine and Stuart Frankel and Benjamin Teague at The Frankel Foundation for Art, Bloomfield Hills; Michael J. Frishberg; Rachel Garbade at Garth Greenan Gallery, New York; Tamsen Greene and Meriwether McClorey at Jack Shainman Gallery, New York; Tim and Susan Hill at Hill Gallery, Birmingham; Eli Gold; Brenda Goodman; Carole Harris; Matthew Angelo Harrison; Patrick Hill; Scott Hocking; David Horowitz, Lida Ferrera, and Susan Thompson at the Solomon R. Guggenheim Museum, New York; David Klein and Christine Schefman at David Klein Gallery, Detroit; Lisa Kohli and Lisa Varghese at Luhring Augustine Gallery, New York; Eleni Koroneou Gallery, Athens; Paul Kotula; Addie Langford; Veronica Levitt at Casey Kaplan Gallery, New York; Kylie Lockwood; Laura Salas Redondo Luna; Leda Lycourioti; Tiff Massey; Mark Masuoka at Akron Art Museum; Charles McGee; Allie McGhee; Lucy Mensah; Jason Murphy; Lida Sigas Nieto at El Apartamento, Havana; George N'Namdi; Lena Solà Nogué; Alex Nogucras and Adrian Schindler at NoguerasBlanchard Gallery, Barcelona, Madrid; Carole and Alex Rosenberg; Lauren Rossi; Salvador Salort-Pons and Laurie Farrell at the

Detroit Institute of Arts; Sikkema Jenkins & Co.; Daniel Sperry and Grace Serra at the Wayne State University Collection, Detroit; Franklin Sirmans, Tobias Ostrander, Maria Elena Ortiz, and Emily Vera at the Pérez Art Museum, Miami; Donna Snowden; Samuel Zell Revocable Trust Collection; Chris Schanck; Juliana Steiner, Alex Valls, and Julianna Vezzetti of Good To Know; Susan Tait; and Charlotte Wagner.

This project would not have been possible without the support of the Cranbrook Academy of Art and Art Museum Board of Governors under the leadership of Jennifer Gilbert, Chair, and our Museum Committee led by Frank Edwards, Chair. I am immensely grateful to the philanthropic organizations that generously supported *Landlord Colors*: the Andy Warhol Foundation for the Visual Arts, the John S. and James L. Knight Foundation, the Maxine and Stuart Frankel Foundation for Art, and the National Endowment for the Arts.

On a personal note, I would like to dedicate this book to the two most important people in my life who patiently supported me through this epic project: to my husband Anthony Marcellini and to Esmé, with love and wonder.

—Laura Mott
Senior Curator of Contemporary
Art and Design

LANDLORD COLORS:
On Art, Economy, and Materiality

"Landlord colors" are the undesirable tones that reside outside the decorum of name brands and popular taste—off pinks and pale greens from previous eras still pulled from the basement stockpile or the stale beige in the large economy-size bucket on the bottom shelf: indifference at a discount. The phrase comes from the conceptual taxonomy of color by John Baldessari and was informed by the artist's young life when he was required to paint the rental properties owned by his father. By economic circumstance, the colors became the dominant backdrop in the tenants' lives. In the context of a place such as Detroit, an exemplar of the American Rust Belt, the term poetically speaks to the overarching material conditions enveloping the city—a situation not of its own choosing.

Intrinsic to the phrase "landlord colors" is the connection between economy and aesthetics: an anticipated cause and effect. Scholarship on both topics often relies on analytic objectivity that allows theoretical tangents to breed and expand; however, such analyses often exist far from the lived experience of precarity. As social and economic crises have increased drastically since the mid-twentieth century, there is an urgency to reach beyond traditional hierarchies of thought, to narrate from the ground up. In response, the project *Landlord Colors* examines five art scenes generated during heightened periods of upheaval: America's Detroit from the 1967 Rebellion to the present; the cultural climate of the Italian avant-garde during the 1960s to 1980s; authoritarian-ruled South Korea of the 1970s; embargoed Cuba from the collapse of the Soviet Union in the 1990s to the present; and contemporary Greece since its financial crisis in 2009.

Landlord Colors investigates these five art scenes—primarily oriented in the cities of Detroit, Turin, Seoul, Havana, and Athens—through the lens of materiality. Instead of macro-narrations in which multitudes of bodies are condensed into the singular, the project privileges material-driven explorations of socioeconomic collapse through individual artistic innovations. Many of these artists engage in various definitions of economy in the careful negotiation of materials and the applied meaning generated through their strategic editing of resources—ranging from material scarcity to excess. They process their surroundings through aesthetic interests predicated on a shared, interpretive visual language and the belief that it communicates to a universality of the human condition. By unearthing micro-histories and vernaculars specific to place, *Landlord Colors* discovers textured and unexpected relationships between artists whose investigations share themes of ingenuity, resourcefulness, and resistance.

Navigating these art scenes will require some time travel; the imagination will need to inhabit places and time periods when materials are first being tested, the paint still wet, the ideas unresolved by canonical history. For instance, what might revisiting the tumultuous cultural moment surrounding early Italian *arte povera* allow us to contextualize about such artworks before they became precious objects conscripted into art history? How do the material tensions seen in the work of South Korean artists orient us to the reality of suppressed freedom during and in the aftermath of the Yushin era? In another location where the ideologies of capitalism and communism persist in battle, how have artists negotiated an insular material culture to become prominent narrators of the Cuban condition? How do Greek artists negotiate twenty-first-century precarities and humanitarian crises while living among the ruins of past ingenuity, the cornerstones of Western civilization? And after Detroit's economic stagnation for over sixty years, how does the work of its artists critically examine the conditions that surround it?

RE-MATERIALIZATION

Despite its crucial role as the tactile and physical embodiment of our artistic, cultural, and economic production, materiality is often neutralized in contemporary art history and academia. This is, in part, indebted to ruptures within modernist art practices of the 1950s and 1960s deemed anti-intellectual, emotional, and intuitive—such as abstract expressionism—which mark the beginning of what we regard as "contemporary art." This is not to imply that materiality was championed in modernism, as materials within its construct often functioned simply as a conduit for formalism, suggesting an experiential transcendence at the hands of the master artist (typically white, male, Western).[1] Actions of disruption were prevalent in the 1960s in both Western and Eastern culture, which saw a surge of radicalization fueled by issues such as liberation from the status quo, vehement opposition to the Vietnam War, race relations, and discontent with the political establishment. Concurrently, it triggered seismic shifts by artists, most prominently within the canon, towards an overtly conceptual art production in which ideas were privileged over aesthetic and material concerns.

In 1967, art historian Lucy Lippard coined the term "dematerialization" to articulate the prevalence of artworks that emphasized the thinking process almost exclusively: "Such a trend appears to be provoking a profound *dematerialization* of art, especially of art as object, and if it continues to prevail, it may result in the objects becoming wholly obsolete."[2] The preference of information over material has only continued to proliferate alongside our dexterity with and dependence on technology. The term dematerialization is now commonly used in the world of finance, in which it refers to the process of physical certificates of investment being destroyed and replaced by an equivalent electronic form.[3]

In this respect, material erasure is often equated with progress. Similarly, parallel timelines are often drawn between artistic interest in conceptual and/or immaterial strategies and the progression of capitalist economies. For example, in her essay "Work Ethic," curator Helen Molesworth summarizes the convergence of art, labor, and economy in mid-twentieth-century America:

> Just as artists relinquished traditional artistic skills and the production of discrete objects, the status of labor and the production of goods in the culture at large were also changing profoundly as the American industrial economy, based in manufacturing, shifted to a postindustrial economy rooted in managerial and service labor. The concern with artistic labor manifested itself in implicit and explicit ways as much as the advanced art of the period managed, staged, mimicked, ridiculed, and challenged the cultural and societal anxieties around the shifting terrain and definitions of work.[4]

An amalgam of the above is Detroit. It is a central protagonist in an American story, yet arguably the postindustrial economy never supplanted the loss of the industrial economy inside the city. The city's American parenthood makes it a participant in the global socioeconomic network, but Detroit has been on its own slow-roll timeline, resulting in an ecosystem specific to its regional condition. This is the nature of crisis; it makes apparent the knots in our efforts for continuity, and it is often in this recognition of failure that we learn the most about the human condition. The political playwright Bertolt Brecht wrote:

> We gain our knowledge of life in catastrophic form. It is from catastrophes that we have to infer the manner in which our social formation functions. Through reflection, we must deduce the "inside story" of crises, depressions, revolutions, and wars.... Existence depends on unknown factors. "Something must have happened," "something is brewing," "a situation has arisen"— this is what they feel and the mind goes out on patrol. But enlightenment only comes, if at all, after the catastrophe. The death has taken place.[5]

The frequency of upheaval and recovery has accelerated over the last half-century primarily due to increasingly global interdependent capitalist economies—some affecting specific industries and regions, with others impacting entire countries. Marxist philosopher György Lukács predicted their expansive reach in the 1920s in *History and Class Consciousness*:

> In the age of capitalism it is not possible for the total system to become directly visible in external phenomena. For instance, the economic basis of a world crisis is undoubtedly unified, and its coherence can be understood. But its actual appearance in time and space will take the form of a disparate succession of events in different countries at different times and even in different branches of industry in a number of countries.[6]

The rapid acceleration of the last century is defined by a wild pursuit of economic progress and measurable growth—often growth at any cost—but it is important to note this is a relatively new phenomenon for humanity, which advanced incrementally between the Roman Empire and the nineteenth century. A unifying concern of the artists in *Landlord Colors* is the interrogation of progress against the realities of lived experience. Two decades into the twenty-first century, we stand in the aftermath of so many crises, and live on the forefronts of others, while localized hits of global problems continue to rise at an alarming rate: volatile economies, volatile politics,

volatile climate. Something is brewing, a situation has arisen.

It is crucial now to pause, to temper the rapid, to reflect. Through all stages of civilization, art has been a means to understand our human experience—how others have lived and what they value. By focusing on the materials that artists mine for meaning, we can extract individual narratives and regard these artworks as cultural documents of their time. Here we can enact what art historian Petra Lange-Berndt describes as *material complicity*, in which we can expand our understanding of an artwork by tracing the provenance of materials beyond simply the artist's intention.[7]

> To follow materials means not to discuss aesthetic issues of quality, expressiveness, or symbolic content, but rather to investigate transpersonal societal problems and matters of concerns. Within this methodology it is paramount to situate artistic practice with historical perspectives and to open meanings of the materials used to their everyday or non-art connotations.... The path one takes is not linear, not clearly divisible into avant-garde, high modernist, postmodern, and so on. Rather, one encounters entangled, anachronistic layers, incorporating references that point beyond exclusively canonical art-historical boundaries.[8]

This method of following the materials provides crucial insight into our periods of focus. Furthermore, *Landlord Colors* foregrounds vernacular interpretations of shared materials, positioning them as principal elements in our visual language. To illustrate this in practice, the start of each section of this essay is dedicated to an interpretative reading of an artist's use of stone—a fundament in art, nature, and industry—as a meditative exercise to trace how each artist relates the material to their local context.

MATERIAL WITNESS: DETROIT (1967–PRESENT)

On a street corner in Detroit in the late 90s, Olayami Dabls picked up a rock that was embedded with a piece of iron. This object became the metaphorical basis for his ongoing outdoor installation *Iron Teaching Rocks How to Rust* (fig. 1, p. 81). Broken stone and natural rock are prominent textures of the city landscape. Together, they had composed the structural foundation of a sprawling city, now regarded by many as rubble. In Dabls' view, the rocks—along with his other materials of paint, mirrors, and found objects—are given magic provided by the iron, which is revered as a sacred metal and medicine in African traditions. There is enough iron in each one of us to make a three-inch nail. We can't live without iron. Blood is its color because of iron. All people on the planet are connected to iron. This connection to a fundamental element of life draws the people here, he says, back to Detroit.

Detroit is French for "strait," a moving body of water connecting two seas. Predestined from the beginning,

it served as a grand junction for purposes and ideals larger than itself: the worker to employment, the industry to prosperity, America to its dream. In the early twentieth century, Detroit was a model city for the desires of the burgeoning middle class; this extended to the country's black population who were searching to improve their conditions within the institutionalized socio-economic oppression

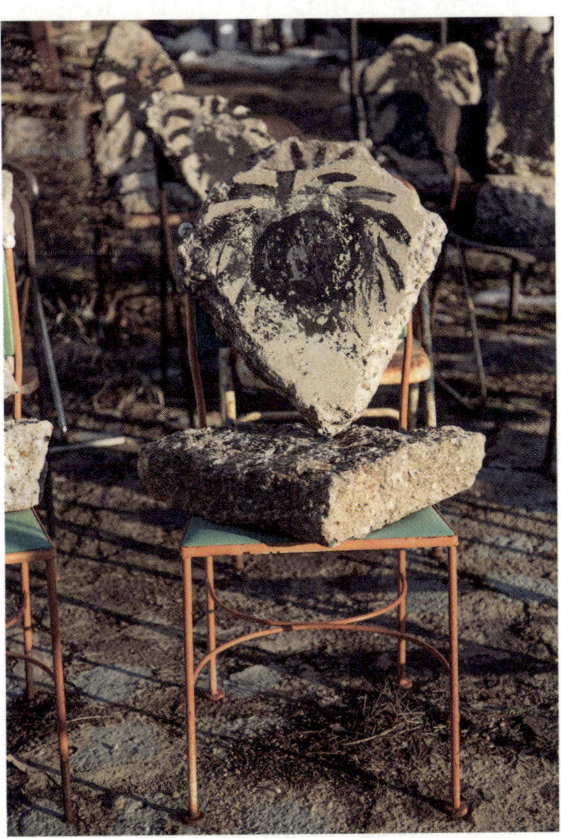

FIGURE 1

Olayami Dabls, *Detention Center* (detail), 2005, rocks, paint, chairs

of the Jim Crow era. The firsthand accounts of black residents who came here as children, and are now in their 70s and 80s, often recite their grandparents' and parents' motivations in a similarly modest script: Detroit was the place you could get a job, educate your children, buy a house, and even own a piano.[9]

Detroit's population peaked at nearly two million shortly before 1950 due its expansive automotive industry and the boom of World War II; however, it was directly followed by an exodus and steady decline of its population in the inner city. Inherently, the factory system leveraged and entrenched disparity. John Watson, a vocal member of the League of Revolutionary Black Workers in Detroit, observed that the workers existed to care for the machine, which received greater consideration than the humans who had become appendages of the factory system.[10] Racial tensions were ongoing both before and after the crest of prosperity in 1950, with uprisings between black residents and police that led to city-wide rebellions in 1943 and again in 1967. Concerning the latter, Detroit's first black mayor Coleman Young narrated the long-winded fallout of this cataclysmic event:

> The heaviest casualty, however, was the city. Detroit's losses went a hell of a lot deeper than the immediate toll of lives and buildings. The riot put Detroit on the fast track to economic desolation, mugging the city and making off with incalculable value in jobs, earnings taxes, corporate taxes, retail dollars, sales taxes, mortgages, interest, property taxes, development dollars, investment dollars, tourism dollars, and plain damn money. The money was carried out in the pockets of the businesses and the people who fled as fast as they could. The white exodus from Detroit had been prodigiously steady prior to the riot, totaling twenty-two thousand in 1966, but afterward, it was frantic.[11]

An objective distance often is deployed when looking at Detroit; it is treated as a case study or a warning, not an actual place filled with real people living in the aftermath of social and economic unrest. Until recently, some declared Detroit to be America's first urban ruin. However, this assumed an entropic condition and positioned the arch of failed capitalism as the sole narrative, despite the fact that cultural production never ceased. Due to automation and the outsourcing of jobs, divestment in Detroit and its people ensued for decades. In 2008, the city was severely impacted by the economic downturn; Detroit's automotive industry verged on full collapse. As of 2018, many "re-"words punctuate headlines about Detroit—renaissance, rebuilding, rebranding—while simultaneously, its cautious longtime residents know the pendulum of progress to be unstable and exclusive.

Detroit yields a broad spectrum of artistic production, however, and one focus of *Landlord Colors* is how artists have negotiated the excessive amount of abandoned material that envelops the city. Starting in the 1960s and 1970s, the anti-aesthetic of broken, raw material has been prominently used by artists to capture the brutal inheritance of its urban landscape. During these decades, as in much of America, the art scene was largely segregated. However, by focusing on material interests, it connects these artists to a shared time and place. Two museum exhibitions—*At Cranbrook: Downtown Detroit* (1979) and *Kick Out the Jams: Detroit's Cass Corridor, 1963–77* (1980)—highlighted the work of Detroit artists from the period. These exhibitions sought to understand the regional scene and were primarily dedicated to artists in the loosely defined Cass Corridor movement, named after the neighborhood where many artists lived and worked. The intensity of the city and the emotional expenditures of living in it were often reenacted in the artistic processes of the movement's key figures: Gordon Newton's assemblages resemble brutal acts of breakage and labor (p. 179); Michael Luchs' prolific series of rabbit silhouettes typically are ensnared in violent ends (p. 155); Robert Sestok's crude sculptural combines feature the discarded remnants of the studio and everyday life. Brenda Goodman's *Self Portrait* series (p. 95) uses tar for its structural composition, a toxic material by-product that can be used industrially in both construction and destruction. In the exhibition review of *Downtown Detroit*, art critic Marsha Miro observed: "If anything, the art these Detroiters make is post-industrial, created as a negation of the notion that industrial progress means human progress. They pick

up industry's pieces and mend them into a new existence as art that has no technological value."[12]

> After the revolution, who's going to pick up the garbage on Monday morning?[13]

Two years after Detroit's rebellion, Mierle Laderman Ukeles asked this question in her *Manifesto for Maintenance Art 1969!* about "maintenance" in Western culture, as capitalism has spurred an insatiable desire for everything to be new, always moving forward.[14] In most hierarchies, the act of maintenance falls to those with the least amount of economic and social mobility. Likewise, this role fell to Detroit's predominantly black population, those who remained and built their lives against the leftover debris of departed industries, civil infrastructures, and former residents. After a trauma, the notion of found material has a different connotation and intentionality relative to the idea of everyday material that flows from a Duchampian legacy. Concurrent with the Cass Corridor movement, painter Charles McGee (p. 159)—the only black artist included in the *Downtown Detroit* exhibition (none were included in *Kick Out the Jams*)—created an impactful series of assemblages and reconstructions during the 1970s: "I think of my recent structures as chunks of Detroit because I'm recycling the actual materials of the city and looking around from a view of things going up and things coming down. Old substances are soaked with history. There's a sense of drama in revitalizing decaying elements by putting them back into an unfolding sequence."[15] Likewise, the reorientation of material is executed profoundly in Allie McGhee's *Ku Klux Klown* (1969) (p. 171), in which a piece of white fabric found on the street is positioned as a Klansman's hood, painted on, and placed next to a petrified banana. McGhee repeatedly uses the banana as a satirical symbol and a formal element in his paintings. The "banana-moon-horn," as the artist dubs it, conjures other potent metaphors beyond its crescent shape and its influence from African art. To follow the material of the banana, a non-native to the West, the economic path of the fruit is traced back to plantations created by US companies in Central and South America. The term "banana republic" is used to describe a single product upon which a country's entire economic output depends—one to which its policies bend towards exploitation, thus drawing parallels to countries sustained on slave labor.

Due to the excessive amount of debris in Detroit, the artists who source it as found material must undertake a mindful editorial process; this is often the result of a studio practice dependent on the near constant act of sorting and collecting from the city. This methodology has continued through successive generations since the 1960s, in part because the city's landscape was never really transfigured by a postindustrial economy. Starting her practice in the late

1970s, Cay Bahnmiller worked obsessively at the distillation and layering of the materials and language of the city (p. 59). In its frenetic clustering, her oeuvre can be understood as one long poetic expulsion of thought and material. Gilda Snowden was similarly prolific; her decades of artistic practice, until her death in 2013, included her role as a seminal mentor for artists who studied at the College for Creative Studies. Snowden's *Constructions* series (p. 167) from the 1980s are embattled, abstract portraits of Detroit life which are imbued with familial history and personally charged objects. Often, an intimacy can be found in Detroit artists' use of found material. In close observation, one begins to understand the city from an individual perspective—their editorial process providing a lens of a microscope instead of a satellite.

These material extractions are complemented by the commandeering of actual physical space, as sections of unoccupied land or abandoned property were activated by artistic intervention as municipal oversight receded and infrastructure collapsed. Founded in the late 1990s, Olayami Dabls' African Bead Museum and the surrounding outdoor installation utilize both owned and forfeited territory, now claimed by Dabls' vortex of energy. Sculptural vignettes populate his installation *Iron Teaching Rocks How to Rust* in which the materials are positioned in conversation with one another. Dabls' installation also exemplifies Detroit artists' reverence for the autonomy of materials, which have their own lifespan outside of human intent. Part of living in the city is an experience of the sublime, as natural elements reclaim the landscape. As Japanese artist Jiro Yoshihara states in his manifesto from

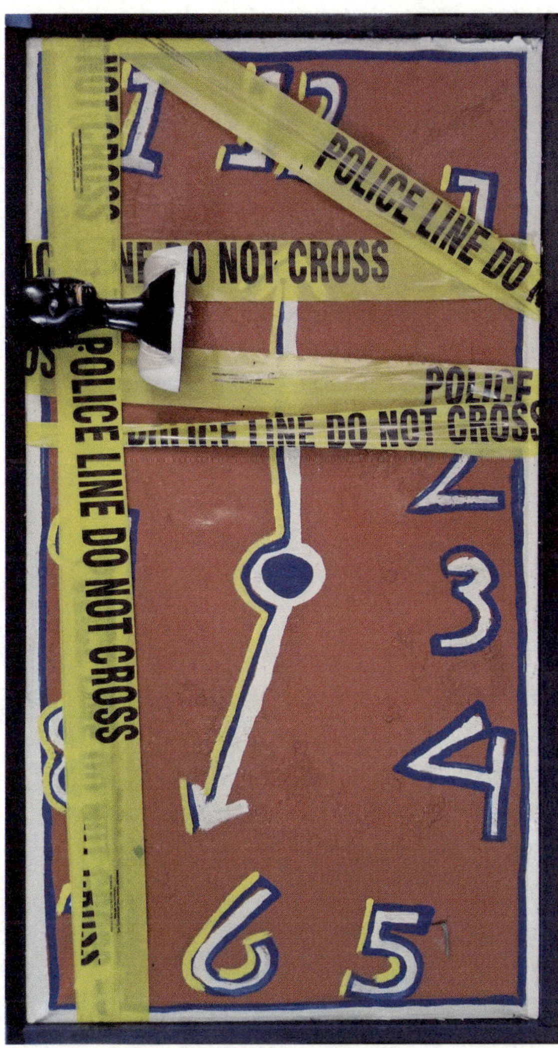

FIGURE 2

Tyree Guyton, *Dark Shadows*, 2017, mixed media

1956: "The fact that ruins receive us warmly and kindly after all, and they attract us with their cracks and flaking surfaces, could this not really be a sign of the material taking revenge, having recaptured its original life."[16]

Since 1986, Tyree Guyton's *The Heidelberg Project*—an iconic, constantly evolving outdoor installation—has been a cacophony of abandoned material reimagined into a cerebral playground for metaphysical ideas, such as time. Throughout the multi-block-long installation, Guyton frequently paints clocks on material scraps, discreetly placing them throughout the surrounding neighborhood (fig. 2). As a serial and continuous part of Guyton's practice, these clocks challenge our notion of "the present." This intervention highlights the human tendency to regard the present as the end of history, when we are, in fact a part of a much longer continuum. Since the 2000s, Scott Hocking has been making large site-specific installations inside abandoned buildings in Detroit. He uses material found on site to recreate monumental objects that draw from ancient forms—the egg, the ark, the crop circle, the pyramid (fig. 3, p. 115). Hocking searches for fundamental questions through these recreations, placing Detroit as one epoch in humankind's long timeline of existential inquiry and negotiation of the sublime. Hocking explains:

Why do we think that these things from the ancient past symbolize the people, but when we look at our contemporary ruins, we can't think how it will be perceived in the future?... We speak different languages, we have different tools, we have different knowledge, but I think the cycles that humans

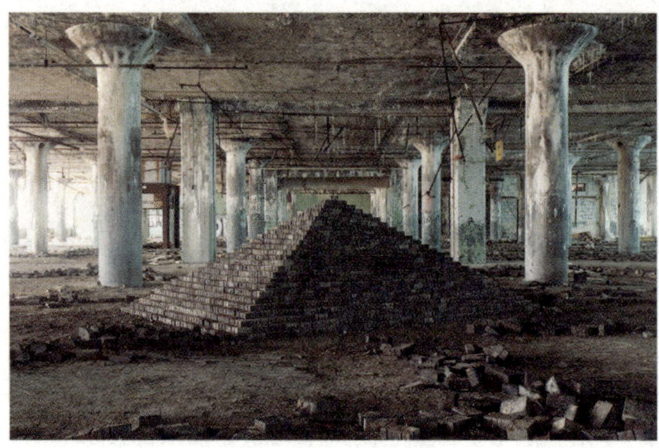

FIGURE 3

Scott Hocking, *Ziggurat, East, Summer* (from the
site-specific installation and photography
project *Ziggurat and Fisher Body 21*, 2007–2009),
2008, archival pigment print

go through are the same all living
things go through. It's a repetitive
circumstance, and to that point, I
think we repeat the same mistakes
as older civilizations. Humanity
has a very short-term memory.[17]

Excessive and accessible abandoned
material throughout Detroit has been
an important resource to its artists,
much like the indigo plant in ancient
India or the desert landscape of the
American Southwest for land artists.
The materials also act as witnesses to
our recent past—remnants of obsolete
innovations, routines, and desires
that are suspended in the present.
The artists who navigate the city for
extended periods of time often work
from a position of a *lived research*,
their accumulation of knowledge
compiled through continuous material investigation. A strait, by definition, is always in motion; likewise,
Detroit is a verb, its artists sustaining
a constant state of rethinking, repurposing, and reinhabiting.

OBSOLESCENCE AS REBELLION: ITALY (1960s – 1980s)

In *Direzione* (*Direction*), created in 1967,
Giovanni Anselmo's use of schist as
material sites the work and its viewer on
a geological timeline spanning millions of
years. Schist is a coarse-grained metamorphic rock with layers of minerals that cleave
into thin irregular plates. The rock is cut
coarsely into the shape of an arrow;
we see the strata of its formation, layers
created slowly through the diligence of
time. Anselmo embedded a compass
into the rock that points us north—to our
shared center, toward a path to follow.
Outside on the streets of Turin, the people
were unmoored as heated voices rose
like kindling, making plans[18] (p. 55).

The Italian avant-garde in the
mid-twentieth century was a regional
art scene with a global impact on
contemporary art. The movement *arte
povera* (literally translated as "poor
art") was coined by art critic Germano
Celant in 1967 to describe a young
generation of artists who created with
natural, industrial, and found materials.[19] Amid the rapid industrialization of post-war Italy, Celant initially
framed the movement as a rejection of
consumer society. Nevertheless, *arte
povera* is often discussed in formalist
and apolitical terms. The positioning of *arte povera* within a social and
political climate has been contentious, in part due to friction among
the artists involved and Celant's curatorial desires to form a cohesive
voice on their behalf. In a critical re-
examination of the movement "From

Vietnam to Fiat-nam: The Politics of Arte Povera," art historian Nicholas Cullinan traces the artists distancing themselves from sociopolitical interpretations to the failed optimism of the political uprisings throughout Europe and beyond in the late 1960s. He carries this estrangement forward through nearly twenty years of domestic terrorism in Italy referred to as the *anni di piombo* (Years of Lead).[20]

In many ways, *arte povera*'s historical trajectory and its shifting quest for political legitimacy mirrors its social context perfectly. The group's inception in the late 1960s is a testament to a period when collective action could be a catalyst for social change. Its dispersal at the beginning of the *anni di piombo* in the 1970s echoes a time when doubt was cast over the aims and ideals of '68, as impatience began to bleed to violence. By the 1980s, its reemergence and historicization acted as a riposte to the ascendancy of the retrograde and market-driven Transavangardia,[21] but one that was careful to reposition itself according to the same vogue for nostalgia, ironically by evacuating its historical and political context.[22]

Arte povera emerged amidst and against a great economic expansion and an increasing Americanization, reaching prominence in the late 1960s and early 1970s with the onset of heightened activism, Vietnam war protests, and sustained social violence that lasted through the mid-1980s. Since the end of World War II, the country had undergone extreme changes, both in terms of industrial production and through the introduction of new technologies dependent on a global economy—a time coined "the economic miracle." Art historian Benjamin H. D. Buchloh suggests that the ethos of the *arte povera* movement enacted a retrieval of obsolescence—i.e., a dedicated interest in materials of the past or the perennial—and a material opposition to what he deemed an American logic of homogeneity of form and culture.[23]

The *arte povera* ethos is articulated compellingly in artist Mario Merz's series of sculptural igloos, in which he composed hemispherical structures of varying scale and material. In *Igloo*, 1971 (p. 173) he makes a dome of steel tubes, attaching a skin of wire mesh to these ribs with C-clamps and neon that spells out "1 + 1 = 2." The structure and materials distill two essential needs for mankind's survival—habitation and communication. More political than most artists associated with *arte povera*, Merz began his career as a medical student before he was arrested in 1945 and imprisoned for one year in Turin for his participation in an anti-fascist group. In the late 1960s, activist language—in both text and form—was layered into *arte povera* works. Some of Merz's neon works that reference the slogans of May 1968 in Paris include *Solitary Solidarity* and *Object, Conceal Yourself*. His first piece of the series,

Giap Igloo, bore a phrase inscribed in neon from the North Vietnamese military strategist General Vo Nguyen Giap: *"Se il nemico si concentra perde terreno se il disperde perde forza"* ("If the enemy masses his forces, he loses ground; if he scatters, he loses strength"). This piece was shown in the exhibition titled *Percorso (Route)*, held in Rome in March 1968; it was curated by Michelangelo Pistoletto, another seminal artist in the movement. The exhibition anticipated the barricades of May 1968 in Paris by constructing walls of cement sacks throughout the gallery space. This series can also be placed within the expanded field of radical architectural inquiry that occurred during the same time, in which the eighteenth-century anthropological construct of the "primitive hut"—the assertion that the ideal architectural form embodies what is natural and intrinsic—was being exhumed in practice. As influences, *arte povera* scholar Carolyn Christov-Bakargiev cites Frank Lloyd Wright's "ecosystemic" model of a nomadic home and Buckminster Fuller's geodesic domes resembling the cells of living organisms.[24]

An important contextualization of *arte povera* is the overall zeitgeist of material focus undertaken throughout Italy by the movement's peers. Concurrent with *arte povera* and Merz's practice were several important radical design and architecture collectives founded in the 1960s. These collectives—including 9999, Superstudio, UFO, Archizoom, and Ziggurat—explored many of the same tenets, operating under ambitious ideologies such as the "refounding of manual labor" and "simple technology."[25] In January 1973, a gathering took place in Milan at the editorial office of the magazine *Casabella* that featured the above collectives alongside architects, designers, artists, and intellectuals, including *arte povera* author Germano Celant and artist Luciano Fabro. The mega-collective titled itself Global Tools, publishing texts and holding workshops from 1973 to 1975. Riccardo Dalisi, a participant in Global Tools, supplied resources and found material to children growing up in Naples's most economically depressed areas and invented everyday objects alongside them and simple architectural structures. He titled these creative actions "technica povera" (poor techniques), which similar to Celant's *arte povera*, carries a positive connotation aligned with a belief in the dignity of the everyday, as the term applies to both man and material.

All of these different factions of the Italian avant-garde are joined by a conviction that the technological machine creates at least as many problems as it is capable of solving.[26] The material manifestations of this rationale were deployed as intellectual weapons. For instance, neon light is a recurring choice among *arte povera* artists such as Merz, Pier Paolo Calzolari, and Gilberto Zorio. Here, twentieth-century technology strong arms the natural element neon, transforming the invisible (inert gas) into the visible (light). A calculated agitation between material

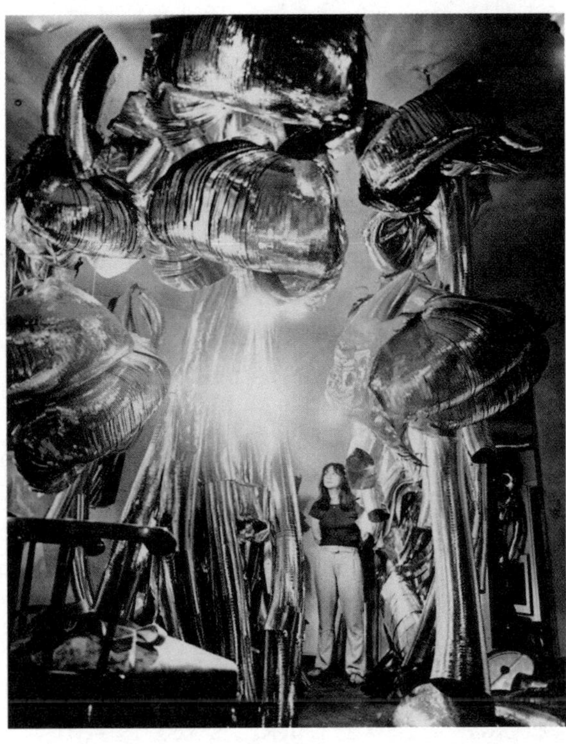

FIGURE 4

Marisa Merz with *Living Sculpture*, Turin, 1966, photograph, installation documentation

and life is also seen in Marisa Merz's seminal work *Living Sculpture* (1966) (fig. 4). First installed in the Turin home she shared with Mario and their daughter, Merz created a monumental reimagination of their domestic space by stapling together pieces of commercially available aluminum and hanging them from the ceilings. Part of the installation was her creation of a chair in aluminum, its jagged edges promising a violent embrace of the body (p. 175). Aluminum was not necessarily a foreign material in the domestic space (canned goods, commercial products), but here it seems to spread like an infestation, suffocating the space and robbing it of protection and comfort. Curator Connie Butler extends

Merz's materiality beyond the domestic and into an expanded framework of the era's aggressive modernization. She cites that in 1965, nearly half of all Italian homes had a television set, the same number who had refrigeration, and "aside from other domestic debris, including a bright blue Olivetti typewriter, the centrality of the TV screen in the documentation images of Merz's *Living Sculpture* is striking."[27]

Furthermore, *arte povera* artists offered an antidote to the object-desire paradigm by investigating imperceptible forces as an artistic material, as in the utilization of the earth's magnetism in Giovanni Anselmo's *Direzione* (*Direction*). In Giuseppe Penone's *Soffio di Foglie* (*The Breath of Leaves*) (1979), the artist illustrates our essential connectivity with the natural world by laying down a pile of myrtle leaves and breathing heavily to leave an impression. Penone offers poetically: "The volume of breath is already a sculpture we produce all of our lives."[28] Now forty years past its inception, and in a society further desensitized to natural disaster, acting with a material carries an important lesson for mankind's relationship to its surrounding world. In a 1969 text titled simply *Arte Povera*, Celant orients these sentiments within the ethos of the time:

This moment tends towards deculturization, regression, the primary and the repressed; toward elementary and spontaneous behavior. It tends toward the primitive elements of nature (earth, sea, snow, minerals, heat, animals), of life (body, memory, thought), and of politics (family, spontaneous action, class struggle, violence, environment).... Poor "art," life or politics, like reality, do not make reference, but offer themselves, through self-presentation, as essence.[29]

EMBODIED MINIMALISM: SOUTH KOREA (1970s–1980s)

Like an oracle, an old television emits a video transmission of a rock from decades ago (p. 187). The present and past coincide; the thing confronts the idea of the thing. The weight of the television is tested against the weight of an actual rock: technology versus nature, foreshadowing a victory. One wonders—if the artist Park Hyun-Ki were alive to see the city of Seoul today, thirty-five years later—whether the distribution would look different....

The term *han* is used to describe a deeply rooted collective psyche that is said to exist at the core of the Korean people—a medley of grief, melancholy, anger, and resentment that defies any direct translation. *Han* is the emotional result of war, division, and oppression of recent generations who lived through Japanese rule (1910–45), the Korean War that divided communist North from capitalist South (1950–53), and the resulting postwar dictatorships. Historian Sandra So Hee Chi Kim explains that within this perpetual state of crisis, "the term *han*

itself emerged as a significant ideological concept during the 1970s" and "some contend that it was during the Park Chung Hee regime that the idea of *han* transformed from a personal sense of sorrow and resentment to a broader, national experience of unrelenting suffering and injustice."[30] Chung Hee's regime ushered in the Yushin era (restoration era), bringing about a twofold transformation: the rampant modernization of South Korea and extreme political repression. It gave rise to the term "developmental dictatorship." The South Korean economy was the top national policy priority, and it was influenced in large part by the United States' need for military and material support for the Vietnam War. Framed as a necessity for reformation, Chung Hee declared martial law that lasted seven years (1972–79), which included the radical suppression of civil rights and public assembly.

Art historian Joan Kee gives an account of the relationship between the Yushin government and the visual arts during the 1970s:

The state was run by a technocracy whose "paramount concerns were effectiveness and performance" and whose policies were intended to mold individual behavior to better serve the economic goals it set. Visual art was by no means exempt from this pursuit of efficacy and achievement. From approximately 1973 the national documentary paintings project—the Korean state's largest continuous visual arts project that resulted in the production of hundreds of figurative oil paintings commemorating various scenes of military and historical glory—expanded to include scenes of economic achievement. The Kukjŏn, the juried National Art Salon held annually in Seoul since 1948, tended to include artworks that featured images of a rapidly industrialising Korea; this was particularly well demonstrated in the many photographs of factories, pipelines, and ships selected to represent Korean art.[31]

The act of giving the canvas over to the space of abstraction instead of pictorial propaganda was applied as a method of resistance. Korean painter Yun Hyong-Keun is renowned for using a wide brush to apply thick bars of dark paint on raw cotton or linen, leaving parts of the organic cloth exposed as the support structure (p. 247). Born in 1928, Yun was incarcerated three times as a political prisoner during Japanese rule, the war, and postwar dictatorships, and he was only able to commit himself to being an artist at the age of forty-five when he was blacklisted from standard employment. After he returned from incarceration in Seodaemun Prison in 1973, all other shades left his palette in favor of the blackish-brown color he created by mixing blue with umber. Yun explained, "The thesis of my painting is the gate of heaven and earth. Blue is the color of heaven, while umber is the color of the earth. Thus, I call

them 'heaven and earth,' with the gate serving as the composition."[32] The raw canvas that remains exposed in his work is as important as the paint; it is a material surface that is meant for creative response and claims artistic ownership of the canvas.

Yun is one of the artists associated with an art movement titled *dansaekhwa* (also referred to as *tansaekhwa*), which translates to "monochrome painting."[33] In stark contrast to Western minimalism, however, some scholars attribute the artists' methods to that of suppressed freedom and limited access to materials. *Dansaekhwa* artworks bespeak a quiet, internal resistance through the use of material choices such as found objects, burlap-wrapped canvases, coarse paint, and ripped paper. A meditative aggression to the surface is notable in *dansaekhwa* artwork, such as Kwon Young-Woo's layers of torn traditional Korean paper (p. 129); Park Seo-Bo's relentless scratching (p. 189); and Chung Sang-Hwa's repeated application and removal of paint from raw canvas (fig. 5). Kee explains that "the artists shared an interest in getting to know the object through the most basic material properties. That interest was so intense as to amount to a kind of belief. Their world was marked by not only the material deprivations experienced in the wake of the Korean War, but also by the realization of imminent dispossession."[34]

While the term was coined by critic Lee Yil, it was a 1975 Japanese exhibition *Five Korean Artists, Five*

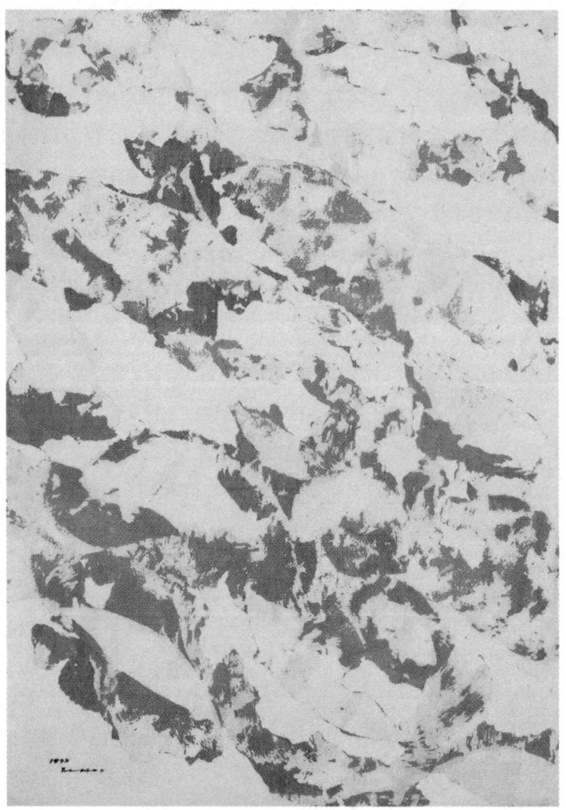

FIGURE 5

Chung Sang-Hwa, *Untitled 73-7*, 1973,
acrylic on canvas

Kinds of White, organized by Korean artist Lee Ufan, that is often credited as the first collective presentation of this type of work.[35] Lee Ufan fled Korea in 1958 after the war and settled in Tokyo, providing an important connection for his Korean peers to a larger art discourse and vice versa. He contributed to both the *dansaekhwa* movement and the Japanese *mono-ha* movement, as a painter and sculptor respectively, the latter developing in the late 1960s from an ethos similar to that of *arte povera*. *Mono-ha* ("school of things") was generated in response to the social, cultural, and political climate of the time and carried a particular investment in

natural and industrial materials. Lee Ufan's *Relatum* series (p. 137) is a rumination on natural and synthetic materials; the rubber is a product of our industrial world, here it is stretched and weighted down by stones that exist autonomously outside of modernity.

Is materiality connected to *han*? Or, can materiality be a part of *han's* articulation when language has failed? In the face of censorship, perhaps these artworks speak in coded communication to the collective. In her book *The Body in Pain*, Elaine Scarry explains our visceral relationship to material objects that carry violent potential: "This is an actual physical fact, a weapon is an object that goes into the body and produces pain; as a perceptual fact, it can lift pain and its attributes out of the body and make them visible. The mental habit of *recognizing* pain in the weapon (despite the fact that an inanimate object cannot 'have pain' or any other sentient experience) is both an ancient and an enduring one."[36] The connection between violence and the material emerges in the work of Ha Chong-Hyun, one of the most prolific artists to emerge from the *dansaekhwa* movement. His work from the 1970s includes found materials such as nails, newspaper, barbed wire, and a kind of burlap used to transport agricultural goods, which was stretched for painting canvases (pp. 106–7). Within a Korean art context these types of materials were non-traditional, rendering them politically charged and positioning them as tools for a radical confrontation with the representational painting promoted by the government. During the Yushin era, Ha Chong-Hyun created a unique method of pushing oil paint through the obverse side of his burlap canvas with varying degrees of pressure, the paint sometimes drying suspended, a record of the force (fig. 6). The process is emblematic of the performative exertion Korean artists used to communicate the sublimated reality of living under the government's military rule. Now in a prominent position in the global economy, South Koreans are negotiating the consequences of a coerced prosperity.

HANDHELD AND UNHOLDABLE OBJECTS: CUBA (1990s–PRESENT)

In Yoan Capote's *Old Speech*, a microphone stands behind two jagged rocks embedded with loudspeakers and wrapped in chains. Rust results from the structures having been submerged beneath the sea for six months. The weight of rocks anchored it down, drowning its potential for use: the voice, silenced (fig. 7).

Like Korea, Cuba is a small nation where competing ideologies of capitalism and communism have played out dramatically over the decades. In the early 1990s, Fidel Castro declared the Special Period in Cuba following the collapse of the Soviet Union (its primary economic partner), the failure of the sugar cane harvest (its primary

FIGURE 6

Ha Chong-Hyun, *Conjunction 79-9*, 1979, oil on hemp cloth

export), and the United States further tightening its embargo (its primary ideological adversary).[37] The resulting economic crisis paralyzed all societal functions: transport, industry, agriculture, etc. Artists not only had to negotiate their own needs for production, but were also influenced by the panic of scarcity that had become part of daily life. Cuban writer Orlando Hernández explains how objects can be regarded with increased intention when the basic needs of a population are withdrawn:

> Objects for cooking, lighting, dressing, objects to facilitate your mobility, the transportation of your belongings, the entertainment of your children, the decoration of your house, so on. In spite of their apparently rudimentary and anti-aesthetic character and their non-professional design, it is necessity that forces people to consume and, for the most part, to invent and produce such objects. Necessity and Poverty. In countries like ours, the inventiveness of this alternative production is vast, diverse, almost infinite.[38]

Within Cuban society, the notion of "everyday" materials has a potent meaning within the framework of socialism, whose promises are grounded in the core essentials of daily livelihood and lifetime sustenance, as opposed to the self-inflicted prosperity of capitalism. By the time of the Special Period, everyday life in

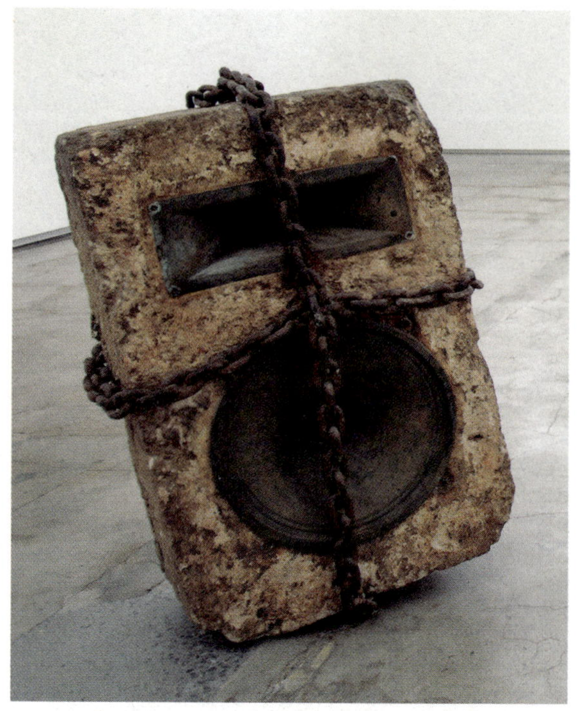

FIGURE 7

Yoan Capote, *Old Speech* (detail), 2010–11, mixed media including coral stone, bronze, iron

Cuba was a tenuous balance between survival and fidelity to the nationalist agenda. There persists a dualistic reality in the Cuban way of life: one in which people work and participate legally, and another sequestered in the black market of side jobs and street deals. These dual existences occur daily and in parallel.[39] Many artists in the early 1990s did not have access to conventional art materials, which required extreme resourcefulness. For Afro-Cuban artist Belkis Ayón, traditional printmaking materials were not available, so she invented them. She would build the printing surface by gluing material onto cardboard, and with palm leaves, seaweed and cut cardboard, she would construct the image through contrasting textures[40] (p. 57). Due to the material conditions of the embargo, the creation of an artwork in Cuba requires a different strategic process. In writing about artist Yoan Capote, curator Hans-Michael Herzog states, "There is a positive aspect to the shortages of the Cuban economy, if in a perverted manner: implementing an artistic idea is a far more difficult and demanding task in Cuba than elsewhere. Capote, therefore, first subjects each of his ideas to intense scrutiny and a lengthy review, before he can start his search for the required materials, which can in turn, become a dynamic feat of its own."[41]

Both as social commentary and out of necessity, contemporary Cuban artists draw from the country's insular material culture—one that excludes most of the global marketplace due to embargoes maintained by the United States. In the 1990s, an interest in a kind of "provisional" art led to several manifesto-driven artistic collectives, such as Gabinete Ordo Amoris,[42] who explored the innovative designs provoked by scarcity, and Los Carpinteros,[43] who created their collective, "to renounce the notion of individual authorship and refer back to an older guild tradition of artisans and skilled laborers."[44] Around the world, this decade saw a rise in artist collectives that corralled different kinds of creative production, all of which recalled the cross-disciplinary format of the Italian avant-garde. These collaboratives expanded the lineage that Duchamp and his readymades put into motion, but with a

socially engaged intentionality rather than an art historical one. Gabinete Ordo Amoris would often exhibit their own work interspersed with the inventions of everyday Cubans, without any delineation of authorship. The primary difference here is that makeshift inventiveness is not born from an individual's exceptional circumstances but the reality of daily existence. As art historian Rachel Weiss writes, "[Cuban] Art of the 'everyday' lives more easily in the everyday, as all avant-garde have dreamed."[45]

An embargo by definition is the hindrance and obstruction of material goods—a literal pen in hand from afar that authorizes localized consequences for both hand and mouth (this is what one cannot use, this is what one cannot eat). Within Cuba, there exists a particular focus on the body as material, in part for its politicized role as the recipient of outside forces, but also because of the limits placed upon it from its own government (this is where one cannot go, this is what one cannot say). Thus, the body has become an important resource, a material of ingenuity in circumstances where dispossession and confiscation are a lived reality. In December 2018, the Cuban government began the process of enacting Decree 349,[46] in which the state demands an approval process over the production of its artists. Amnesty International's summation characterized it as follows: "Under the decree, all artists, including collectives, musicians and performers, are prohibited from operating in public or private spaces without prior approval

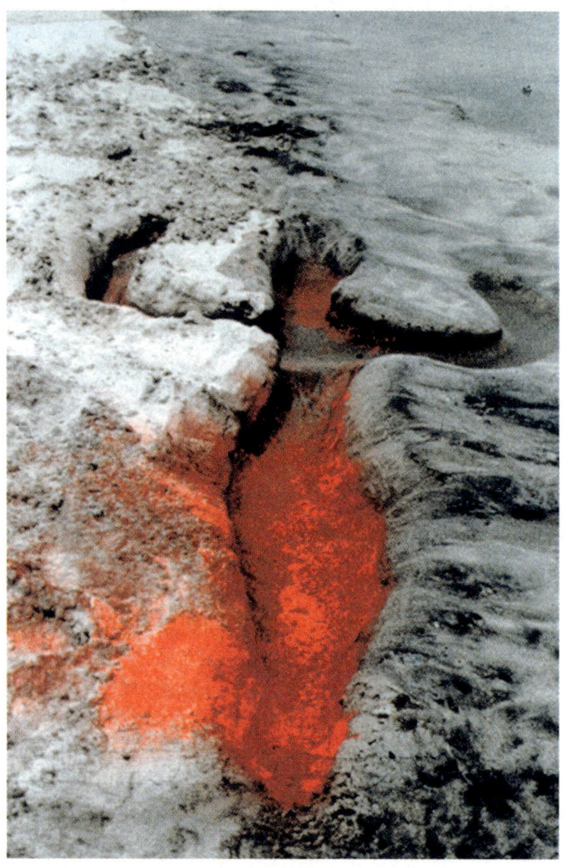

FIGURE 8

Ana Mendieta, *Untitled: Silueta Series, Mexico, From Silueta Works in Mexico, 1973–77*, 1976, color photograph

by the Ministry of Culture. Individuals or businesses that hire artists without authorization can be sanctioned, and artists that work without prior approval can have their materials confiscated or be substantially fined."[47] Among the artists arrested in December 2018 for attempting to protest the decree was Tania Bruguera, an internationally recognized Cuban artist who is based in both New York and Havana. An early Bruguera piece, *El peso de la culpa* (*The burden of guilt*) (p. 63), was first performed as an unofficial part of the Sixth Havana Biennial in 1997. Staged inside her house for an intimate audience, a barefoot Bruguera performed in front of a large Cuban flag made of human hair. Wearing the headless carcass of a lamb, she slowly and ritualistically ate from a pile of Cuban earth in front of her along with water and salt. The work is based on the rumored history of the enslaved indigenous Cuban peoples' suicides during the Spanish occupation. The artist explains, "The only way that some of them could rebel—as they didn't have any weapons and they weren't warriors by nature—was to eat dirt until they died."[48] Bruguera's artistic practice is part of an expanded investigative use of the body by Cuban female artists. For example, Susana Pilar uses herself as a conduit for the collective experience of Cuban women, primarily of the African diaspora. In the performance *Contact (In Homage to Ana Mendieta)* (2015), she collaborates with Afro-Cuban religious subcultures in a ritual of dance and community to resurrect the spirit of seminal Cuban-American artist Ana Mendieta (fig. 8). Within a culture predicated on absence and presence—who has stayed, who has left, who is heard, who is silenced— the use of body as material is an insistence of relevance, a demand of its presence. The feminist theorist Judith Butler expands on this idea:

In both the Latin and Greek, matter (*materia* and *hylè*) is neither a simple, brute positivity or referent nor a blank surface or slate awaiting an external signification, but is always in some sense temporalized....

To speak within these classical contexts of *bodies that matter* is not an idle pun, for to be material means to materialize, where the principle of that materialization is precisely what "matters" about that body, its very intelligibility. In this sense, to know that significance of something is to know how and why it matters, where "to matter" means at once "to materialize" and "to mean."[49]

At the moment of writing this text, the fate of Decree 349 is unknown. However, its very existence reinforces how the artist is seen as a potential threat. Material, object, body—all susceptible to control.

Contemporary Cuba today functions on tense dichotomies between official and unofficial markets, entrepreneurialism and ideals; a complicated terrain the artists themselves have to negotiate between their country and a global art world. Economic deregulation and the introduction of twenty-first-century technology also play a role in the contemporary life of the country. The Cuban dilemma is captured poetically in Wilfredo Prieto's sculpture *Miren el tamaño de este mango* (*Look at the size of this mango*) (2011) (p. 215), a work indebted to the *arte povera* lineage of the deft and strategic placement of objects. The mango, native to Cuba, is strapped to an imported smartphone with a rubber band. If we are to trace the material complicity of these two objects, we are taken from locally sourced agriculture to the global production complex, from inland to offshore. Look at these two small items that can fit in your hand—somehow they speak to larger concepts of allegiance, sustenance, information, ingenuity, survival, and the future. Look at this small island—somehow it encapsulates so many tensions at the core of the human experience.

ON LIMBS AND VACUITY: GREECE (2009–PRESENT)

In ancient Greece, marble was used to render the Gods into human form. Today, the marble medians in front of the university have grown jagged from protesters breaking off fragments to hurl at police. In the work of Andreas Lolis, the material is carved into exacting replicas of cardboard, Styrofoam, and wooden scraps, and then assembled into a makeshift shelter. The structure reconstitutes the living conditions of immigrants who are stranded in Greece, having fled to its shores to escape: the marble, hard and cold, instead of protective (p. 151).

On the island of Hydra, there is a very small slaughterhouse built into a jagged rocky slope overlooking the Aegean Sea that stirs below. The Greek island is named after the mythological multiheaded monster that has the power of limb regeneration. In battle, when one head was chopped off, the Hydra would regrow two. The drama of the landscape invites mythmaking, with a rock kingdom of houses that interrupt the eye-bleaching blue of the sky above and sea below. Henry Miller described Hydra as "wild and naked perfection." The path to the slaughterhouse is under direct sun, far from port, where inquisitors on foot walk primarily in isolation. The slaughterhouse has been converted into a site for contemporary art by the DESTE Foundation. In the summer of 2017, it exhibited the sugared and severed left hand of Kara Walker's seminal monument *A Subtlety*[50] (fig. 9). The artwork was originally created in 2014 for the molasses-drenched Domino Sugar factory in Brooklyn, where the hand was attached to a grand, seventy-five-foot-long sphinxlike body made of sugar. The statue combined two distinct racist stereotypes assigned to black women: a kerchief-wearing mammy and an overtly sexualized caricature with prominent breasts, buttocks, and vulva.[51] Sugar as material references the tragic three-hundred-year history of American sugar plantations whose operation depended upon slave labor. But here, on the island, the hand has been violently severed from its body like a talisman or a keepsake from another land. The slaughterhouse is like a vitrine, just large enough for the left hand; thus, it is difficult to imagine its body of origin. The sugar—a foreign and incompatible substance in extreme heat—melts here. The hand loses its shape along with connection to its body, no trace of its history. The reality of the African diaspora is poetically communicated with this severance, a sentiment shared by Detroit's predominantly black population.

Sculptures missing their limbs, extracted from their origin stories and landscapes, are often presented in museums primarily as formal studies. The severed hand of *A Subtlety* is a reversal of Greek antiquity now disseminated around the world. Ancient Greece authored much of the Western imagination: democ-

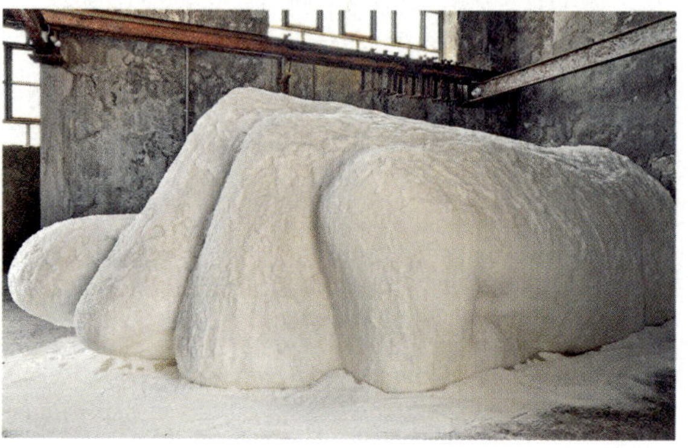

FIGURE 9

Kara Walker, *Figa*, 2014, installation view, DESTE Foundation Project Space, Slaughterhouse, Hydra, Greece, 2017

racy, medicine, geometry, Platonism, *Antigone*, and *The Odyssey*. The independent Greek state we know today was established only in 1830 and was preceded by roughly four centuries of rule by the Ottoman Empire. The Empire at its peak consisted of what are currently parts of Southeast Europe, Southwest Asia, and North Africa. These populations and ethnic groups roamed throughout the territory; for this reason there was no coherent sense of a nationality for hundreds of years.

The authors of the Greek enlightenment in the nineteenth century depended on the perceptions of the rest of Europe where Philhellenism was in vogue, i.e., the idealism of ancient Greek culture and intellect. The modern Greek state reconstituted and enforced these ideals, making a separatist edit of its history.

Today, Greece has been on the forefront of the twenty-first-century global economic crisis that began in 2009, while simultaneously emerging on the frontline of Europe's humanitarian crisis as refugees emigrate from the Middle East and Africa. As explained by Natalie Zervou in "Fragments of the European Refugee Crisis:"

> This tumultuous history combined with Greece's position on the southeastern borders of the European continent contributed to a general anxiety among the Greek people regarding their place in Europe, and their desire to resist orientalization.... The increasing influx of immigrants from non-Western countries is oftentimes presented by right-wing party adherents as jeopardizing not only the perceived 'unity' and 'homogeneity' of the Greek nation-state, but also ultimately Greece's position in Europe.[52]

Simultaneously, the Greek art scene, particularly Athens, has been asked to decipher its country's condition. As the Acropolis looms in the background, what does contemporary Greek art say about the human project today? Athens was the co-site for *documenta 14* in 2017, where viewers outside a central venue were greeted with noncommissioned graffiti: "Enjoy the Ruins." The responses to the staging of *documenta* in the city ranged from wariness to resistance. Its execution was infrastructurally fraught from the beginning, a parallel to the dichotomy between the economic stability of the primary host, Germany, and the mica-like fragility of its subject, Greece. Also presented in 2017, the 6th Athens Biennale, titled *Waiting for the Barbarians*, was displayed in vacated structures in the Omonia neighborhood—new ruins against the old. Curator Nayia Yiakoumaki explained, "From postwar depression and civil-war damage to a society of false prosperity, the buildings are emblematic of what's happened in Greece over the years."[53]

This idea of *false prosperity* runs throughout cultural dialogue in the country. It is the identity crisis of the crisis, one that arises from the constant act of looking back while simultaneously driven to keep pace with growth expectations demanded by actual and abstract overlords: the European Union and globalization. In a work with many renditions, artist Dora Economou sources pumice stone from a small Greek island that has been fully converted into a quarry leased by a French company. She roughly carves and paints them into brightly yellow lemons (pp. 90–91), mirroring the sunny visual disposition overlying the country's exploitative structure. The situation in Greece has summoned a reassessment of its own timeline. As philosopher Bruno Latour explains, "The adjective 'modern' designates a new regime, an acceleration, a rupture, a revolution in time. When the word 'modern,' 'modernization,' or 'modernity' appears, we are defining, by contrast, an archaic and stable past."[54] What are the metrics for modernity: is it subjective—a mindset, a declaration—or structural and systemic achievements? Provocatively, writer Yorgos Tzirtzilakis applies Latour's logic in his 2010 essay "Crisis and Mourning in the Contemporary Greek Culture:" "This is why the crisis brings out a collective truth which reveals, in its own way, that 'we have never been modern.… Modernity has never begun.' Therein lies the special character of contemporary art in Greece."[55]

Greek artist Socratis Socratous investigates this arch of political intentionality through intervention in civic spaces, wherein contemporary narratives of Athenian life play out. Thematically, Socratous frequently uses the garden in his work as a context for mankind's quest to order and transplant nature for the purposes of human progress. Greece's National Garden was commissioned in 1838 by Queen Amalia, a monarch imported from Germany for the then newly formed Greek state to further solidify and propagate a European national identity in the aftermath of the Turkish-Greco War. The artwork's articulation of Greek nationalism also underscores the agenda to define its physical borders, which resonates with the immigration crises the country now faces. In his work *Stolen Goods* (2009–15) (p. 223), Socratous removes plant life from the National Garden illegally, taking tree limbs, blossoms, and leaves, and casting

them in gold, copper, bronze, and silver. The temporality of the natural order is frozen in time. Curator Elena Parpa explains: "Executed at the height of Greece's financial crisis, when numerous scandals revealed a corrupted political system that systematically embezzled public funds, Socratous's piece poetically emulated an analogous gesture pointing at the way a country with claims to a glorious past that laid the pillars of democracy in marble temples and agorae, was now brought to the brim of destruction by various acts of stealing."[56]

To slow down—to mediate on materials and their history—is its own form of resistance. Now, in the twenty-first century, progress addresses the communal, primarily through advances in technology, yet the same threat of isolation is at stake. The work of Andreas Angelidakis relies on the suspended space and time of the internet, which he shapes and edits as material. He speculates on technology's potential, in an embodied world of social media and real-time snapshots, to serve as our culture's ancient ruins in the future (p. 53). In his video work *Vessel*, he utilizes the classic Greek ceramic pot form as a screen to tell the story of Diogenes the Cynic[57] from the fifth century BC and to scroll a Facebook newsfeed. In this reversal of logic, ancient Greece tells the story of the internet. The subtitles ask: *Were these vessels the screens of the ancient world? Will future people study our ancient screens?*

Just before the turn of the twenty-first century, the nation-state in many ways quickly started to lose its importance as the diffusion of media and technology created a new societal paradigm. This permits people to be connected, but remain detached. In "Everyone Is South of Something" curator Lorenzo Bruni explains, "[We have] an autonomous mental geography, divided from the physical one, and created a consumption of knowledge [that] has destroyed every boundary that limits information to what can be found in a national newspaper."[58] Contemporary Greece is emblematic of how we live out our lives in a world without walls in parallel to our physical one, yet the real violence still lands in the latter. Paradoxically, our systems are held up by phantom limbs because they lack transparency; economies collapsing on a constant loop. Perhaps returning our attention to the physical—to bodies that lumber rather than levitate, to materials with limits—is the wisest path forward.

FIVE STONES:
THE LANGUAGE OF
MATERIAL

A piece of rubble, a slab of earth, a weight, an anchor, a weapon—five artists, five stones.

The brief vernacular interpretations at the start of each section of this essay reflect on the artwork of Olayami Dabls, Giovanni Anselmo, Park Hyun-Ki, Yoan Capote, and Andreas Lolis. Each offers a contextual storytelling of their specific place and time—Detroit, Turin, Seoul, Havana, and Athens, respectively. However, through a shared material—a stone—these works also articulate a universality of visual communication, an interpretive language that within the field of contemporary art has grown in fluency. The language of materials, in this context, is generative. The regional avant-garde movements post-World War II (with critics ready to name them) learned from each other through an increasingly communicative art world. Thus, the rock as an art object now has a lineage.

Artworks operate as cultural documents, coded and challenging, that speak to the inherent complexity of the mind often more so than didactic or linear narratives. Furthermore, we have an ability, through the materials, to evaluate what has shifted since the artwork left the artist's hands, when it enters into the world and became vulnerable to the contexts of time, politics, and seismic cultural shifts. Petra Lange-Berndt expands:

> Material generally denotes substances that will be further processed; it points to the forces of production at the time. From a critical perspective, the term "material" describes not prime matter but substances that are always subject to change, be it through handling, interaction with their surroundings, or the dynamic life of chemical reactions.

It is therefore a political decision to focus on the materials of art: it means to consider the processes of making, and their associated power relations, to consider the workers—whether they are in factories, studios or public spaces, whether they are known or anonymous—and their tools and spaces of production.[59]

For instance, a material to investigate as an articulation of the above is a piece of clothing. In Michelangelo Pistoletto's seminal *arte povera* work *Venus of the Rags* (1967), the artist places a classical statue of the Roman goddess of love, beauty, and fertility facing away from the audience—her sanctum—and toward a pile of unkempt street clothes. Therein the deity confronts the reality of the everyday. In considering its cultural context, its displacement parallels the call to arms of the workers' movements in Italy at the time. In a similar strategy, Cuban artist Reynier Leyva Novo produces large-scale textiles inspired by a type of welcome rug made with recycled and second-hand clothes commonly found in Cuban homes. These rugs address how spaces of daily life are politicized by economy in Cuba. For *Landlord Colors*, Novo created a 16-by-16-foot rug made of clothing from Cuban immigrants who now live in the United States—collected in Miami, handmade by paid workers in Cuba, and then exhibited in Detroit (p. 181). In addition to the local economic implications of

scarcity, the transportation format mimics the illogical structure of the global marketplace while underscoring the fashion industry as a prominent consumer of resources and producer of waste. In her series *White Out* (p. 157), Detroit artist Tiff Massey explores the textile industry's relationship to American slavery. Historically, fabrics were imported from the East to the colonial United States to clothe Americans and their slaves, with gingham becoming a signature fabric worn by enslaved women. In these works, Massey alters the gingham pattern to create parallel lines, a revisionist history enacted by subverting material by hand.

Another material to trace is rust, the result of oxygen and water—elements essential for human life—interacting over time with iron, an essential material for human ingenuity. Athens-based artist Zoë Paul is invested in both the recent and historic lineages of materiality that range from ancient utilitarian forms to industrial waste, examining how they compose contemporary Greek civilization. In one ongoing series, Paul sources rusted refrigerator grills from a scrapyard on the Greek island of Giali now owned and quarried by a foreign mining company (p. 195). Reused as found templates for her weavings, she applies the rich tradition of Greek craft onto the debris of the industrial-technological production the country performs for the rest of Europe. Detroit textile artist Carole Harris purposefully rusts the textiles she uses, even though it is widely equated with failure—it is what happens when humans remove their care from an object (p. 109). However, Harris values the aesthetic it creates: "People were always painting over rust. Through my travels, I found that [practice] didn't happen around the world. Others weren't so ready to cover up what is natural…. Things do break down and erode, and I see a kind of beauty in that erosion."[60] Ha Chong-Hyun has a similar intimate fascination with the barbed wire he first collected in the early 1970s, then viewed only through the legacy

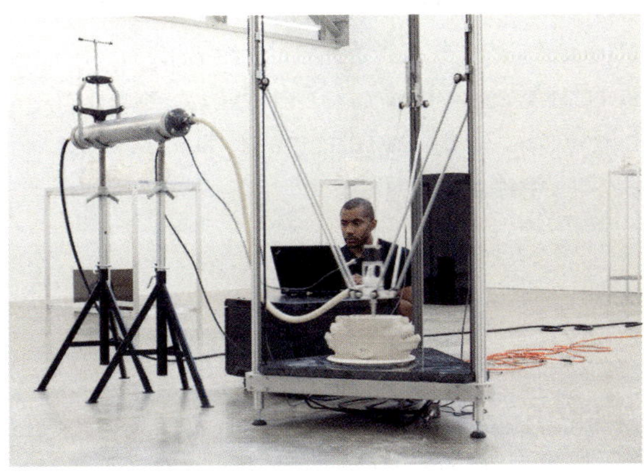

FIGURE 10

Matthew Angelo Harrison, *Dark Povera Part 1*, installation view, Atlanta Contemporary, 2017, handmade 3-D printer, African mask replica, automotive clay

of war. However, as the material gave way to rust and he to age, it slowly took on a new metaphorical patina informed by the passage of time.[61]

As illustrated in the materials above—stone, clothing, and rust— narratives with detailed specificity are extracted by following their provenance and intentionality. This lexicon of materials contributes to an

expansive and referential vocabulary utilized by contemporary artists. In the context of *Landlord Colors*, it lends a continuity of ideas between disparate places and times, each negotiating a crucial challenge to humanity. An example of *material fluency* can be found in the practice of Detroit artist Matthew Angelo Harrison, whose sculptural investigations include the creation of his own hand-made 3-D printing devices that make reproductions of existing objects, such as authentic and forged African masks (fig. 10). Formerly a clay model maker for the Ford automotive company, he refers to his practice as *dark povera*, an intersection of the material ethos of the *arte povera* movement through an African-American perspective. He invites the loss of material information through repetitive printings, the act of production becoming an erasure. As an evolution from the Italian movement, Harrison engages in what he deems a "post-industry" practice, in which technology is not the antagonist, but rather an essential tool to examine his own cultural paradigm.

Interestingly, John Watson of the League of Revolutionary Black Workers in Detroit represented the American black liberation movement at an international anti-imperialist conference organized in Rome in 1968. On this trip he also visited the city of Turin, the birthplace of the *arte povera* movement.[62] Turin's automotive industry played a pivotal role in the Italian economic miracle of the 1950s and 1960s, attracting hundreds of thousands of immigrants to the city, particularly from the rural southern regions of Italy—Turin was essentially the Italian equivalent of Detroit.[62] Perhaps through the work of Matthew Angelo Harrison, however, we can see that the spiral moves slightly forward. Imagine John Watson in that room in 1968, strategizing for the protection and freedom of the black worker in Detroit. Harrison stands now as his beneficiary, dexterously crafting art history with any material he chooses in hand.

Cycles upon cycles, prosperity then crisis. Cycles upon cycles, thought then action. In 2016, Detroit theater collective The Hinterlands staged a play called *The Radicalization Process* that was a retelling of Sophocles's *Antigone* from 441 BCE through the actions of the radical political activist movements of the 1960s and 1970s. Sophocles' story perennially resonates across time because Antigone sacrifices herself in the name of her principles in a struggle against tyranny. The play is an articulation of why we are looking back at these particular episodes of collapse, all five held within the brief span of a single human lifetime. There is another cycle, one from artist to artist, which extends the lifeline of humanity. These artists are our narrators—both living and dead—often trying to communicate the same core lesson, attempting to maintain the forward momentum. In the play, the actors recite a battle cry thrice, screaming what is at stake, careening between the ancient past, the recent past, and the present:

"The only war that matters is the war against the imagination; all other wars are subsumed in it."

"The only war that matters is the war against the imagination; all other wars are subsumed in it."

"The only war that matters is the war against the imagination; all other wars are subsumed in it."[63]

1   Petra Lange-Berndt, "How to Be Complicit with Materials," in *Materiality*, ed. Petra Lange-Berndt (London: Whitechapel Gallery; Cambridge: The MIT Press, 2015), 13.

2   Lucy R. Lippard and John Chandler, "The Dematerialization of Art," in *Materiality*, ed. Petra Lange-Berndt (London: Whitechapel Gallery; Cambridge: The MIT Press, 2015), 176.

3   Will Kenton, "Dematerialization (DEMAT)," *Investopedia*, updated April 25, 2018, https://www.investopedia .com/terms/d/dematerialization.asp.

4   Helen Molesworth, "Work Ethic," in *Work Ethic*, ed. Helen Molesworth (University Park: Pennsylvania State University Press, 2003), 25.

5   Bertolt Brecht, "On the Popularity of the Crime Novel," quoted in Ernest Mandel, *Delightful Murder: A Social History of the Crime Story* (London: Pluto Press, 1984), 72.

6   György Lukács, *History and Class Consciousness* (Cambridge: The MIT Press, 1972), 72–73.

7   Lange-Berndt, "How to Be Complicit with Materials," 13–16.

8   Lange-Berndt, 16.

9   Carole Harris, interview by Laura Mott and Taylor Renee Aldridge for *art21 magazine*, May 2017.

10   Michael Stone-Richards, "Scenes on Post-Humanism: Rilke with Gunther Anders in Detroit" (presentation, Symposium: A Portrait of the Post Human?, Cranbrook Art Museum, Bloomfield Hills, MI, December 7, 2018).

11   Coleman Young and Lonnie Wheeler, *Hard Stuff: The Autobiography of Mayor Coleman Young* (New York: Viking, 1994), 179.

12   Marsha Miro, "Detroit: The Scrappiness of Survivors," *Detroit Free Press*, December 2, 1979, 7E.

13   Mierle Laderman Ukeles, "Manifesto for Maintenance Art 1969!," *Arnolfini*, September 2018, https://www.arnolfini.org .uk/blog/manifesto-for-maintenance -art-1969.

14   Bartholomew Ryan, "Manifesto for Maintenance: A Conversation with Mierle Laderman Ukeles," *Art in America*, March 18, 2009, https://www .artinamericamagazine .com/news-features/interviews /draft-mierle-interview/.

15   Charles McGee, quoted by Roy Slade, introduction to *At Cranbrook: Downtown Detroit* (Bloomfield Hills: Cranbrook Academy of Art Museum, 1979), 9.

16   Jiro Yoshihara, "Gutai Manifesto, 1956," in *Materiality*, ed. Petra Lange-Berndt (London: Whitechapel Gallery; Cambridge: The MIT Press, 2015), 33.

17   Laura Mott, "Coyotes, Movies, and Myths: A Conversation with Scott Hocking," *Big Car*, August 4, 2016, https: //www.bigcar.org/interview-with -scott-hocking/.

18   During the academic year 1967–68, demonstrations occurred in twenty-six out of thirty-three Italian universities, and by March 1968, an estimated half-million students were on strike.

19   While a definitive list was never published by Celant in his manifesto-like texts on *arte povera*, a core thirteen artists have been the definitive focus in art history since the late 1960s: Giovanni Anselmo, Alighiero Boetti, Pier Paolo Calzolari, Luciano Fabro, Jannis Kounellis, Mario Merz, Marisa Merz, Giulio Paolini, Pino Pascali, Giuseppe Penone, Michelangelo Pistoletto, Emilio Prini, and Gilberto Zorio.

20   During the Years of Lead, roughly between 1968 and 1988, 428 murders were attributed to political violence in the form of bombings, assassinations, and street warfare between rival mili- tant factions in Italy.

21   Coined by the critic Achille Bonito Oliva, Transavanguardia literally means "beyond the avant- garde" and was an Italian movement that was part of an international revival of expressionist painting in the late 1970s and 1980s.

22   Nicolas Cullinan, "From Vietnam to Fiat-nam: The Politics of Arte Povera," *October*, no. 124 (Spring 2008): 29–30, https: //www.mitpressjournals.org/doi /10.1162/octo.2008.124.1.8.

23   Benjamin H. D. Buchloh, foreword to *Arte Povera: Selections from the Sonnabend Collection*, by Claire Gilman (New York: Colombia University, 2001), 7.

24   Carolyn Christov-Barkargiev, *Arte Povera* (New York: Phaidon, 1999), 26.

25   Sara Catenacci and Jacopo Galimberti, "Deschooling, Manual Labour, and Emancipation: The Architecture and Design of Global Tools, 1973–1975," in *Collaboration and Its (Dis) Contents: Art, Architecture, and Photography since 1950*, ed. Meredith A. Brown and Michelle Millar Fisher (London: The Courtauld Institute of Art, 2007), 104.

26   Catenacci and Galimberti, 119.

27   Connie Butler, "Marisa Merz: Alien Culture," in *Marisa Merz, The Sky Is a Great Space*, ed. Connie Butler (New York: DelMonico Books/Prestel, 2017), 21–22.

28   Interview, Giuseppe Penone at Ikon Gallery, 2009, https://www.youtube.com/watch?v=q0-UNHJKRN8.

29   Germano Celant, *Arte Povera*, trans. Paul Blanchard (Milan: Electa, 1985, revised 1998), 119–23.

30   Sandra So Hee Chi Kim, "Korean Han and the Postcolonial Afterlives of 'The Beauty of Sorrow,'" *Korean Studies*, no. 41 (2017): 253–79, https://muse.jhu.edu/article/665890.

31   Joan Kee, "Why Performance in Authoritarian Korea?," *Tate Papers*, no. 23 (Spring 2015), https://www.tate.org.uk/research/publications/tate-papers/23/why-performance-in-authoritarian-korea.

32   Joan Kee, *From All Sides: Tansaekhwa on Abstraction* (Los Angeles: Blum & Poe, 2015), 6–7.

33   While there is debate among scholars concerning the artists who constitute the participants in the movement, a generous list includes Cho Yong-Ik, Chung Chang-Sup, Chung Sang-Hwa, Ha Chong-Hyun, Heu Hwang, Kim Guiline, Kwon Young-Woo, Lee Dong-Youh, Lee Ufan, Park Seo-Bo, Suh Seung-Won, and Yun Hyong-Keun.

34   Joan Kee, *From All Sides*, 10.

35   Joan Kee, *Contemporary Korean Art: Tansaekhwa and The Urgency of Method* (Minneapolis: The University of Minnesota, 2013), 2.

36   Elaine Scarry, *The Body in Pain: The Making and Unmaking of the World* (New York: Oxford University Press, 1987), 16.

37   Holly Block, "Remembering Why," *Art Cuba: The New Generation* (New York: Harry N. Abrams, Inc., 2001), 7.

38   Orlando Hernández, "The Gabinete Otro Amoris," Diango Hernández (website), http://www.diangohernandez.com/the-gabinete-ordo-amoris-by-orlando-hernandez/.

39   Holly Block, "Remembering Why," 8–10.

40   Marilyn A. Zeitlin and Gerardo Mosquera, *Contemporary Art from Cuba: Irony and Survival on the Utopian Island* (Harlem: Delano Greenidge Editions, 1999), 129.

41   Hans-Michael Herzog, introduction to *Yoan Capote*, by Charmaine Picard (Milan: Skira Editore S.p.A, 2016), 20.

42   The core collective members were Diango Hernández and Francis Acea.

43   The original members of Los Carpinteros were Marco Antonio Castillo Valdés, Dagoberto Rodríguez Sánchez, and Alexandre Arrechea.

44   Los Carpinteros website, http://origin.www.skny.com/artists/los-carpinteros.

45   Rachel Weiss, *To and From Utopia in the New Cuban Art* (Minneapolis: University of Minnesota Press, 2011), 1.

46   The extent to which Decree 349 will be implemented or subdued is unknown at the time of writing this text, completed in December 2018.

47   "Cuba: New Administration's Decree 349 Is a Dystopian Prospect for Cuba's Artists," press release, August 24, 2018, Amnesty International, https://www.amnesty.org/en/press-releases/2018/08/cuba-new-administrations-decree-349-is-a-dystopian-prospect-for-cubas-artists/.

48   José Muñoz, "Performing Greater Cuba: Tania Bruguera and The Burden of Guilt," in *Holy Terrors: Latin American Women Perform*, ed. Diana Taylor and Roselyn Constantino (Durham: Duke University Press, 2003), 401–15.

49   Judith Butler, "Bodies That Matter," in *Materiality*, ed. Petra Lange-Berndt (London: Whitechapel Gallery; Cambridge: The MIT Press, 2015), 121.

50   The full title of the piece commissioned by Creative Time in 2014 is *A Subtlety or the Marvelous Sugar Baby: A Homage to the Unpaid and Overworked Artisans Who Have Refined Our Sweet Tastes from the Cane Fields to the Kitchens of the New World on the Occasion of the Demolition of the Domino Sugar Refining Plant*.

51   Antwaun Sargent, "Interview: Kara Walker Decodes Her New World Sphinx at Domino Sugar Factory," *Complex*, May 13, 2014, https://www.complex.com/style/2014/05/kara-walker-interview.

52   Natalie Zervou, "Fragments of the European Refugee Crises: Performing Displacement and the Re-Shaping of Greek Identity," *TDR: The Drama Review* 61, no. 2 (Summer 2017): 32–47.

53   Cathryn Drake, "On The Ground: Athens," *Artforum*, February 10, 2017, https://www.artforum.com/slant/cathryn-drake-on-the-ground-in-athens-66502.

54   Bruno Latour, *We Have Never Been Modern* (Cambridge: Harvard University Press, 1993), 17.

55   Yorgos Tzirtzilakis, "Pasa Dynamis Adynamia," *South as a State of Mind*, http://southasastateofmind.com/south-remembers-pasa-dynamis-adynamia-yorgos-tzirtzilakis/.

56   Elena Parpa, "Socratis Socratous," *The Breeder*, http://thebreedersystem.com/artists/socratis-socratous-artist-page/.

57   An irascible and contrary figure in ancient Greece, Diogenes the Cynic lived with extreme simplicity, often depicted as reclining in a large overturned pot as a makeshift house on the street of Athens. http://penelope.uchicago.edu/~grout/encyclopaedia_Romana/greece/hetairai/diogenes.html.

58   Lorenzo Bruni, "Everyone Is South of Something," *South as a State of Mind*, http://southasastateofmind.com/article/everyone-is-south-of-something/.

59   Lange-Berndt, "How to Be Complicit with Materials," 13.

60   Laura Mott and Taylor Renee Aldridge, "On Rust: Roundtable Discussion #1," *art21 magazine*, May 8, 2017, http://magazine.art21.org/2017/05/08/on-rust-roundtable-discussion-1/#.XBlRTmhKgdU.

61   Ha Chong-Hyun, interviewed by Laura Mott, September 4, 2018, Seoul, South Korea.

62   Dan Georgakas and Marvin Surkin, *Detroit: I Do Mind Dying: A Study in Urban Revolution* (Cambridge: South End Press, 1998), 62.

63   This quote was used in the play written by The Hinterlands but comes from a poem by Diane di Prima, "Revolutionary Letter #75," in *Revolutionary Letters*, 5th ed. (San Francisco: Last Gasp of San Francisco, 2007), 103–4.

Andreas Angelidakis trained as an architect, although he works primarily across the disciplines of contemporary art, curation, and architectural criticism. In the artist's entry for *documenta 14*, writer Nicholas Korody aptly defined the combination of the personal, the civic, and the creative intersectionality of Angelidakis' practice: "His work emerges from the experience of being in place: in Greece, in climate change, in architecture, in psychoanalysis, in the internet, in a body."[1] Central to his investigation is the landscape of contemporary Athens, which he describes as a sort of nightmare of modernist failures—a city suffering from minimal governmental planning, corruption, and alarming population growth over the last century. The definition of ruin is expanded within the twenty-first-century discourse of Angelidakis' practice: nature's eternal contributions (weather and time) and mankind's inherent fallacies (war and politics) are joined by the incredibly expansive virtual world we have created over the last quarter century. Angelidakis is on the forefront of negotiating the future, particularly as increasingly new technologies raise questions about authenticity, memory, and cultural inheritance.

In the video work *Building an electronic ruin*, Angelidakis explores the internet as a parallel world being built and abandoned. Set in the virtual space of Second Life, architecture that the artist creates is not vulnerable to age, gravity, or natural disaster. When Angelidakis sets fire to his constructions in this landscape, it is of no consequence. Second Life was once full of users, but by 2011 was essentially deserted, like many unused portals, platforms, and websites. His avatar traverses a desolate virtual landscape. Angelidakis offers that Facebook, Instagram, and all other future incarnations will quickly follow the same fate, becoming our version of the ancient ruins of Athens and Rome.

L.M.

1   Nicholas Korody, "Andreas Angelidakis," *documenta 14*, https://www.documenta14.de/en/artists/945/andreas-angelidakis.

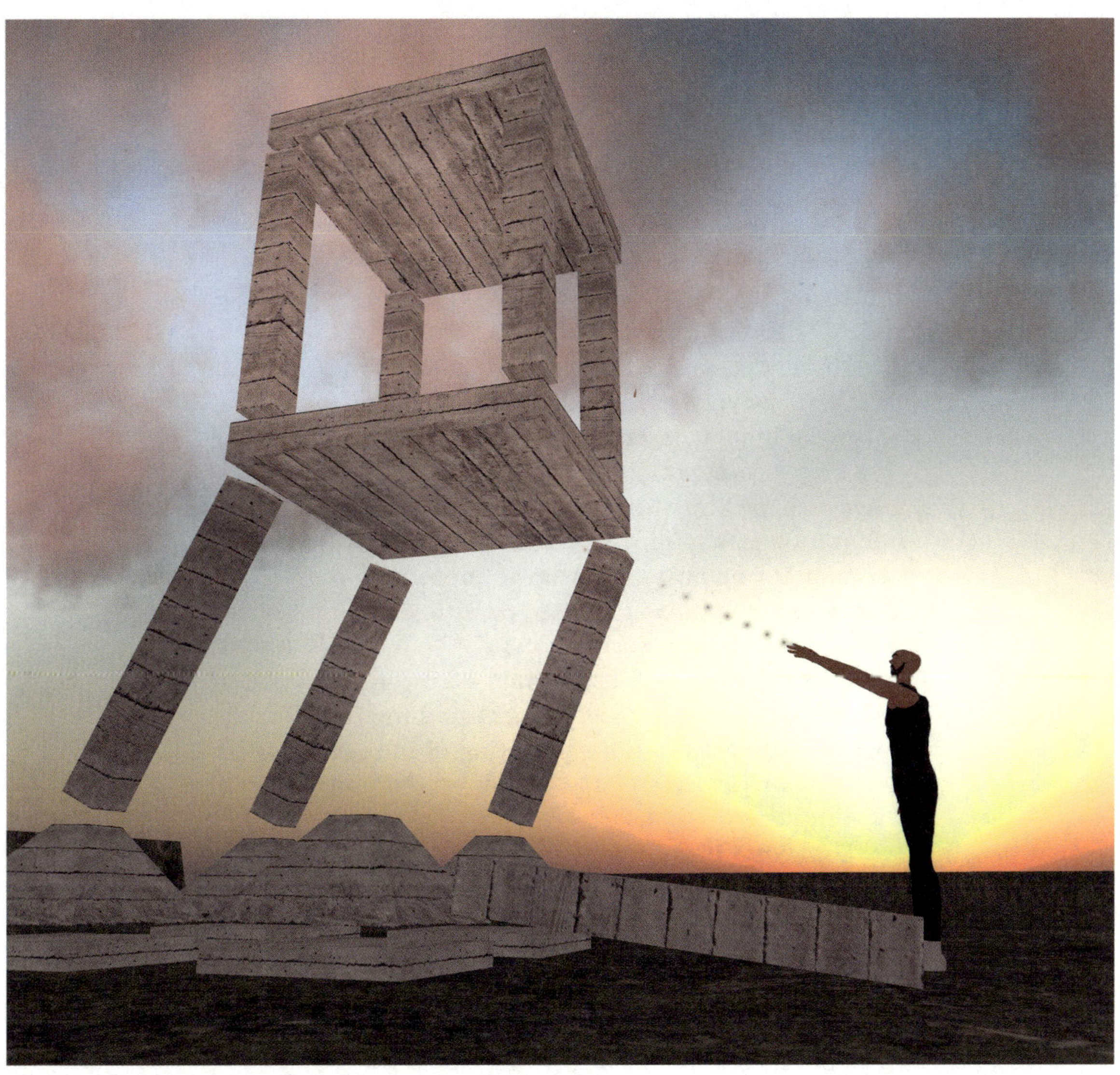

Building an electronic ruin, 2011, video still   cat. no. 1

A seminal work in the *arte povera* movement, *Direzione* (*Direction*) was first exhibited in Turin in late 1967 amid the tumult of student protests at the city's university. The work marked a new path that Giovanni Anselmo had taken just two years earlier, when he rejected the closed nature of his previous drawings and paintings in favor of a more open-ended art practice. No longer thinking of his art as "crystallized," Anselmo considered his new works as "devices" to reveal the "energy that surrounds us."

Direzione consists of a large, flat triangular slab of schist, a type of rock that is formed by metamorphism at high temperatures and under great pressure that aligns minerals into thin layers. A small compass embedded in the surface of the rock determines the orientation of the piece as it lies on the floor with its vertex pointing north. Anselmo's interest in rocks, like *arte povera*'s approach to materials in general, is in its transformative process and potential. The rock's matrix is, according to Anselmo, composed of "formerly vegetable or reptile or, at any rate, something organic and animated, before the transformation of the earth's crust buried many aspects of life and drew them away from the light."[1]

Direzione instantiates two earthly phenomena for the viewer: gravity through its sheer weight and the magnetic field to which the compass, and the otherwise inert work, responds. *Direzione* opens the reception and experience of art to the larger world, rendering the invisible visible. By revealing latent energies and invisible forces, it privileges the viewer's sensory perception and phenomenological experience. By doing so, the artist resists interpretive closure and uses material to connect both the object and its perceiving subject to worldly forces.

A.B.

1   Rosalind Krauss, "Giovanni Anselmo: Matter and Monochrome," *October*, vol. 124, Postwar Italian Art (Spring, 2008), 125–36.

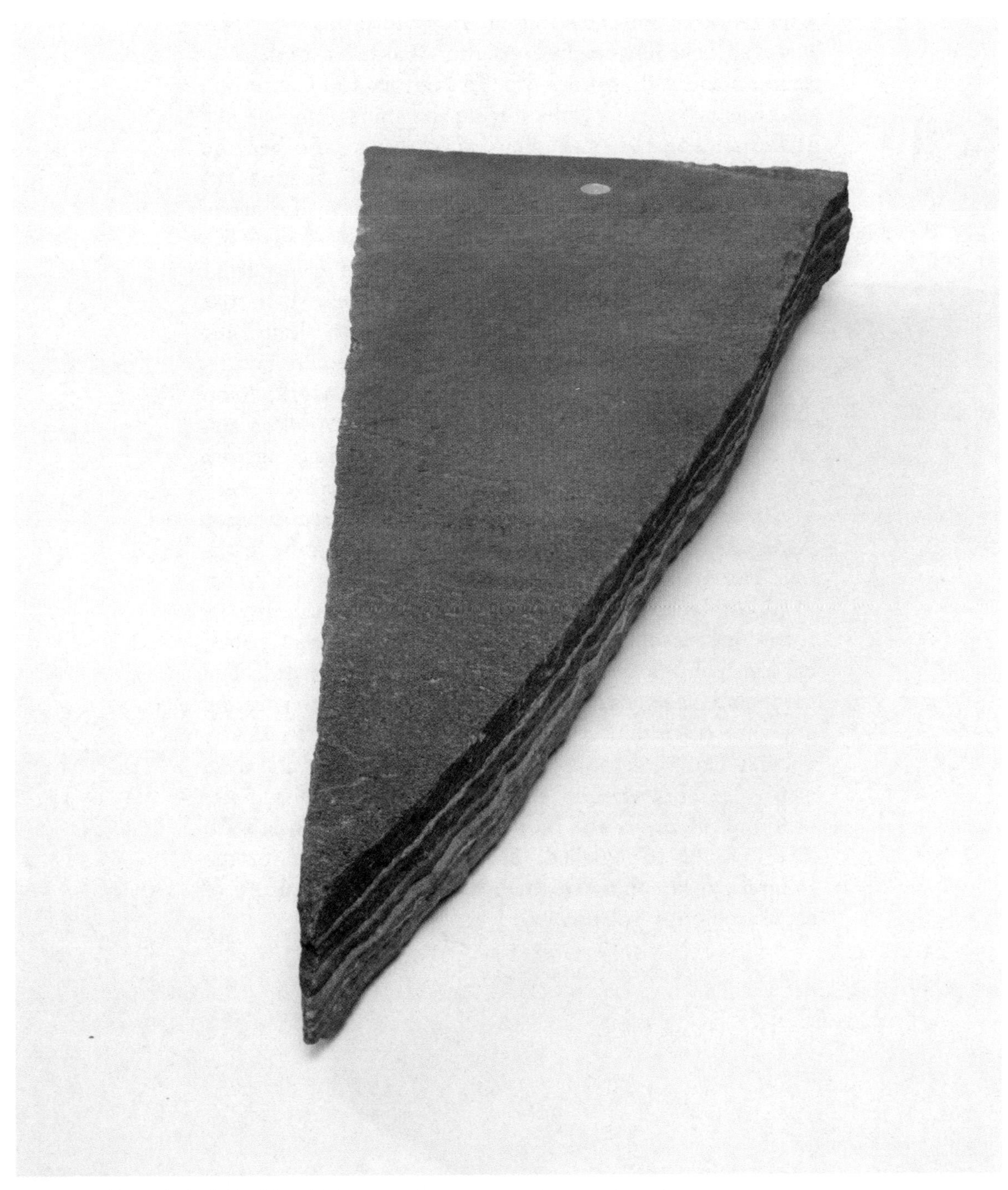

Direzione (*Direction*), 1967–70, schist, magnetic compass, glass   cat. no. 2

BELKIS AYÓN

The work of Belkis Ayón provides interpretive imagery that reveals insight into the Abakuá, a male-only secret society that originated in Nigeria and Cameroon and was brought to Cuba during the transatlantic slave trade (sixteenth to nineteenth century). Ayón became particularly interested in the history of Abakuá rituals while a student in the 1980s studying the art of Cuban cult culture. Even though others warned her about the serious implications that could result from her inquiry into private spiritual practices, the artist was able to learn intricate details about their historical and cultural mythologies and to create her own iconography based on their legends. Through her work, Ayón speculates and interprets the myths of the Abakuá and specifically identifies narratives of violence against women that are perpetuated by patriarchal power.

In the work *Ya estamos aquí* (*We are already here*), Ayón has rendered seven figures who appear to be in ritual. The artist's ability to work through various gradations of black, gray, and white is made possible by her technique of adhering and partially removing sandpaper, carbon, palm leaves, seaweed, and cut cardboard on a cardboard base. Ayón developed this technique during a severe economic collapse in Cuba referred to as the Special Period, a time when very few materials were available. This scarcity encouraged the improvised use of found materials and more distilled working methods. The layering of materials becomes a metaphor for the inherent opaqueness of the Abakuá and the culture of secret societies in Cuba.

T.R.A.

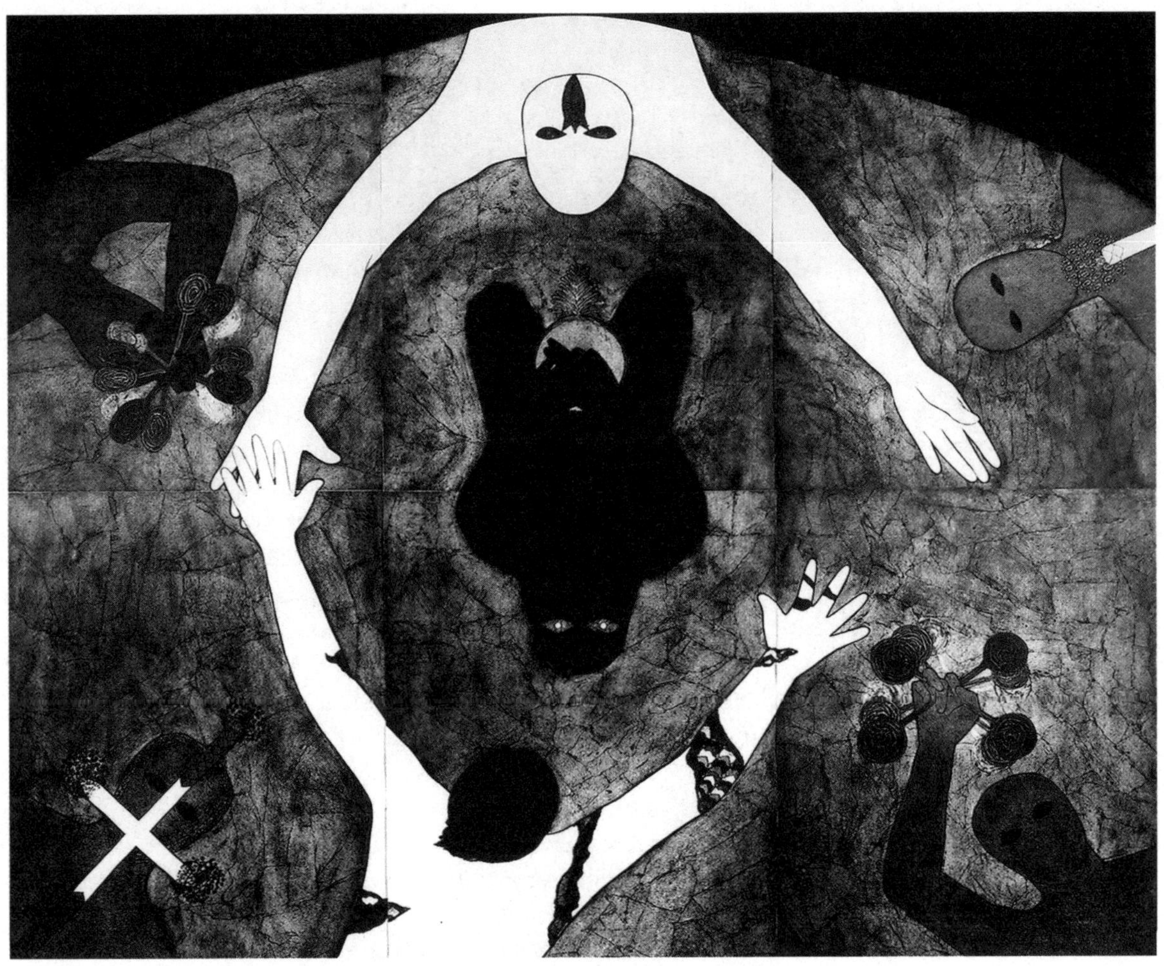

Ya estamos aquí (*We are already here*), 1991, collagraph   cat. no. 3

Although primarily a painter, Cay Bahnmiller had a lively and literate mind that extended her interests to music, literature, and history. Her kinetic assemblages reflect a myriad of influences. She often collaged fragments of text, found objects, and raw materials into her artwork, repurposing their meaning and associations with rich symbolism. *Der Imker* (*The Beekeeper*) is a mixed-media construction on wood that teems with autobiographical and historical references with heightened anxiety; the layering of material is so dense it hampers one's ability to make sense of it all. Populating this piece is the bric-a-brac she discovered at garage sales, secondhand stores, and while walking the streets of Detroit. A battered figurine of a foppish boy poised atop a shovel dominates the foreground at center, while to his left a light switch cover rests as a useless artifact. Spools of thread and yarn, suggestive of domesticity or women's work, are bound to the surface in a thick paste. Torn pages of poetry by Emily Dickinson, whom Bahnmiller adored, line the perimeter and hang inside; the assemblage acts as a barricade to protect her heroine from external forces.

Der Imker is likely a profound manifestation of trauma. Bahnmiller created the work immediately following a violent assault she experienced when walking alone one night on the streets of Detroit. There are potent emotional cues, starting with a message the artist scrawled in the upper right corner: "Just call me Lucky." This sentiment is reiterated in the poker chips that litter the work's caustic terrain. More broadly, the work is a personal expression of societal issues that plagued residents living in the city at the time.

R.M.

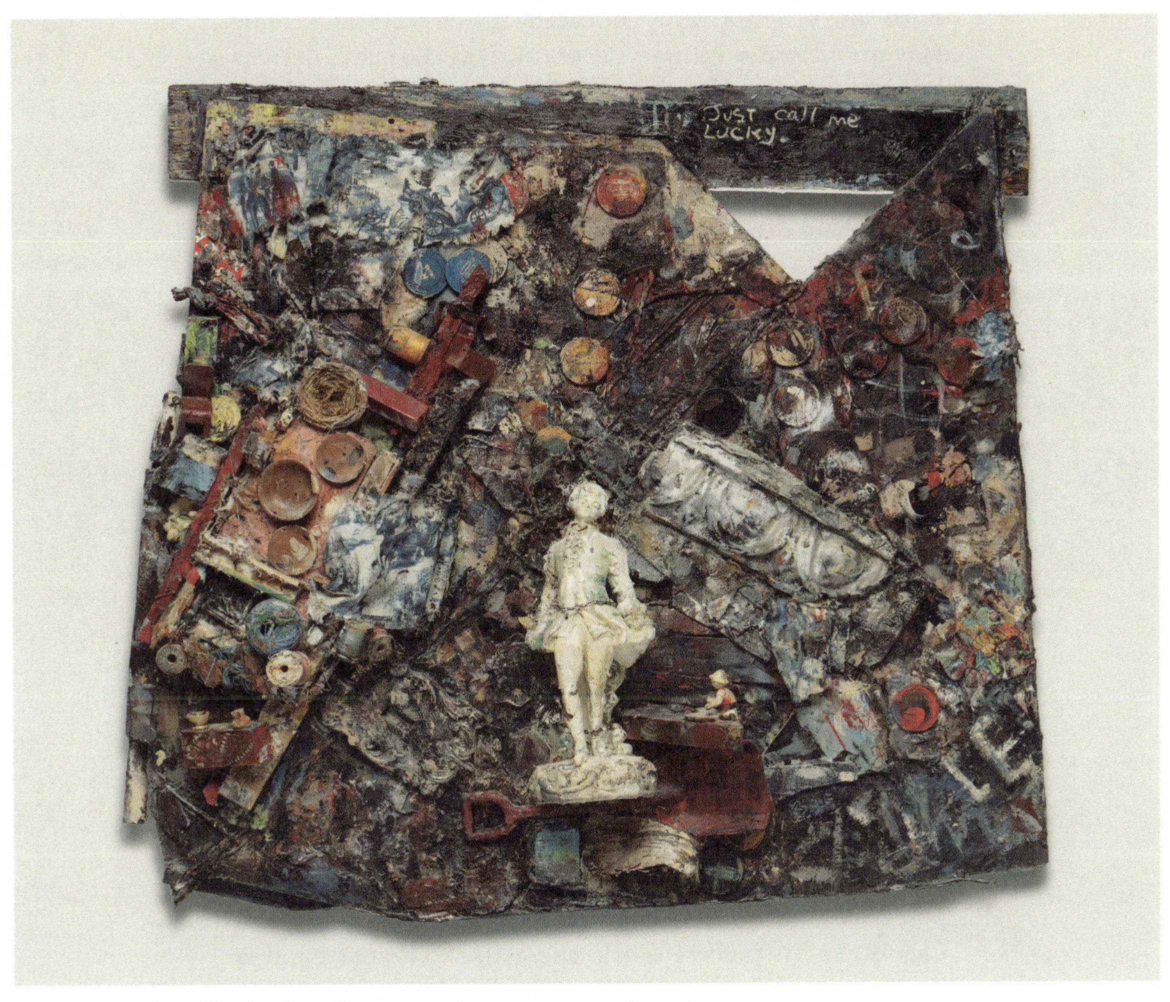

Der Imker, 1993–96, mixed media construction on wood   cat. no. 4

Born in Virginia and educated in Detroit and New Haven, interdisciplinary artist Kevin Beasley derives his creative impulses from US industrial histories, status symbols among black American youth, and sonic expressions that are birthed out of African American musical traditions. *Landlord Colors* presents a selection of works made in 2014 for which he took up the alchemical-like act of mixing polymer and a reactant to produce foam that he combined with resin and found objects. As an example of his monolithic inventions, *Untitled (chest pack)* is a seemingly deflated battery charger with cables extending from its case, reaching outward like two arms dangling onto the floor. Two additional works—*Untitled (street shirt one)* and *Untitled (street shirt two)*—use distressed clothing in combination with other materials, such as a pillowcase, a glove, and human spit.

Together, the works are assemblages of abandonment—evidence of a living world that once functioned rigorously and abundantly, but that is no longer active. As Beasley has shared, he "define[s] a critical facet of sculpture as its relationship to the body" and that he "never liked seeing sculpture hanging from the ceiling [because] it always pertains to an act of violence, given the history of lynching in America."[1] Beasley anticipates the unknowns that come along when audiences encounter his pieces. While the artist's labored hand is present, what is absent is the value to humanity of the object's initial use.

T.R.A.

1   Katherine Brinson, "Artist Kevin Beasley on Installing His Work at the Guggenheim," Guggenheim Museum Blog, August 26, 2015, https://www.guggenheim.org/blogs/checklist/artist-kevin-beasley-on -installing-his-work-at-the-guggenheim.

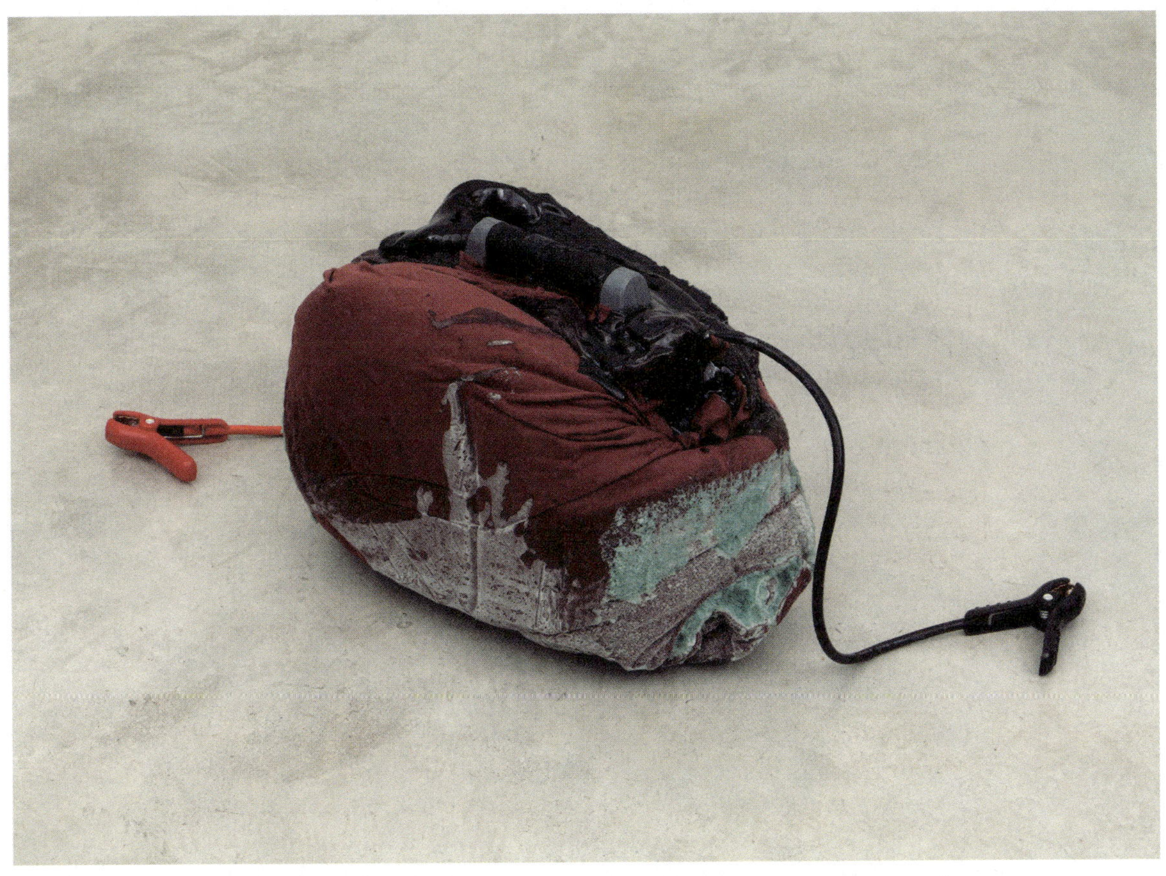

Untitled (chest pack), 2014, urethane foam, resin, long sleeve shirt, battery charger   cat. no. 5

El peso de la culpa (*The burden of guilt*) is one of Tania Bruguera's iconic works, originally performed at her home in 1997 at the same time as the Sixth Biennial of Havana. It has since been restaged in different parts of the world. As the audience entered the space, Bruguera stood barefoot with a dead sheep wrapped around her neck and a Cuban flag woven with human hair hanging behind her. The performance consisted of the artist drinking small amounts of soil mixed with water, which references a pre-Columbian suicide ritual. Bruguera explains, "Eating earth, which is sacred and a symbol of permanence, is like swallowing one's own traditions, one's own heritage, it's like erasing oneself. It's electing suicide. What I did was take this historical anecdote and update it to the present."[1] At its core, the piece is a political comment on Cuba's precarious economic situation during the 1990s, during which food shortages reached such height that a popular local saying developed: "We are eating soil." The phrase comes from the context of the Special Period, when the Soviet economy that supported Cuba disappeared and the country was defenseless in the face of the international market and its sanctions.

The piece emerged from a time when Cuban-born artist Ana Mendieta was a central influence on Bruguera's thinking and methodology, as seen in her intersection of earth and body as material. Both artists conjure mythic and metaphoric ties to the natural world as a way to negotiate societal conditions of displacement, identity, and subjugation. Bruguera extends her investment in the human condition into activism, as evident in her "Manifesto on Artists' Rights" presented to the United Nations in 2012, and exhibited as part of *Landlord Colors*.

A.G.F., L.M.

1   Octavio Zaya, *Cuba: los mapas del deseo* (Vienna: Kunsthalle Wien, 1999), 239–57.

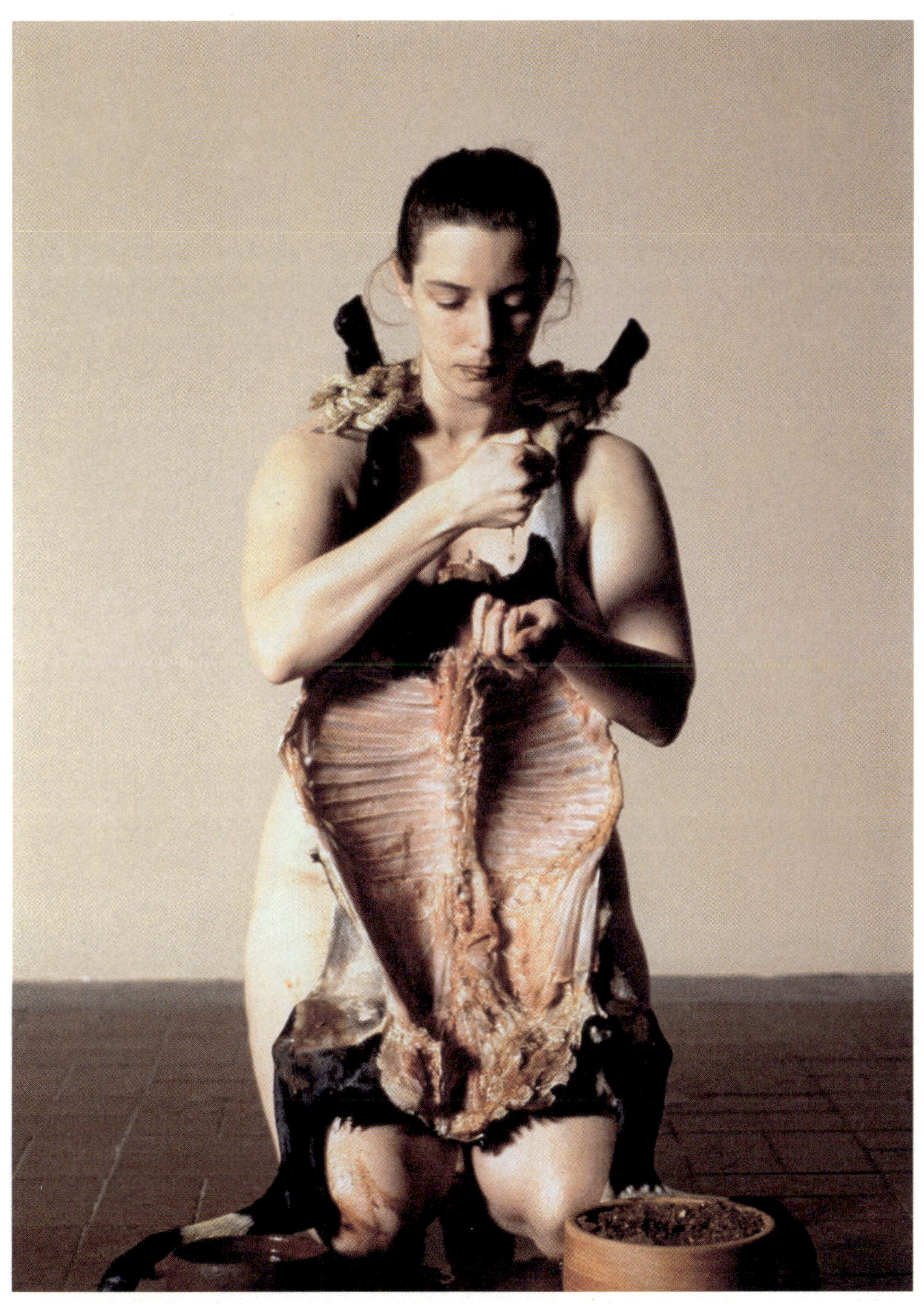

El peso de la culpa (*The burden of guilt*), 1999, photograph, performance documentation   cat. no. 8

TANIA BRUGUERA

MANIFESTO
ON ARTISTS' RIGHTS

*Originally presented at the United Nations in Geneva,
Switzerland, December 6, 2012.*

Art is not a luxury. Art is
a basic social need to which
everyone has a right.

Art is a way of building
thought, of being aware of oneself and of others at the same
time. It is a methodology
in constant transformation for
the search of a here and now.

Art is an invitation to questioning; it is the social
place of doubt, of wanting
to understand and wanting to
change reality.

Art is not only a statement of
the present, it is also a call
for a different future, a better
one. Therefore, it is a right
not only to enjoy art, but to
be able to create it.

Art is a common good that
does not have to be entirely
understood in the moment one
finds it.

Art is a space of vulnerability
from which what is social

is deconstructed to construct
what is human.

Artists not only have the
right to dissent, but the duty
to do so.

Artists have the right to dissent not only from affective,
moral, philosophical, or
cultural aspects, but also from
economic and political ones.

Artists have the right to
disagree with power, with the
status quo.

Artists have the right to be
respected and protected when
they dissent.

The governments of nations where
artists work have the duty
to protect their right to dissent because that is their
social function: to question and
address what is difficult to
confront.

Without the possibility to dissent, an artist becomes an

administrator of technical goods, behaves like a consumption manufacturer and transforms into a jester. It is a sad society where this is all social awareness creates.

Artists also have the right to be understood in the complexity of their dissent. An artist should not be judged first and discussed later. Artists should not be sent to jail because of proposing a "different" reality, for sharing their ideas, for wanting to strike up a conversation on the way the present unfolds. If the artist's proposal is not understood, it should be discussed by all, not censored by a few.

If one publicly expresses and evinces ideas in a different way from that of those in power, governments, corporations and religious institutions too easily declare that one is irresponsible, wanting to use guilt and incite the masses to violent reactions as their best defense strategy, instead of processing criticism and calling for public debate. Nothing justifies the use of violence against an idea or the person suggesting it.

Governments have the duty to provide a space for self-criticism in which they are accountable for their actions, a space where the people can question them. No government is infallible; no human being—even if elected—has the right to talk for all the citizens. No social solution is permanent, and it

is the artists who have the opportunity and the duty to suggest the imagery of other social alternatives, of using their communication tools from a space of sensitive responsibility.

Artists suggest a meta-reality, a potential future to be experienced in the present. They suggest experimenting a moment which has not yet arrived, a situation of "what if that were this way." Therefore, they cannot be judged from spaces in the past, from laws trying to preserve what is already established.

Governments must stop fearing ideas.

Governments, corporations (today they are like alternative governments), and religious institutions are not the only ones with a right to build a future; this is the right of citizens, and artists are active citizens. That is why artists have the right and the responsibility not only to think up a different and better world, but to try to build it.

Artists have the right to be artivists (part artists/ part activists), because they are an active part of civil society, because art is a safe space from which people can debate, interpret, build, and educate. This space must be defended because it benefits us all: art is a social tool.

Governments should not control art and artists. They should protect them.

Artists have the right not to be censored when gestating their work or during the research process of conceiving it. Artists have the right to create the work they want to create, with no limits; they have the duty to be responsible without self-censorship.

Society has the right to have its public spaces as spaces for creativity and artistic expression, since they also are collective spaces for knowledge and debate. Public space belongs to civic society, not to governments, corporations, or religious institutions.

Freedom of artistic expression does not emerge spontaneously. It is something one learns to reach, leaving behind pressure, emotional blackmail, censorship, and self-censorship. This is a difficult process that should be respected and appreciated.

Artistic censorship not only affects artists but the community as well, because it creates an atmosphere of fear and self-censorship paralyzing the possibility of exercising critical thinking.

To think differently from those in power does not make you irresponsible.

In moments of high sensitivity (wars, legislative changes, political transitions), it is the duty of the government to protect and guarantee dissident, questioning voices, because these are moments in which one cannot do away with rationality and critical thought, and it is sometimes only through art that many emerging ideas can make a public appearance. Without dissent there is no chance of progress.

Socially committed artists talk about difficult moments, deal with sensitive topics, but, unlike journalists, they have no legal protection when doing their work. Unlike corporations, they have no significant economic backing. Unlike governments, they have no political power. Art is a social work based on a practice that makes artists vulnerable and, as is the case with journalists, corporations, and governmental or religious institutions, they have the right to be protected because they are doing a public service.

The right to decide the value of an artistic statement is not a right of those in power. It is not the right of governments, of corporations, of religious institutions to define what art is. It is the right of artists to define what art is for them.

Art is a complex product without a single and final interpretation. Artists have the right not to have their oeuvre reduced or simplified as a schematic interpretation which may be manipulated by those in power to provoke and, consequently, result in public offenses directed to the artists, so as to invalidate their proposals.

To create a space for dialogue and not for violence against works of art questioning established ideas and realities, governments should provide educational platforms from which artistic practice may be better understood.

We must be cautious about the increasing criminalization of socially committed artistic creation under the rationale of national security and the need to control information because of political reasons with the purpose of censuring artists.

There are many types of strategies for political censorship. Political censorship is not only exercised through direct political pressure, but through censuring the access to economic support, creating a bureaucratic censorship postponing production processes, marginalizing the visibility of a project by drawing artists away from legitimization and distribution circuits; controlling the right to travel, deciding who has the right to talk on what subjects; and, at times, even using "popular sensitivity" as censorship. All these are decisions taken and conducted from political power so as not to be challenged.

On the other hand, there are artists who are internationally acknowledged and admired because of being artivists in their countries of origin and who, at a given time, for one reason or another, migrate and establish themselves temporarily in other countries where they find a new type of censorship, a censorship that relegates, pigeonholes, and sets them inside a limited mental geography where they are only allowed to talk critically of the country they come from and not the country to which they have arrived. This is a situation of censorship in which artists are relegated to being uni-dimensionally political: a used political object.

The process of discovering a different society, the inner negotiation required to understand the place of arrival and the place one has left, is inherent to the contemporary condition, which is, increasingly, a migrant condition. This is a condition that artists embody and on which they have the right to express. After all, a national culture is the hybridization of the image those who do not live in the country have of it and all present day-by-day build, wherever they have originally come from.

We cannot ask artists, whose work is to question society, to keep silent and resort to self-censorship once they cross a territorial border.

Artists have the right not to
be fragmented as human beings
or as social beings.

Artistic expression is a space
to challenge meanings, to defy
what is imaginable. This is
what, as times goes by, is recognized as culture.

A society with freedom of artistic expression is a healthier
society. It is a society where
citizens allow themselves to
dream of a better world where
they have a place. It is a society that expresses itself better, because it expresses itself
in its entire complexity.

There is no other type of
practice in the public sphere
providing the qualities of
the space created by art.
That is why this space must
be protected.

Governments have the duty to
protect all their citizens,
including those who may be considered uncomfortable because
they question government
or what is socially established.

Critical thinking is a civic
right that becomes evident
in artistic practices. That
is why, when threatened,
we should not talk of censorship, but of the violation
of artists' rights.

JAMES LEE BYARS

The Death of James Lee Byars (1982/94) is a performance the artist created to presage his departure from the earthly plane: a gold-leafed room, glass sarcophagus, five crystals, and the instructions: "quietly lie down and quietly get up." In many ways, his entire artistic practice was predicated on unhinging from his physical self, and his infamy became more dominant than any artwork he produced. He was the beneficiary of many contradicting descriptors, all somewhat true: a nomadic seer, a dandified trickster, a minimalist mystic. However, he was born flesh and blood in Detroit in 1932, growing up in what was once Paradise Valley, a low-income neighborhood that has few remaining landmarks from that time. Later, he attended Wayne State University and studied philosophy and art. It is said for his senior thesis in 1955 that Byars made an installation of large stones inside his family home after removing the doors, windows, and furniture. Several years later in 1958, he saw a Mark Rothko painting at Cranbrook Art Museum that led him to hitchhike to New York City to meet the artist. He landed at the Museum of Modern Art, where upon arrival with his portfolio in hand, a curator instantly purchased two drawings for the collection.[1] Suspicious and captivating, Byars' life and art practice continues to span the world, reading like an epic novel, until his final end in Egypt in 1997—the mortal one at least.

Gold is a dominant material within Byars' oeuvre, and he often wore reflective gold suits in his performances: the phantasmagoric Detroit hustler. *The Philosophical Nail* is a reliquary sanctifying a gold-leafed nail and offering potent conceptual threads that are surprisingly parallel. The splendor of the world, the desire of man: gold conjures up references as fantastical as alchemy and as practical as its universal role as economic currency—it is deathless in this regard. Ubiquitous instead of rare, the nail is essential to build everything that surrounds us, yet it also acts as the tool that incites transcendence beyond our corporeal bodies, through the coffin or the cross.

L.M.

1   James Elliot, *The Perfect Thought: The Works of James Lee Byars* (Berkeley: University of California Press, 1990), 72–73.

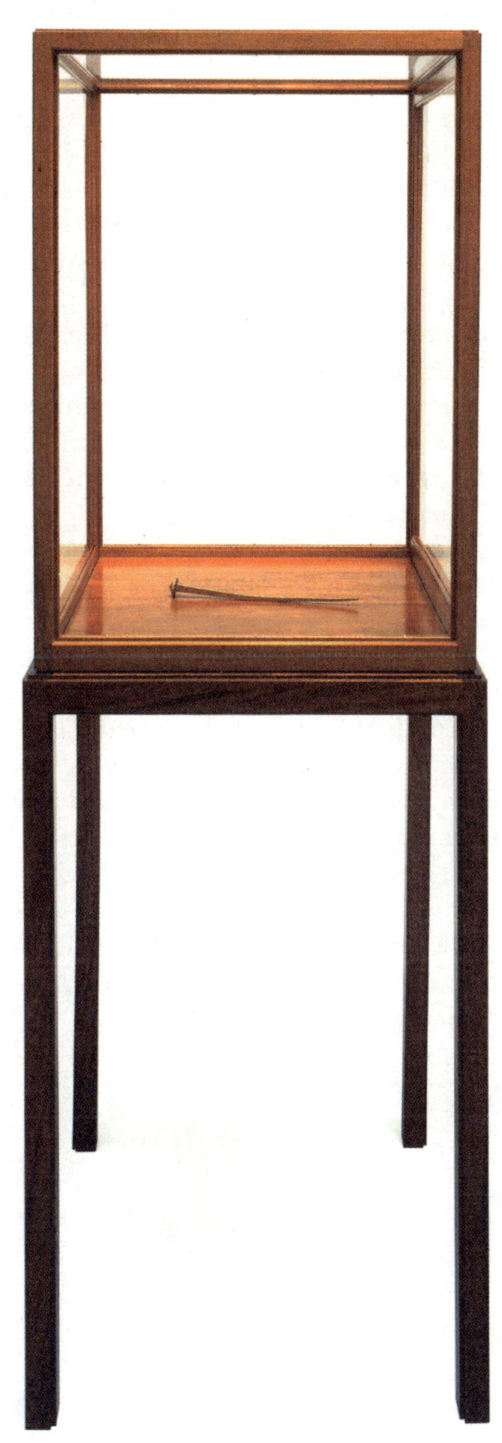

The Philosophical Nail, 1986, gilded iron   cat. no. 10

PIER PAOLO CALZOLARI

Rife with material experimentation since the 1960s, Pier Paolo Calzolari's expansive practice, like the mischievous Roman gods, tests nature's power to enact transformation. Working across multiple disciplines, he has sourced fire, ice, and air through their human-corralled equivalents: kerosene, Freon, and helium balloons. He often pairs the organic with the technological to set up narrative encounters that emerge from their adjacent associations. These evocative material compositions elicit an experience of the familiar, and yet uncanny, through the isolation of what is both mundane and essential to the human experience. Dichotomies emerge—the natural and industrial, the elemental and manufactured, the temporal and permanent—that alternately lend themselves to legible and poetic interpretations.

In *Non (studio per grande opera "Non")*, the neon tubing relays a dissonant statement against a single tobacco leaf. Neither terse nor emphatic (lacking capitalization and punctuation) the informal script and its central placement suggest a rumination on itself: I am not natural. Where the fluorescent light illuminates the leaf's desiccation and alludes to its eventual disintegration, the fibrous material's curling form cradles the industrial element. Yet, tobacco itself is a divisive material, a natural resource cultivated by a global industry to propagate indulgence and dependence. Nature always keeps its own autonomy—it exists with or without us. However, we might regard both materials with equal distrust.

L.M., I.G.W.

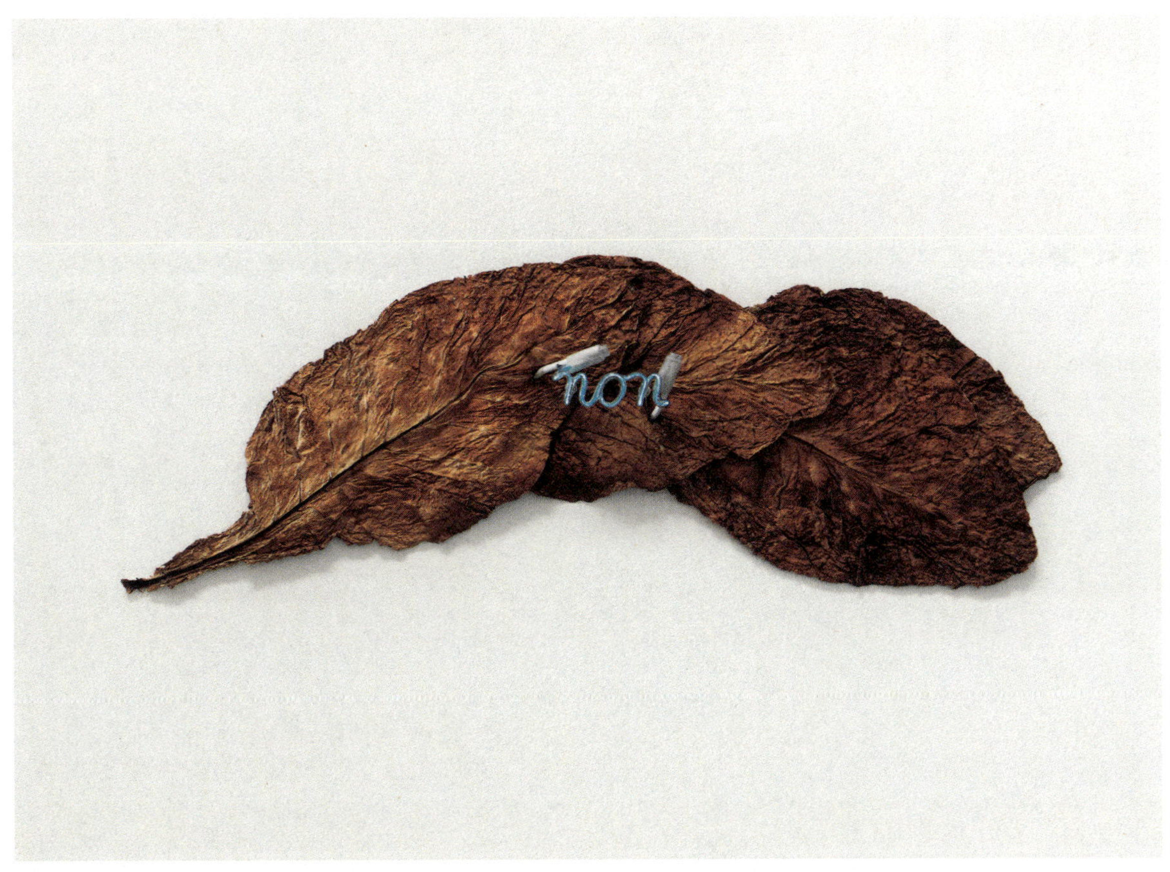

Non (studio per grande opera "Non"), 1969–70, Virginia tobacco leaves, blue fluorescent tubes, transformer   cat. no. 11

YOAN CAPOTE

While many artists of his generation fled the country, Havana native Yoan Capote chose to remain in Cuba through the Special Period of the 1990s, learning how to adjust and thrive within its constraints.

For *Island (see-escape)*, Capote selected a material found in abundance on the island—fishhooks—tapping into both the fishing tradition of Cuba and its recycling culture. Sorting hooks for his father during his childhood, the artist's personal experience is also a common one. At first glance the work is a traditional seascape, one of many representations of the sea in Cuban art. It is only upon close inspection that one sees the dramatic waves are dangerously sharp. With a team of assistants, Capote laid out approximately 500,000 fishhooks to compose the sea, incorporating collective labor into the creative process to depict the Cuban condition. The romantic image abruptly dissolves into peril; the open waters turn into an impassable border.

The work reveals the two-sided nature of Cuba's relationship to the sea, both physically and metaphorically. The sea provides a primary source of food for the island, but it is also the dangerous course many migrants have taken for a freedom that lies beyond. The panoramic seascape cultivates a common material to create a conceptual portrait of Cuba. *Island (see-escape)* portrays intimate and collective fears, becoming a political stance and a powerful ode to the resilience of the Cuban people.

L.C., L.M.

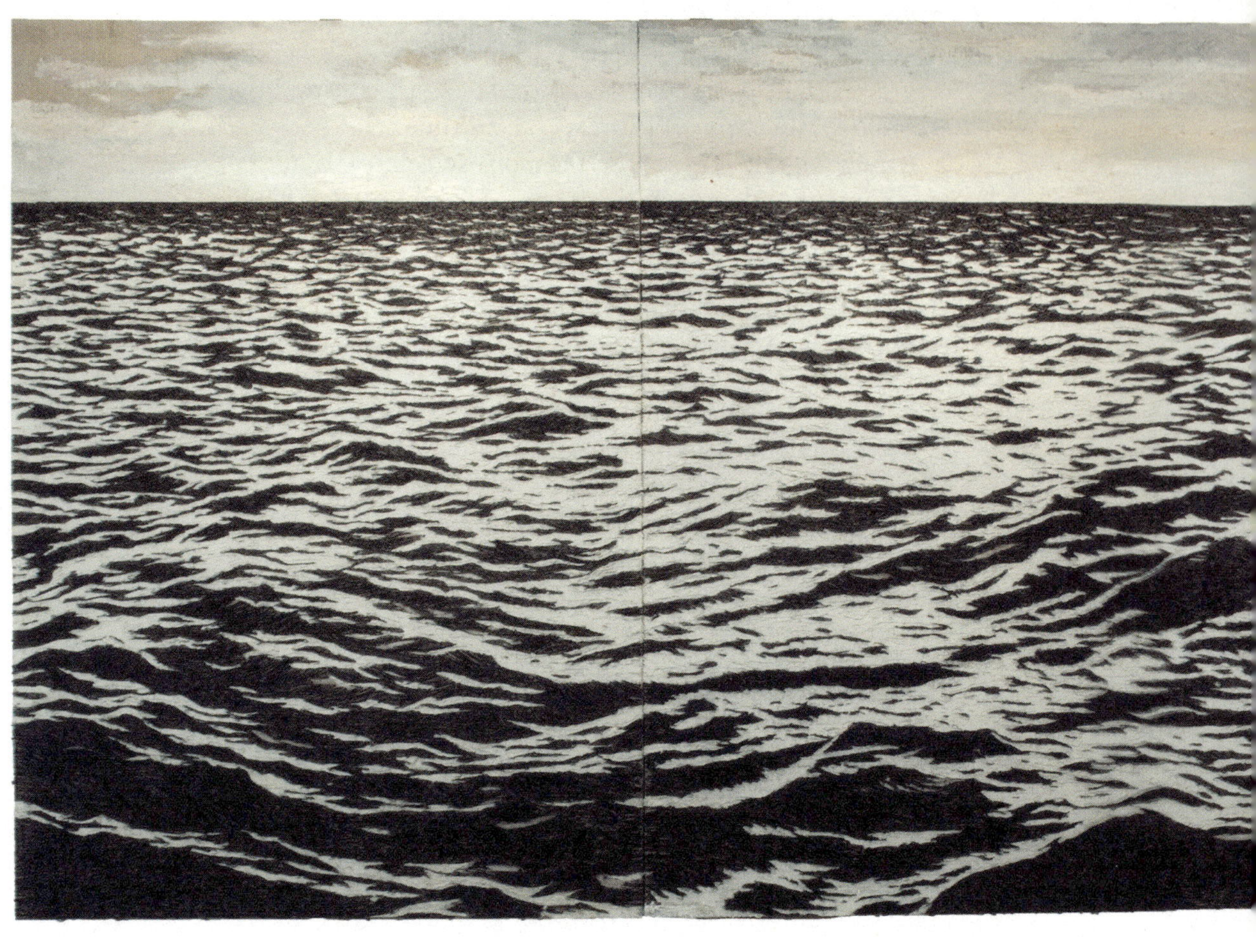

Yoan Capote, *Island (see-escape)*, 2010, oil, nails, fish hooks on jute on panel   cat. no. 12

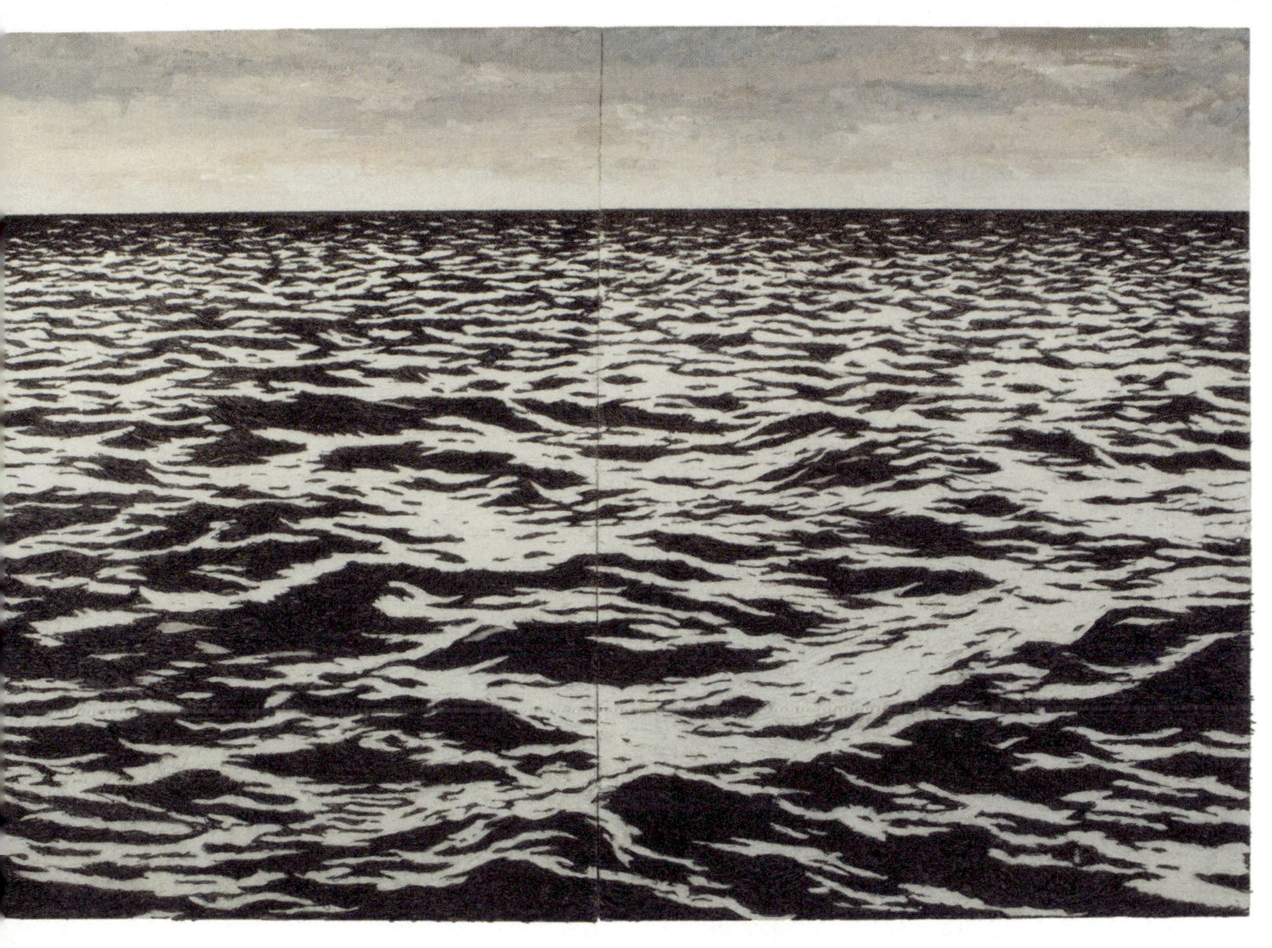

Elizabet Cerviño operates across all media disciplines that relate back to the body, her own or its proxy. As she explains, "Depending on the idea, the body can be performance, environment, installation, object, 'painting,' or just a gesture that tries to say a word and ends-up in a sound."[1] Cerviño's performative lineage begins with the rituals of the earliest civilizations and extends to her direct forebears of performance art, such as Janine Antoni, Carolee Schneemann, and Ana Mendieta. Her works are often driven by a mediation with natural materials using gestures that are subtle and fragile to create a contemplative space for the audience. Her choreography is often cursory and action-oriented, relying on the surrounding context for meaning. For instance, previous "scripts" simply direct her body's entrance and departure from an artwork:

> *Stand Up or Change Posture*: After 13 minutes partially covered with dirt from the earth, I stand up, and once I've taken a standing position, I keep that posture for a while and then I leave.

> *Rest*: Seated on a chair, my whole naked body has been covered with red brick powder that almost imperceptibly falls. For an hour I breathe, simulating a desert landscape, until I rise up.

As a Cuban artist, notions of absence and presence, the visible and invisible, are potent themes in relation to national identity. In addition to displaying one of her large-scale paintings with a surface oxidized by iron, Cerviño creates a performance for *Landlord Colors* dedicated to the ephemeral nature of material, including the body.

L.M.

1   Elizabet Cerviño, artist statement, 2019

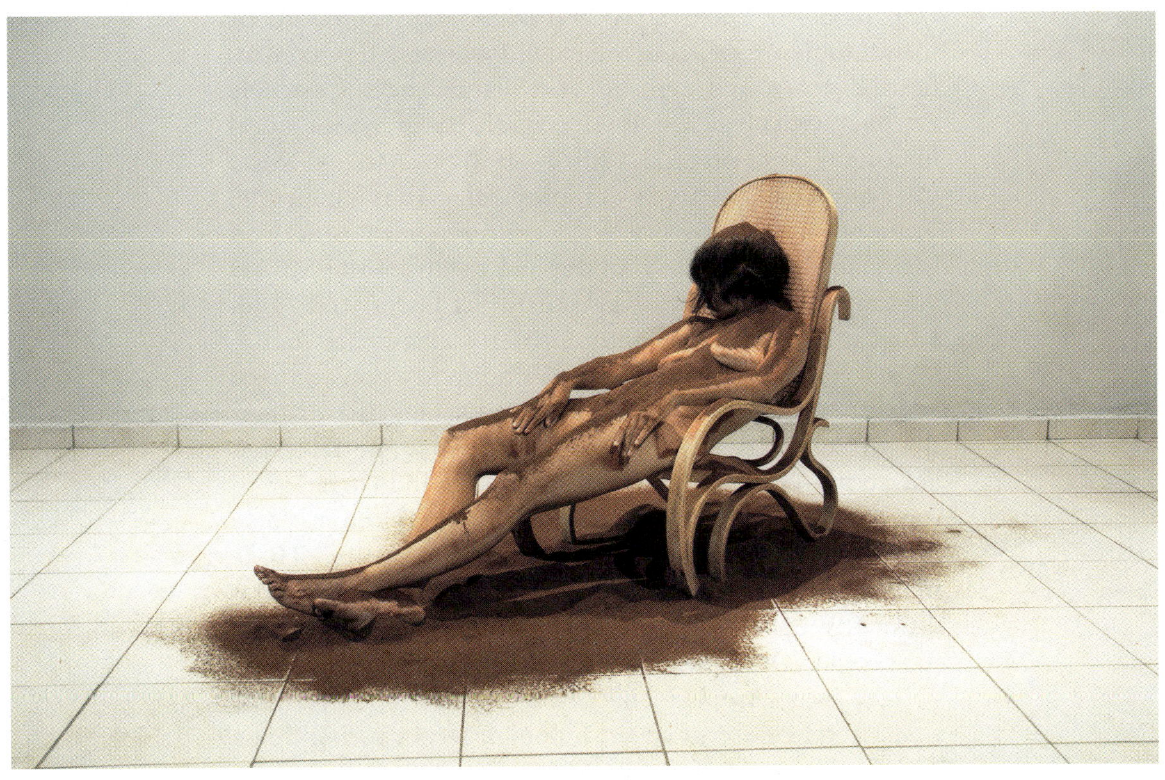

Descanso (Rest), 2010–11, photograph, performance documentation

Iron Teaching Rocks How to Rust, a large-scale outdoor installation made from discarded objects, has continuously grown and evolved on Detroit's near west side for over two decades. In the tradition of griots—oral historians and cultural leaders in West Africa—artist Olayami Dabls weaves complex tales that blend 500 years of African history with contemporary American life. Dabls, who is the founder and owner of the MBAD African Bead Museum, has transformed nearly one-and-a-half city blocks and four formerly abandoned buildings with his site-specific environment, now dubbed "African Town" by the community. The artist primarily works with four highly evocative materials that are common in the city's natural and industrial environment: rock, iron, wood, and mirror. They are also imbued with meaning in African spirituality. These materials relate to the African *Nkisi* figure, which traditionally serves as a totem protecting a village and its people. Dabls uses them to transfigure inanimate objects into complex characters in an elaborate fable that stretches across several plots of land overlooking a major urban freeway in the Motor City.

The installation is an eighteen-part story of the colonization, assimilation, and deterioration of African culture in the United States. In such early vignettes as *Iron Tried to Trick the Young Artist* and *Iron Teaching Rocks Table Manners,* iron symbolizes the European oppressor and is also a representation of the industrialization of Detroit. Lessons about the precarious nature of language, knowledge, and identity unfold across the sprawling installation.

R.M.

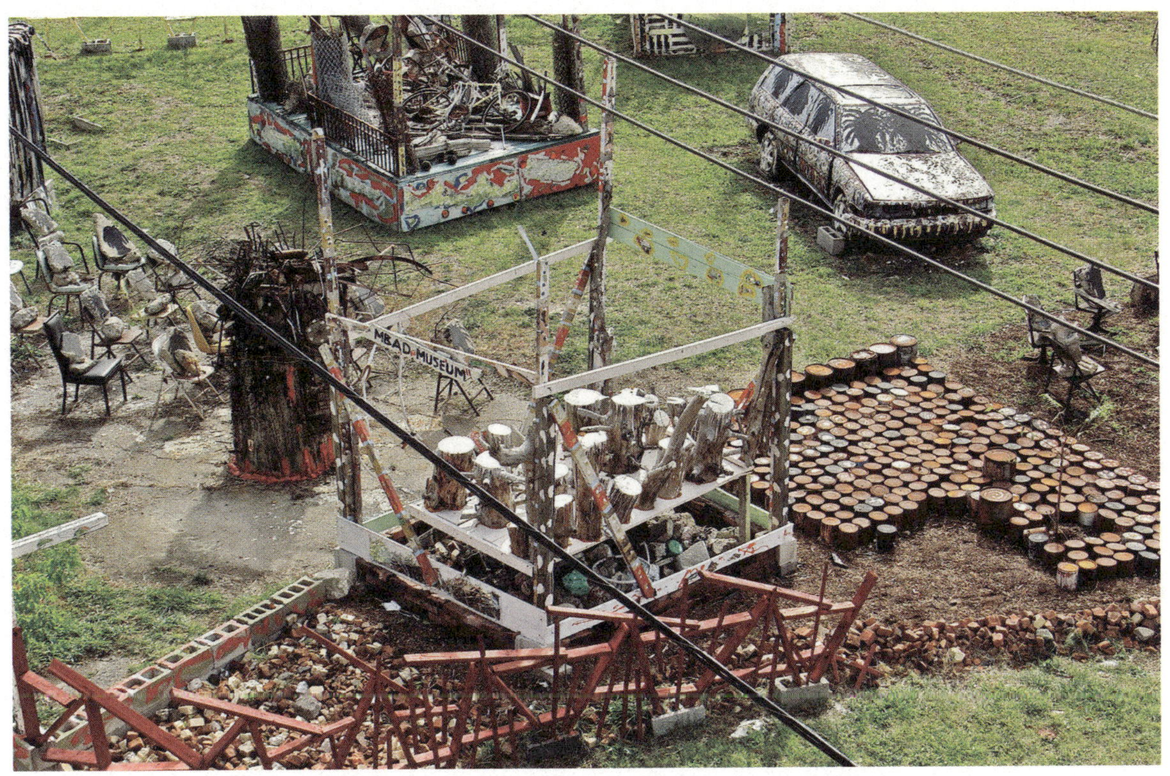

Iron Teaching Rocks How To Rust (detail), 2000–present, iron, rock, wood, mirror, paint

RICCARDO DALISI

Riccardo Dalisi is an architect, designer, and artist invested in disrupting calcified modes of creating and experiencing space. A student in Naples under the tutelage of architect Francesco Della Sala, he emerged in the midst of the disintegration of rationalist modern architecture in Italy. Dalisi was a participant in the Italian radical architectural scene of the 1960s and early 1970s, becoming a leading voice in the discipline's development parallel to the Italian *arte povera* initiative. In 1973, he co-founded the Global Tools initiative that explored design's potential as a retort to the burgeoning success of modern Italian design and the human indifference of contemporary design. A part of the "anti-design" debate, he argued for imagination as the creative force in space-building rather than consumerist or functionalist interests.

Following the 1972 publication of his seminal text "La tecnica povera in rivolta" ("The poor technique of revolt") in the journal *Casabella*, he began a series of design experiments in communities across Naples. Often incorporating folklore, historical materials, and a childlike perspective into his design and sculptural practice, Dalisi's disruptive works seek to produce an "architecture of unpredictability." Initiating a sociological experiment, he collaborated with Neapolitan children from working-class neighborhoods. Using models designed by his architectural students, he encouraged the children to make their own objects and to take ownership of their interpretations. Their ensuing creations, born out of cheap—or poor—materials, privileged the relational over the functional. These objects upend capitalist experiences of space and spatial design by foregrounding the experience of making. Dalisi's instructions for creating papier-mâché chairs with kids from Naples in the early 1970s will be resurrected and a new chair will be created for this exhibition with children from Pontiac, Michigan.

A.B., I.G.W.

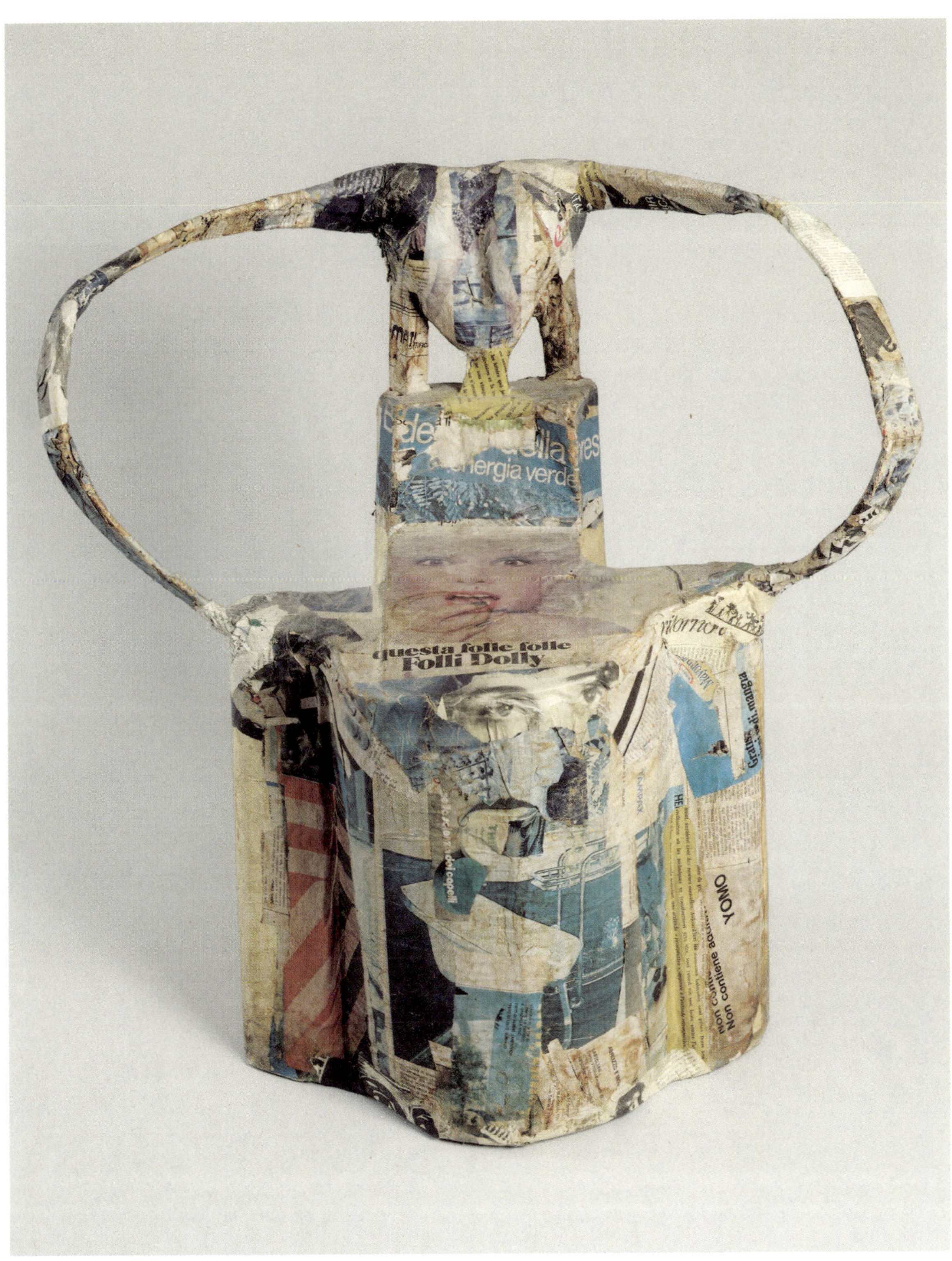

Trône (*Throne*), 1973, paper, glue, wood

MINIMAL TECHNOLOGY:
The Function of the Approximate in the Universe of Precision

Originally published in Casabella, *no. 386, February 1974, 43–45, in participation with Filippo Alison and Dino Rossi.*

Immense egg shells, tensi-structures, blown-up coverings, mobile homes, orientable environments, transportable villages, ecological films, pulsating diaphragms, flexible forms, spaces like interchangeable clothing, starry spaces, the sputnik, etc., etc. One has the impression that the relationship between "possible" and "imaginable" is being turned around, that what is possible will in the end engulf what is unimaginable.

Despite the levels that have been reached, in addition to the euphoria of the "precision mentality," there is a growing criticism and justified preoccupation. The technological machine is creating at least as many problems as it is capable of solving. To its expansion there corresponds a progressive destruction of the "approximate," of everything which, over the centuries, has been built, from the most minute furnishing to the city, the landscape.

Technological development can do many things, but it has been demonstrated that its historical function is closely tied to the ways it is managed, to its objectives, to its immediate and long-range goals. Where such technological development is not linked to the fundamental objective of the advancement of man and of his actual emancipation, there advances a special form of alienation.

But the solution is not only in the possibility of precautionary checks, in the total strategy of goals, in the basic political notions. The solution also lies in the preparation of suitable methods and systems in a series of disciplines and of orientations capable of keeping the central core of problems in focus. There is no sense

in isolating, even for a limited
time, the technological debate
from the debate on the fundamental questions: for what purpose and why. There is no sense
in keeping the "new" strictly
distinct from the "old," as if
they were separable categories,
nor is it meaningful to divide
production from use, the export
from the common man, advanced
technology from everyday's
technology. If one keeps these
polarities clearly in mind, the
miraculous, almost adventurous
aspect of certain modern technologies disappears from that
emotional surface of the collective imagination which speculation and profit often employ.

The efforts of technological
research concerning results must
be accompanied each step of the
way by the effort to perfect the
goals and to discover adequate
means of enlarged participation.

If we don't separate the
euphoria of the "new" from the
study of that which is "minimal," then will essential and
definite distinctions emerge
which touch, at bottom, problems
of another order. Suspension
bridges, tensistructures, special reticula were already
known, in their elementary principles, among primitive peoples.
The "new" is neither in the
discovery of constructive principles, nor in the quantitative
proportion, nor in the spa-
tial-figurative concept. The
whole gamut of the centuries and
the countries of the world are
dotted with extraordinary works.
What is new is that breath
or "precision," clarified

by Koyre, which the ancients
refused to follow. It is in
mechanized systems that there is
established between product
and producer, between product
and user, a distance strewn with
an ever larger chain of inter-
mediaries. In this unbridgeable
gap man becomes a passive consumer, and the technological
designer becomes a link between
the productivity of profit and
the consensus-makers, the hidden
persuaders, and the moulders
of false needs. But the study
of the ancient or of the primitive is transformed into a
reflexion on our profound needs,
and on the possibility of dis-
tinguishing parallel modes of
technological research.

One is aware of the need to
insert, between technological
research and the study of antiquity, an attitude of radical
inquiry, a concentrated reflection on the force of participation, on the communal capacities
of creativity and on the free
development of the imaginative
intelligence.

To return to an almost ritual
state of research, of research
united to the social-therapeutic
force of creative work—this
is not a need of the so-called
avant-garde alone.

The myth reminds us that
the search for the proper steel
for the sword of Siegfried was
relentless, and that this search
was carried out using the
primeval forces of the earth
(the dwarves), in the deep
caves. When one speaks of
removing myth, of demystification, the reference is to the

superficial aspect, to the hypnotic power of form and of the technological level, to the danger of falling into psychologically aberrant cult forms.

The mythical virtue to which I referred is the maximum level of consciousness of a problem where results and goals, emotion and reason, individual virtue and communal power are equally present. "Radical" or "minimal" technology aims at being such a moment of synthesis: the material value of technology, a theoretical value identified with manual work, with the "sensuousness" of creative force, the communal potency of creative work. To use a material in its elemental state, such as a leaf of a newspaper, a piece of obsolete wood is in some sense to rediscover its hidden, less artificial virtue. Together with new materials, through an intensive research operation one can reestablish contact with the original value of matter from which derive work and form, productivity and language.

Athens-based artist Dora Economou relies on explorations of scholarly territories—art history, literature, economy—in relation to physical ones—the street, the city, the island. Part of her process is making her way through the world with a heightened perception, open to the potential of objects she discovers in her path. She explains, "I don't go out scavenging for things, they find me. But it takes a certain learned skill to get to recognize them…. Trials leave traces of memories on matter. In crime series, the forensic surgeon reconstructs the crime and recovers the murderer by tracing evidence of the lethal weapon on the tissue around the wound. Technically, there can be no murder without a body, but I could be a murderer without committing a crime."[1]

THE HORROR, THE HORROR is a seemingly jovial object of a crudely sculpted lemon in bright yellow, an extension of an earlier work, *The dark, the dark*. The title undermines the aesthetic and asks us to question further; in fact, they are the last words of the dying antagonist Kurtz in *Heart of Darkness*, Joseph Conrad's novel on the cruelty of imperialism. The sculpture is made of pumice stone that Economou collected from Gyali, a small island in Greece converted into a quarry that is the main source of income for Nisyros, the main island nearby. The pumice quarry is leased by a French company and is one of many examples in which Greece's natural resources are leveraged financially for their European neighbors, now creditors following the 2009 government-debt crisis. The reidentification of the lemon denotes an acidity applied to the native stone that speaks to the pervasive feeling of national exploitation.

L.M.

1   Dora Economou, "Dora Economou: Predeal," *The Breeder*, May 2014, http://thebreedersystem.com/exhibition-details/dora-economou-solo/.

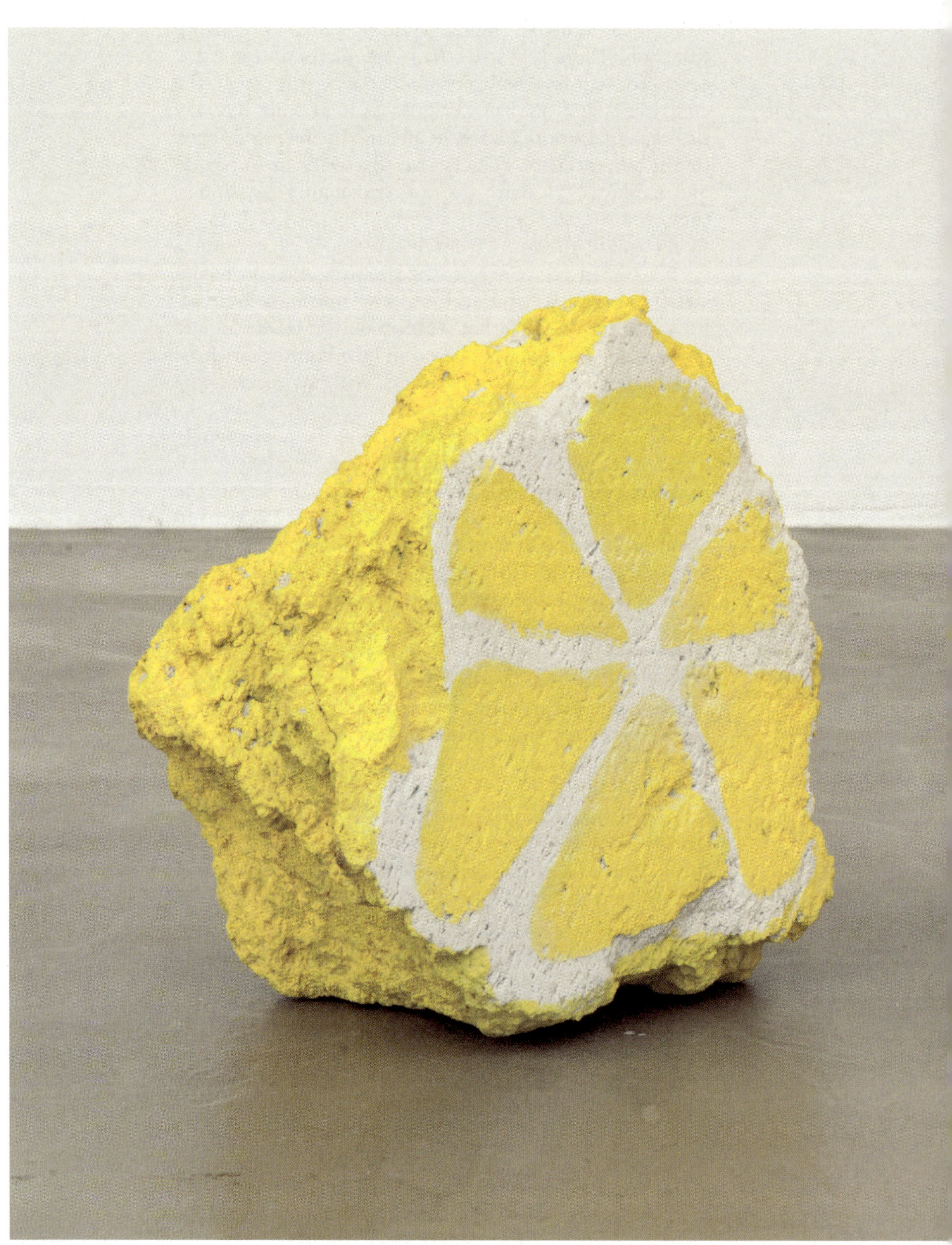

Dora Economou, *The dark, the dark*, 2015, pumice stone, paint

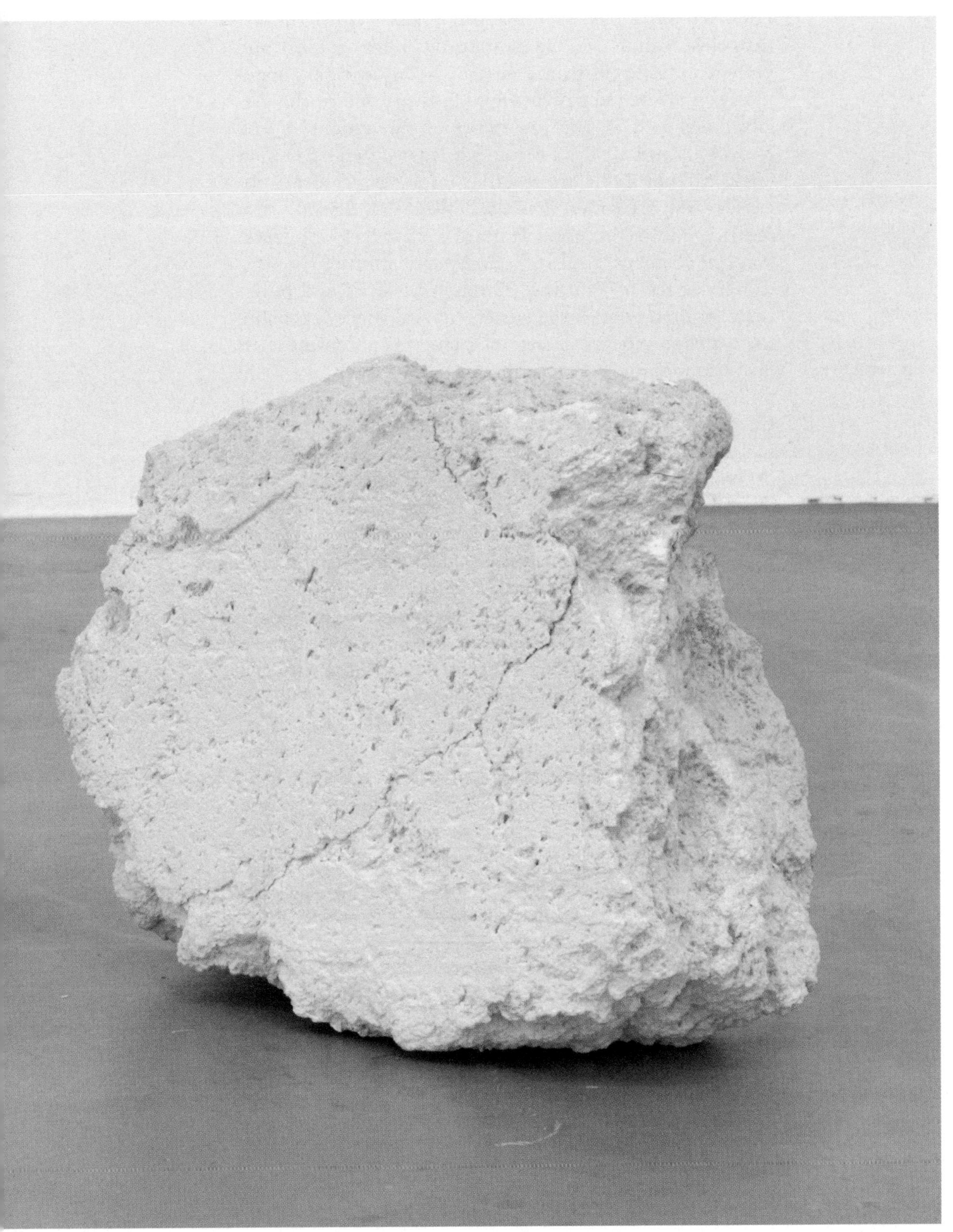

Lucio Fontana has an impactful place within the art historical canon for his punctured holes (*buchi*) and violent cuts (*tagli*) to the surface of his works, particularly in stretched canvas. Fontana was one of the artists enveloped in the *art informel* movement of the late 1940s and 1950s, a term that was coined by French critic Michel Tapié to describe informal gestural processes and artworks that eschewed the figural, geometric, and structural. Fontana's *Concetto Spaziale* (*Spatial Concept*) series is a demystification of the illusionary space of painting. Through his cuts and punctures, Fontana opens the surface to real space, exposing the canvas's inherent material quality as an object with no autonomous communication of its own, yet rife with conceptual potential. The vast interpretations of the series are chronicled in its wildly varied trajectories in scholarship: the destruction of art history; fetishistic psychoanalytic theory; projections of "the void;" and the political context of fascism, among others.

Art historian Anthony White positions Fontana's work within the context of Italy's declining postwar economic miracle: "They embody a genuine desire for overcoming the drudgery and grind of industrialized labor. The 'Cuts' propose a utopian moment of uplifted grace that nevertheless remains entirely contained within the materiality of muscular energy."[1] *Concetto Spaziale, New York 7* is perhaps a crowning example of this argument, in which Fontana's use of brass—an industrial material—elicits connections to the rise against a societal mindset predicated on mass production, a critique that also seeded the *arte povera* movement, then on the horizon. Less stylized and surgical than the precise cuts incised on Fontana's monochromatic canvases, the harsh cuts in brass conjure a visceral experience of a real wound sustained.

L.M.

1   Anthony White, *Lucio Fontana: Between Utopia and Kitsch* (Cambridge: MIT Press, 2011), 241.

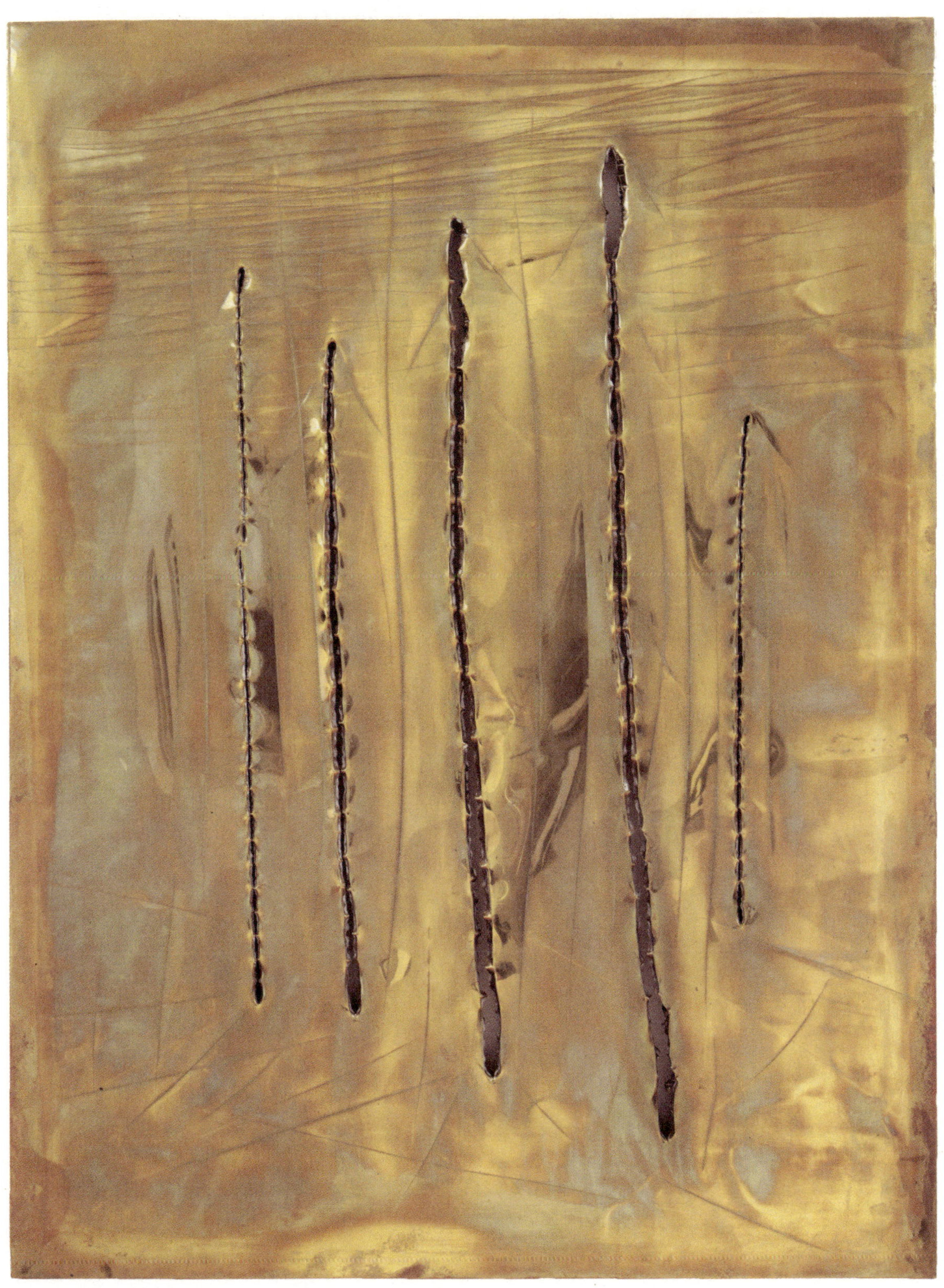

Concetto Spaziale, New York 7, 1962, brass   cat. no. 17

When Brenda Goodman moved her studio to the Cass Corridor neighborhood of Detroit during the 1970s after graduating from the College for Creative Studies, the classically trained painter became motivated to explore her interior psychologies through scavenged material. Goodman relocated to New York City in 1976, a time when a fraught economy and prolific crime were palpable in both cities.

Created in 1977 as a series of four, the *Self Portrait*[s] become portals into the unsettling energies of the urban built environment. They are haunting representations of the artist that capture an emotional and lucid moment in time. The almost life-sized cone sculptures made of tar, canvas, feathers, and wire allude to a process of cocooning against vulnerability. The bound sculptures are tightly wrapped with telephone wiring and string, with erect wooden sticks at the base. In 1980, these works were exhibited in the seminal exhibition *Kick Out the Jams: Detroit's Cass Corridor 1963–1977* at the Detroit Institute of Arts. In 2003, Goodman returned to the self-portrait, this time through painting. The artist has said of this series, "I want to remove the veils between myself and the viewer, and communicate the palpability of needs met, of needs unmet, of needs never met." The precedent provided by the *Self Portrait* series indicate a trajectory of Goodman's work that continues to be a core interest for the artist.

T.R.A.

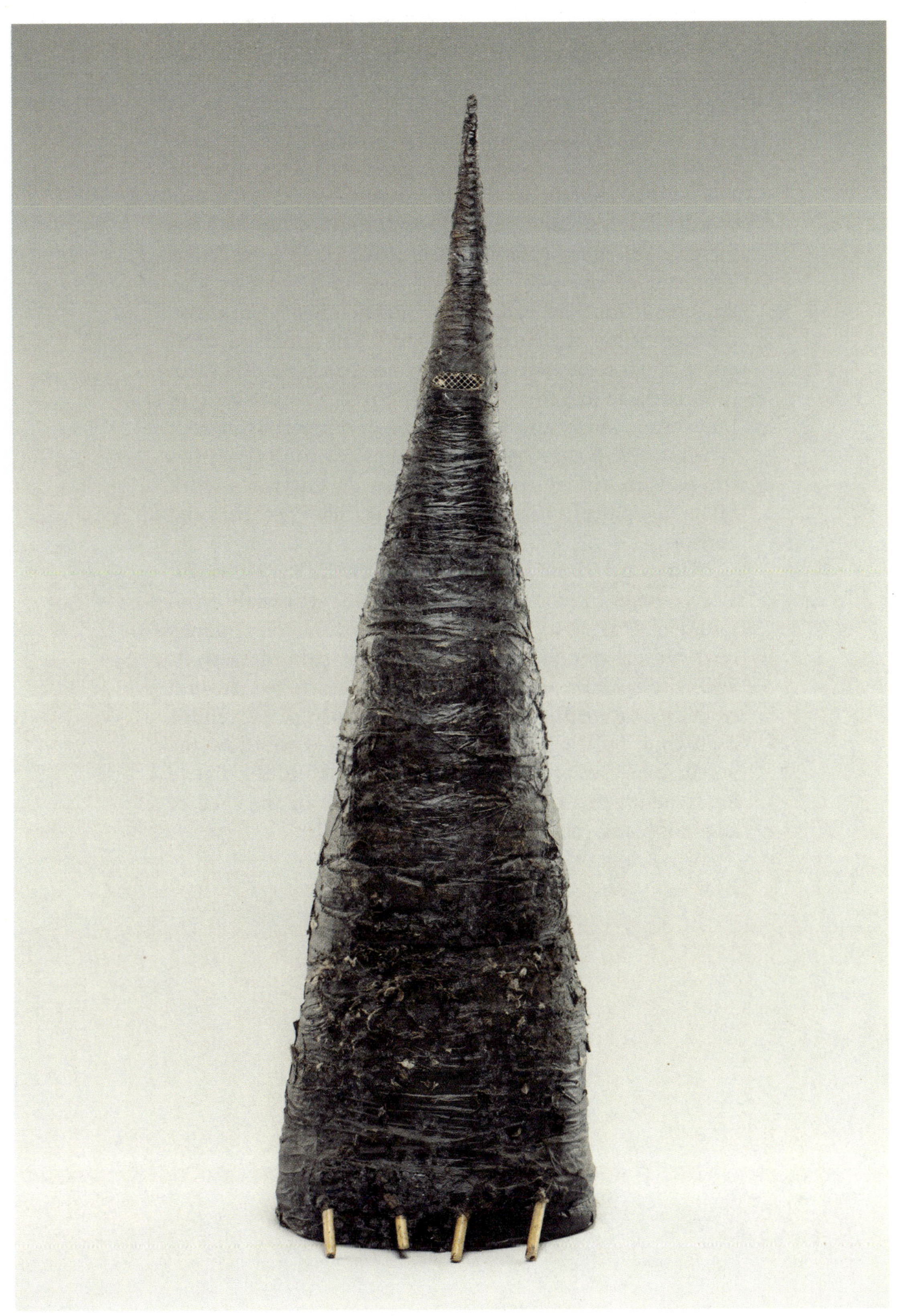

Self Portrait, No 1, 1977, canvas, feathers, tar, wood, wire   cat. no. 18

TYREE GUYTON

Caged Brain is a potent example of Tyree Guyton's art that speaks directly to the lived experiences of African Americans in post-industrial America. Over the past fifty years in Detroit, public education and basic city services have continually eroded. The school-to-prison pipeline and neighborhood blight became crises that disproportionately affect black inner-city youth. Guyton uses just two materials to convey his feelings on these urban issues: a rope and a birdcage. The tangled mess of discarded rope is materially suggestive of bondage and the traumatic effects of racism inflicted upon the mind and body. The birdcage references the forced captivity and domestication of a creature born to be free. *Caged Brain* is reminiscent of Maya Angelou's autobiographical coming-of-age poem "I Know Why the Caged Bird Sings," which describes the way creativity can free the mind. Guyton's work takes a confrontational stance against institutional authority.

Guyton is best known for his *Heidelberg Project*, a large-scale outdoor installation made primarily from found objects, that spreads across several city blocks near his childhood home on the east side of Detroit. The site-specific environment was destroyed several times by city officials and vandals, only to be rebuilt each time by the artist, who has refused to allow his voice to be suppressed. His work is about the battle for freedom of expression, perseverance in the face of adversity, and the triumph of human will.

R.M.

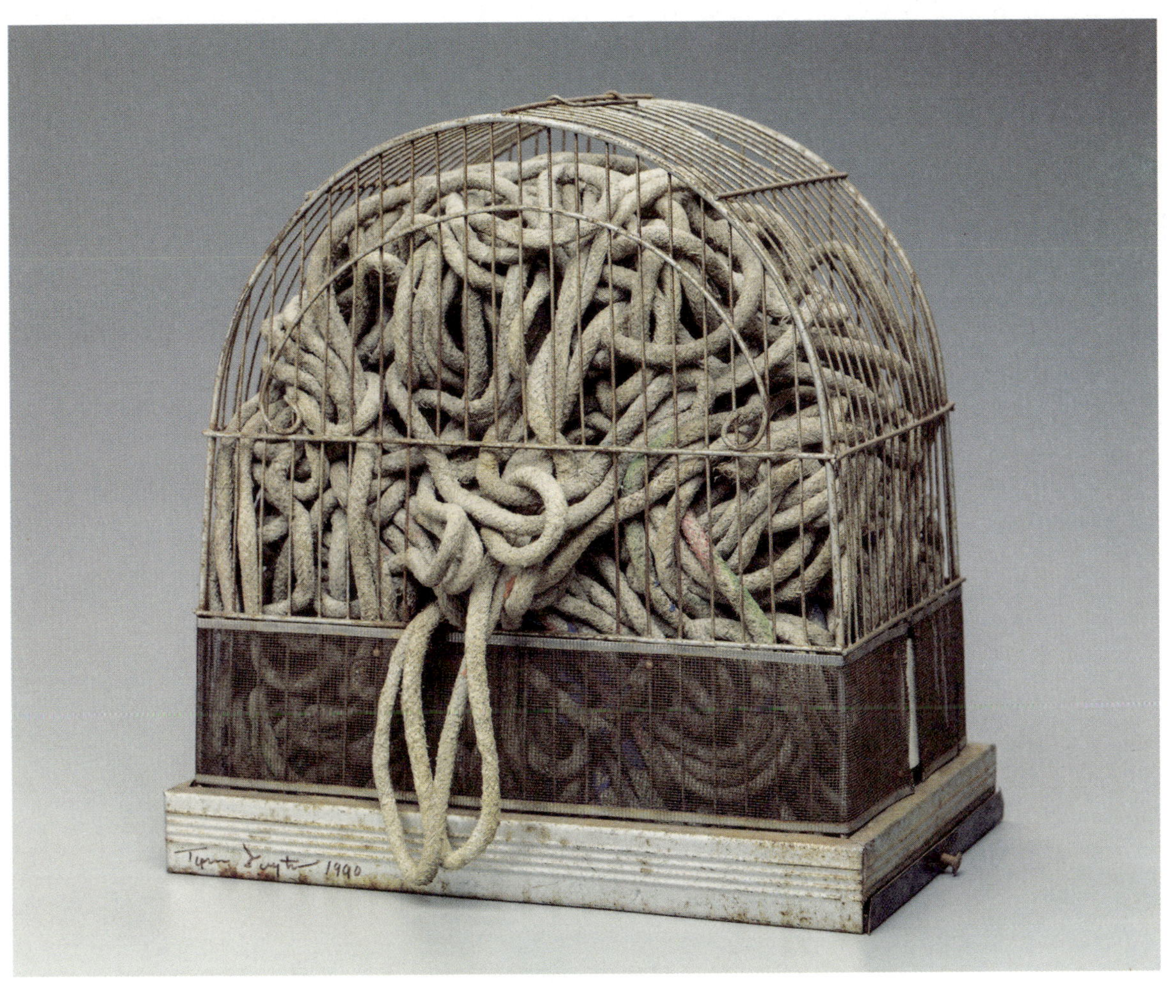

Caged Brain, 1990, mixed media   cat. no. 21

MARSHA MIRO

DETROIT: THE SCRAPPINESS OF SURVIVORS

Originally published in the Detroit Free Press,
December 2, 1979, 7E.

Here we are again. Back thrashing about in the wickets of Detroit art. Is there or isn't there?

Detroit has artists, that's become more sure. Roy Slade, president of Cranbrook Academy of Art, found 21 hanging out in the lofts, corridors, and galleries of the city. He selected them from many others for his current exhibition, "At Cranbrook: Detroit Artists," which is occasion for these musings.

But is there something that could be labeled Detroit art?

Slade couldn't find a neat package of it. Instead, he settled on this answer in his show's catalog: "In the work of Detroit artists, there appears to be a tenuous and tentative bond: that of assemblage. Consciously or unconsciously, the artists share the commonality of putting things together, whether objects, colors, shapes, forms, textures, materials, images or ideas."

Writer Sarah McFadden, in the August issue of Art in America, found art in Detroit. After a whirlwind tour of the locals and an evening at Bookie's for punk rock, she dubbed these artists "anti-formalist" and "industrial expressionists," because they make art identifiable "with the city's scarred industrial environment."

By that mouthful, she seems to have meant that Detroit artists' work is expressively or emotionally based, not concerned primarily with formal aesthetic relationships, and that it is related to industry by use of its materials.

What of these explanations?

Anti-formalist—Detroit art is that. Robert Sestok did a series of collages two years ago that pushed formal order to the hilt, complicating it with its own logic to the point where works became highly emotional once again.

Detroit art is very expressionistic and emotional. The city's core group—usually identified as Sestok, Michael Luchs, Gordon Newton, Jim Chatelain and sometimes John Egner—isn't known for racking intellect for inspiration. Theirs is an intuitive, psychically charged art.

But is it industrial Art? I don't think so. That is only a small aspect, and an easy assumption given Detroit's history.

If anything, the art these Detroiters make is post-industrial, created as a negation of the notion that industrial progress means human progress. They pick up industry's pieces and mend them into a new existence as art that has no technological value.

John Hallmark Neff, former curator of modern art at the Detroit Institute of Arts, understood. "The best Detroit art is an art of survivors," he said.

It's scrappy. The edges are built on brinkmanship, with survival always the motivator. But this type of survival is less the bread-and-butter sort and more the sort a jazz musician wrings out of his last high note. It's survival of the creative soul—art grown from the barest necessity.

If anyone has touched on the fuse that might have set off the artists, it is Susanne Hilberry, who was associate curator of modern art at the DIA and now runs her own gallery in Birmingham.

She says of them, "They were creating in a largely destroyed city, just after the violence of the first 1967 riots. These people were cognizant of what they had witnessed, and they continued to observe its effects."

The chilling reality of Army tanks patrolling city streets, snipers shooting from the roof of Saks in the New Center, and looting everywhere made Detroit seem the site of another civil war. If you survived those moments, when the whole fabric of urban life was in shreds and notions of law, order, justice, and material abundance were in question, if you survived such confrontation, you sit forever uneasy.

This place was not conducive to an art about visual perfection or luscious color relationships, harmony, progress, and order. What thrived was discord and tension. In those years, the art was more virulent, crude and outwardly violent. Today, the demons seem a step removed but nonetheless present.

The work in the Cranbrook show is recent. Two pieces, one by Steven Foust, the other by Naomi Dickerson, were made at the museum for particular sites. Only a few artists don't seem to belong—John Slick, Lois Teicher and Mel Rosas.

Though the trash cans and the alleys recorded in Rosas' drawings seem appropriate subjects, his work is too concerned with skillful drawing to have the emotional abandon typical of the others.

David Barr's painted Masonite constructions are assemblages, but their unique coloration is less like dull Detroit color and more international.

The quality of the rest of the art is surprisingly strong and consistent. Seeing the work in the white museum spaces somehow removes a bit of its threat.

Slade opens the show with the work of Egner, Newton, and Luchs. Newton, the most reclusive of the group, has been known to produce three dissimilar artworks at once. The first may echo Rauschenberg, another may be unadulterated Newton, and the third may look plucked from the sky. He doesn't provide the normal connections from one set of works to another, or stylistic similarities, but uses his objects as vehicles for communicating his ideas about survival.

Demise is staved off inside his gray, barricaded cities this time. He draws them as fantasies of untenable space, with a cloud, set immovably above, blasting arrows. He builds them out of wood, too, as eccentric conglomerates of minimal architecture, spruced up HUD housing and visions of Armaggedon. He rarely provides hope.

Egner, who was educated at Yale, has in his small wood-strip structures managed, with power and tenderness, to combine his East Coast polish with his Wayne State obsessions.

His wall constructions are splotched with blobs of colored paint that would normally fit on a wider surface, but here they make the sculpture feel larger, more like a painting, as color bleeds off edges.

Luchs is back with his rabbit sculptures made of refuse trapped in wood. They are sacrificial lambs now, Trojan horses that he is ripping apart, shooting to smithereens, in an act of exorcism. This image, which has become his icon and symbol of urban withdrawal, is being purged from his art so he can move on. It is a transition.

Robert Sestok's assemblage of horizontally strung cans, bottle tops and junk becomes a metaphor for the transformation of nature's geology into one of stratified industrial waste.

Jim Chatelain, in his paintings of a still-life and tumbling bowling pins, continues to make a virtue out of being awkward, off-center and off-color.

Naomi Dickerson is one of those people who can turn a single drawn line into a poignant plea for creativity. Even the monofilament thread she has strung here from floor to ceiling to outline rectangles and to order empty spaces becomes the most tender and tentative of lines.

If you handle broken glass as others shape clay, you're not only brave and bound to make something unexpected, but a Detroiter working materials with a lethal safety quotient. And you are probably Paul Webster. He uses glass to activate space and to light corners, windows and walls with quiet control.

Paul Schwarz continues to fracture the buildings of

the world. Here the Chrysler
Building seems broken into
an impenetrable surface
of black and white geometrics.
One wonders where the
gravity went.

The show continues through
Jan. 20 at Cranbrook, 500 Lone
Pine Rd., Birmingham. Hours:
1-5 p.m. Tuesday-Sunday.
Admission is $1.50; students $1.

Ha Chong-Hyun's work is distinguished within the *dansaekhwa* movement for his masterful ability to extract the conceptual and emotional potency of everyday materials. For example, through barbed wire, nails, coil, and hemp, he speaks in an almost preternatural form of communication that heightens the level of relevance in the object-human paradigm. The canvas becomes a raw stage, as he typically isolates a single material for the rapt attention of an audience to contemplate. This seemingly simple act is in fact loaded with cultural connotation. He referred to the debilitating use of barbed wire as an active agent in war, to contain prisoners during the Korean conflict and later to imprison pro-democracy advocates. His process of using the material extracts its inherent qualities, as he explained, "when I cut or burn my hands on the wire barbs, I know I am in the work."[1] Ubiquitous throughout the world to the same effect, it is meant to ensnare and draw blood, a material that fulfills the threats of warring ideologies. Today, it runs like overgrowth along the border between North and South Korea.

Ha's critical thinking on materiality extended beyond the canvas and into discursive forms to understand Korean artistic methods and situate them among their global contemporaries. From 1969 to 1974, Ha chaired the short-lived, but seminal, group called the A.G. (or Avant Garde) that published texts referencing international artists and held well-attended exhibitions. However, many of Ha's techniques, such as pushing paint through hemp sacks repurposed as canvas, stand as unique expressions of ingenuity specific to the Korean context—a form of minimalism that cannot be subsumed by the Western canon.

L.M.

1   Kim Bok-Young, "From Materiality to the Corporeal: The Late Conjunction Works of Ha Chong-Hyun," *Misul segye*, no. 153 (August 1997), 46.

Ha Chong-Hyun, *Untitled 72-(A)-1*, 1972, barbed wire on panel　cat. no. 22

CAROLE HARRIS

Artist Carole Harris utilizes her decades of experience as both a graphic and interior designer to create nontraditional textiles. She undertakes experimental processes that extract the richness and depth of natural materials that have undergone a physical transformation. *In a Silent Way* exemplifies Harris' method of burning and "rusting" fabrics, pushing the boundaries of what constitutes beauty and how one can learn to find aesthetic pleasure in an industrial landscape. Harris collects bits and pieces of metal on walks along the streets of downtown Detroit and uses a homemade solution to accelerate the oxidation process of the metal that she rests atop the fabric in order to stain it in rich shades of ochre.

The rhythm and vibrancy of the intuitive art form of jazz influences her improvisational process of stitching and pattern-making. *In a Silent Way* was titled after a 1969 album of the same name by American jazz trumpeter, composer, and bandleader Miles Davis. The album was considered to be a defining moment in his career and was characterized as an eclectic, nontraditional project with a down tempo—a minimalist vibe not unlike Harris's own piece. Prior to this textile, her work has been similarly musical—her patterns highly rhythmic, creating a sense of movement—but this work is more subtle and contemplative. For Harris, the process of hand-stitching that she has developed is a form of meditation that she finds to be quieting.

R.M.

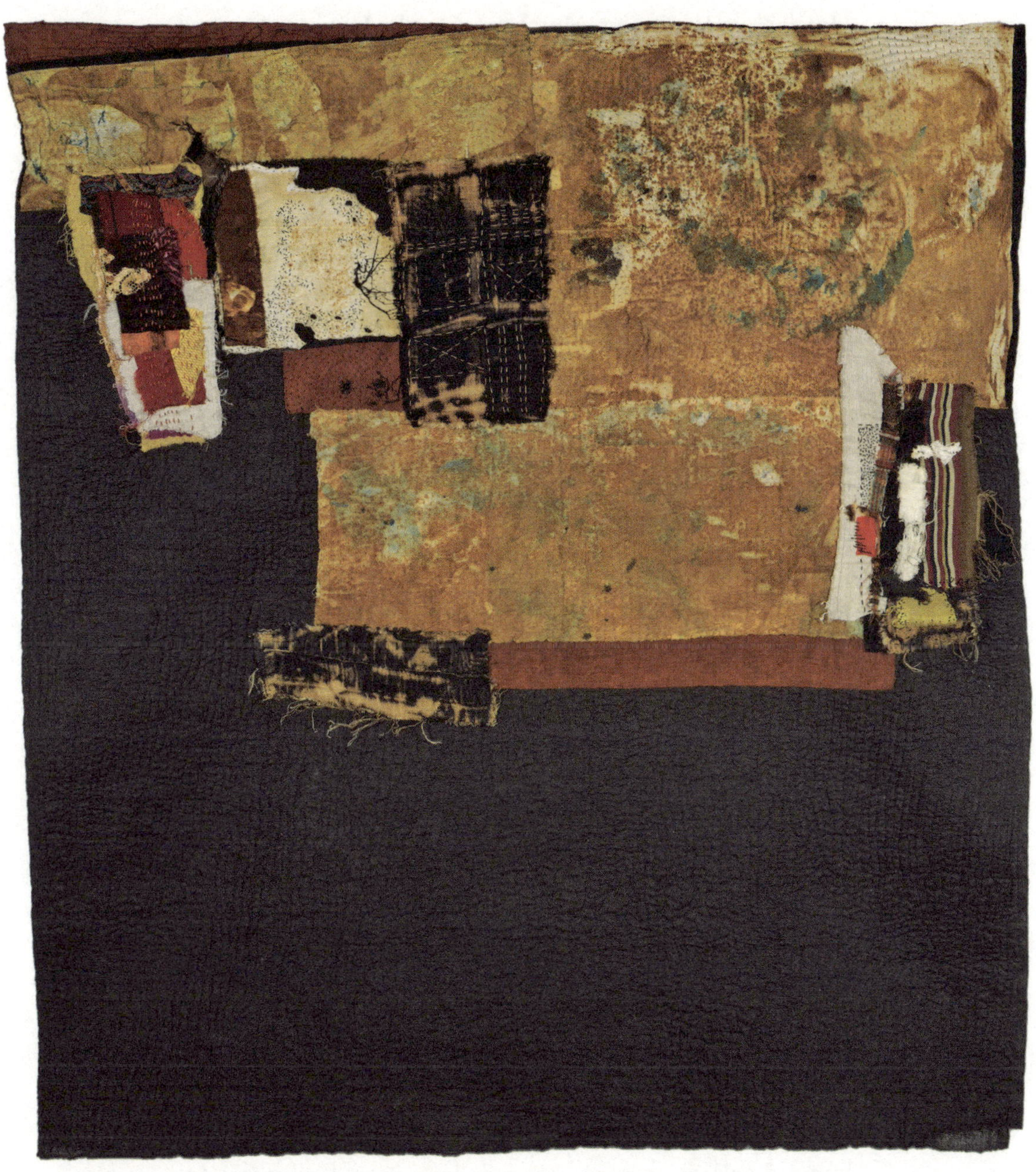

In a Silent Way, 2017, fiber, rust   cat. no. 24

Until recently, artist Matthew Angelo Harrison's day job was as a clay sculptor for the Ford Motor Company. One of his main professional concentrations was in prototyping, often relying on his ability to alter an object slightly for a new intention. The act of recontextualization is integral to his artistic practice, which often includes self-engineering his own apparatuses for production. Among his innovations, Harrison constructs low-resolution 3-D printers to make replicas of preexisting objects, such as African masks, that have lost much of their connection to cultural heritage. Over repetitive printings and cumulative degradations, the original form loses detail and becomes altered beyond recognition; a new autonomous form has been created. In an inverse strategy, he also entombs found sculptures in thick blocks of resin, like an arthropod suspended in amber, creating a synthetic intervention that prompts questions of origin and authenticity. He explains, "I'm attracted to the possibility of an individual's identity being lost in abstraction over time—abstraction through different mediums and interpretations—and ending up with a kind of surveillance of what the identity was."[1]

As an extension of this thinking, Harrison surveys his relationship to the art historical canon and refers to his practice as *dark povera*, "dark and poor," as an homage to and provocation of the *arte povera* movement seen through the lens of the black experience. He sees parallels between the political context of postwar Italy and that of Detroit, yet inserts notions of identity to accompany the movement's material ethos. Working from the *Landlord Colors* checklist, Harrison creates a context-specific installation within the museum that uses materials complicit to his Detroit life—modeling clay, African masks, bulletproof glass—among shared forms and materials referencing the *arte povera* artworks on view.

L.M.

1   Laura Mott and Taylor Aldridge, "On Rust: Roundtable Discussion #2," *art21* magazine, May 8, 2017, http://magazine.art21.org/2017/06/15/on-rust-roundtable-discussion-2/#.XFfCzWn9mM8.

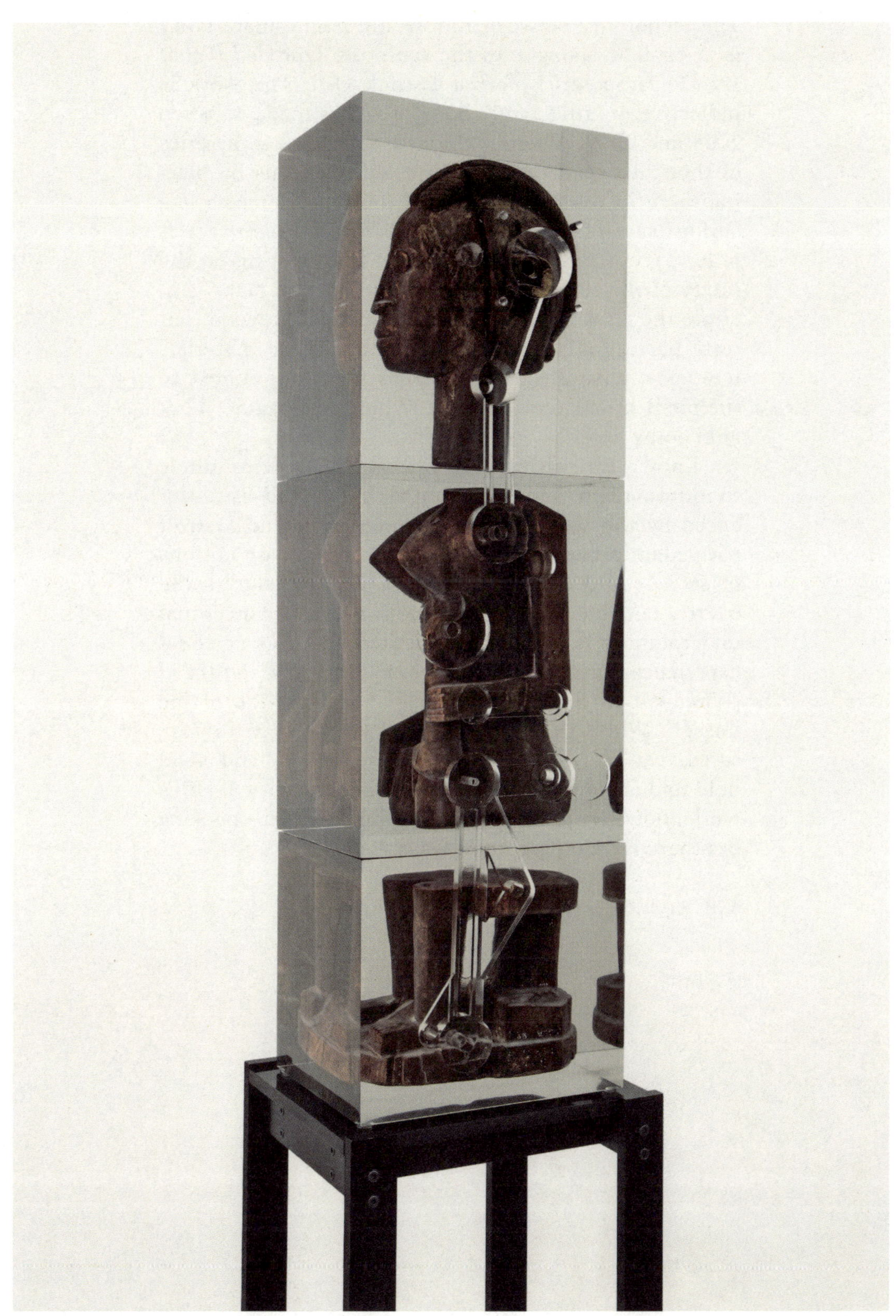

Dark Silhouette: Watcher, 2019, polyurethane resin, anodized aluminum, acrylic

The dichotomy between robust and fragile materiality is in explicit dialogue in the sculpture *Untitled (What We Do Is Secret)* by artist Patrick Hill. The work is indicative of Hill's larger body of works made between 2008 and 2009, wherein the artist engaged in a series of thought experiments that tested materials by placing them in tension. This construction of objects is a performance of stress and balance: black weights act as pillars, preventing a sheet of glass from resting on the safety of the floor, while two thin concrete slabs penetrate the glass to support a large splinter of wood that rests horizontally between the slabs. These materials now exist absurdly far from their function, almost to the point of existential angst: What am I again? What am I doing here?

Known for pairing the hard and the soft to allude to minimalism and the human body, Hill is influenced by the work of performance artist and Detroit native James Lee Byars. Like Byars, he takes up notions of secrecy and concealment as a way to address the overtly tangible and obvious. However, this conceptual underpinning is also complemented by Hill's personal experience with chronic illness. Similarly, *Untitled (What We Do Is Secret)* asks for consideration of the unseen. While the glass has not yet cracked or ruptured, we know that the concrete, wood, and steel hold undue weight against it—we are concerned. Hill's work allows for a rumination on the tensions, opposing or otherwise, that are not always visible.

T.R.A., L.M.

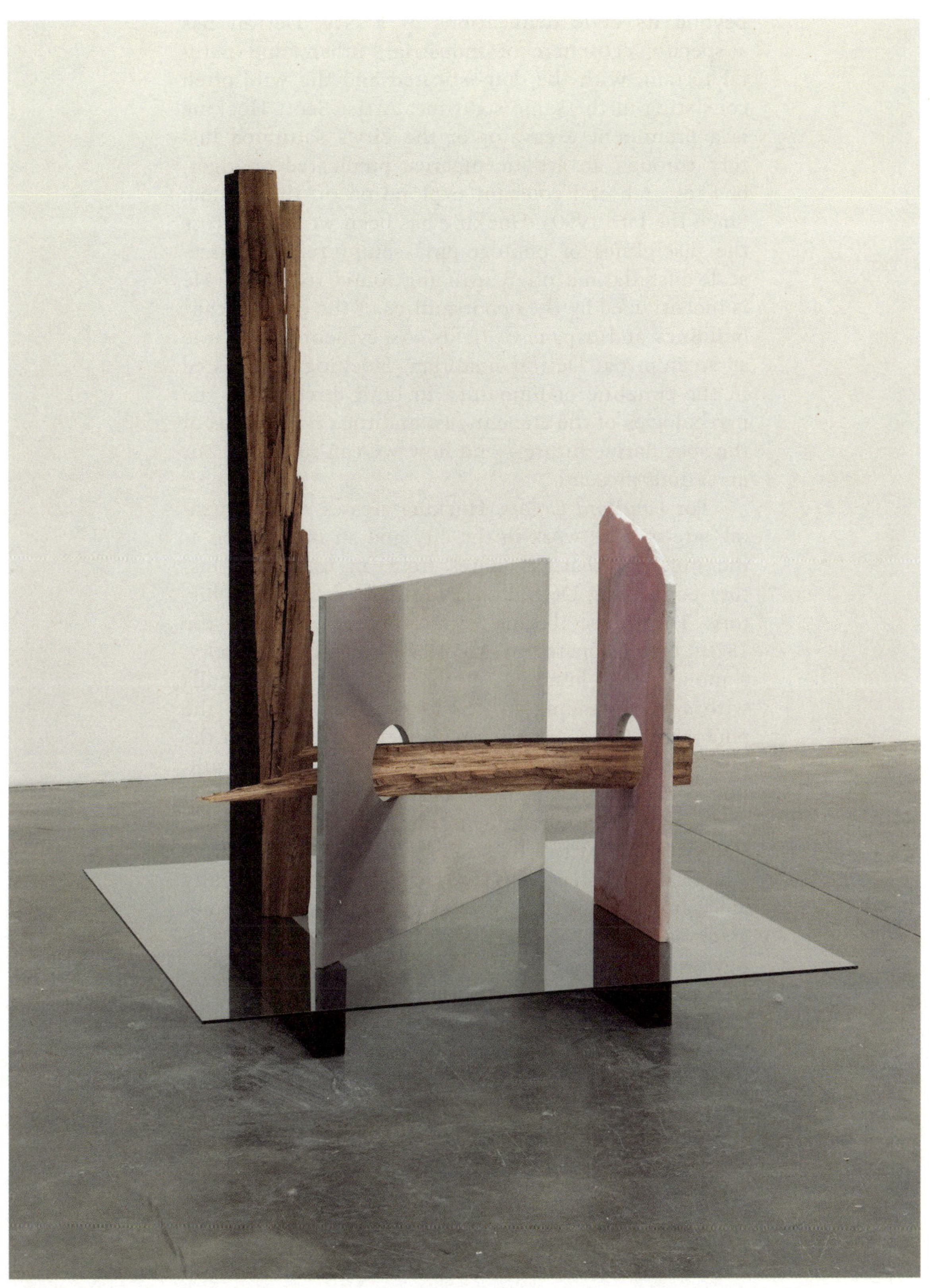

Untitled (What We Do Is Secret), 2009, wood, glass, aluminum, marble, steel, concrete, dye, ink, epoxy
cat. no. 26

Beyond its civic delineations as a city, Detroit has a specific ecosphere of industrial, urban, and natural terrain, with the domesticated and the wild often coexisting in the same sightline. Artist Scott Hocking is a prominent excavator of the city's saturated history through an artistic practice predicated on rigorous research and constant exploration on the ground. Since the late 1990s, Hocking has been working across the disciplines of photography, sculpture, and large-scale installation, often utilizing found materials. He is incentivized by the opportunities of the city's vacant buildings and expansive fields. As evident in his role as an informal Detroit historian, Hocking is invested in the timeline of humanity in both directions—the mythologies of the ancient past and the civilizations of the speculative future—and how we can negotiate our precarious present.

For *Landlord Colors*, Hocking creates a monumental, site-specific work in the city and an installation at the museum that originates from an unearthed history connecting Detroit to a seminal event in US history. The project begins with a photograph from the 1870s that resonates in America's collective memory: a mountain of hundreds of thousands of bison skulls with a man standing atop as its conqueror. Today, the photograph is a devastating reminder of the plight of the bison population, which reportedly numbered sixty million at the start of the nineteenth century and was decimated to near extinction by its end. The government-led slaughter was part of its strategy to destroy the Native Americans' primary food source, which successfully aided in their destruction to similar effect. The photograph is associated heavily with the American West; however, it was in fact taken in Detroit, where the bison bones were sent by train to be crushed and processed to be used by various industries. One such product was a paint pigment called "Bone Black" that is applied to large industrial equipment. Despite more than a century of economic collapse in Detroit, this business still survives today. Bone Black is the primary palette of Hocking's monumental sculpture that reconsiders this seminal image from a contemporary perspective.

L.M.

(see *Landlord Colors: Material Detroit*, p. 249)

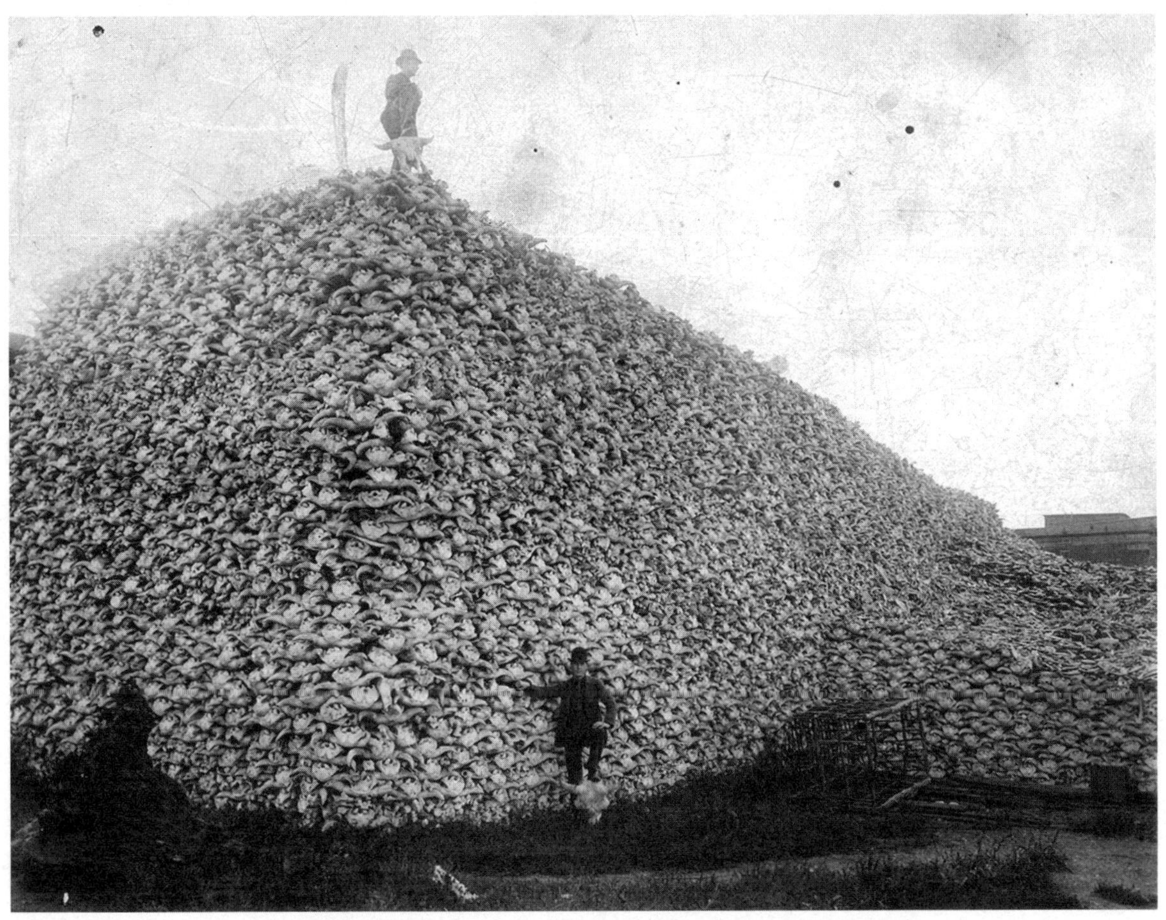

Research for *Bone Black*, Michigan Carbon Works, Detroit, 1892, photograph   cat. no. 27

JANNIS KOUNELLIS

In the sculptural work of Jannis Kounellis, the careful arrangement of organic and inorganic material depicts a powerful allegory of human presence in the natural world. *Untitled* (1968) is an installation of two materials processed and utilized by global economic trade, particularly during the twentieth century: coal and jute bags. As the world's largest source of energy, coal has acted as both the engine and the ruin of progress. Since Kounellis first used coal as an artistic material at the end of the 1960s, our relationship to the combustible rock has grown increasingly acrimonious due to its detrimental effects on man and nature, from the black lungs of miners to the red alerts of air pollution, among others. Second only to cotton, jute is one of the most affordable and widely used fibers globally. Kounellis said he used the sacks as found material due to their connection to maritime commerce, ubiquitous in harbors the world over. He expands: "A sack is also something which contains something else. A ship, a labyrinth, a burlap sack are things which are grandiosely maternal. They are protective, they surround you and, therefore, possess a profound credibility."[1]

While Kounellis is a seminal figure of the Italian *arte povera* movement, the aesthetics and economies of the sea recall his birthplace, Piraeus, the port of Athens. Before his death in 2017, Kounellis returned to Athens in 2012 with an exhibition at the Museum of Cycladic Art, which included a large installation of jute sacks filled with coal. He stated he was mindful of the reformulation of his material choices and how, years later, they were pertinent to Greece's current economic and social crisis.

L.C., L.M.

1　Mario Codognato and Mirta d'Argenzio, *Echoes in the Darkness: Writings and Interviews 1966–2002* (London: Trolley Books, 2002), 317.

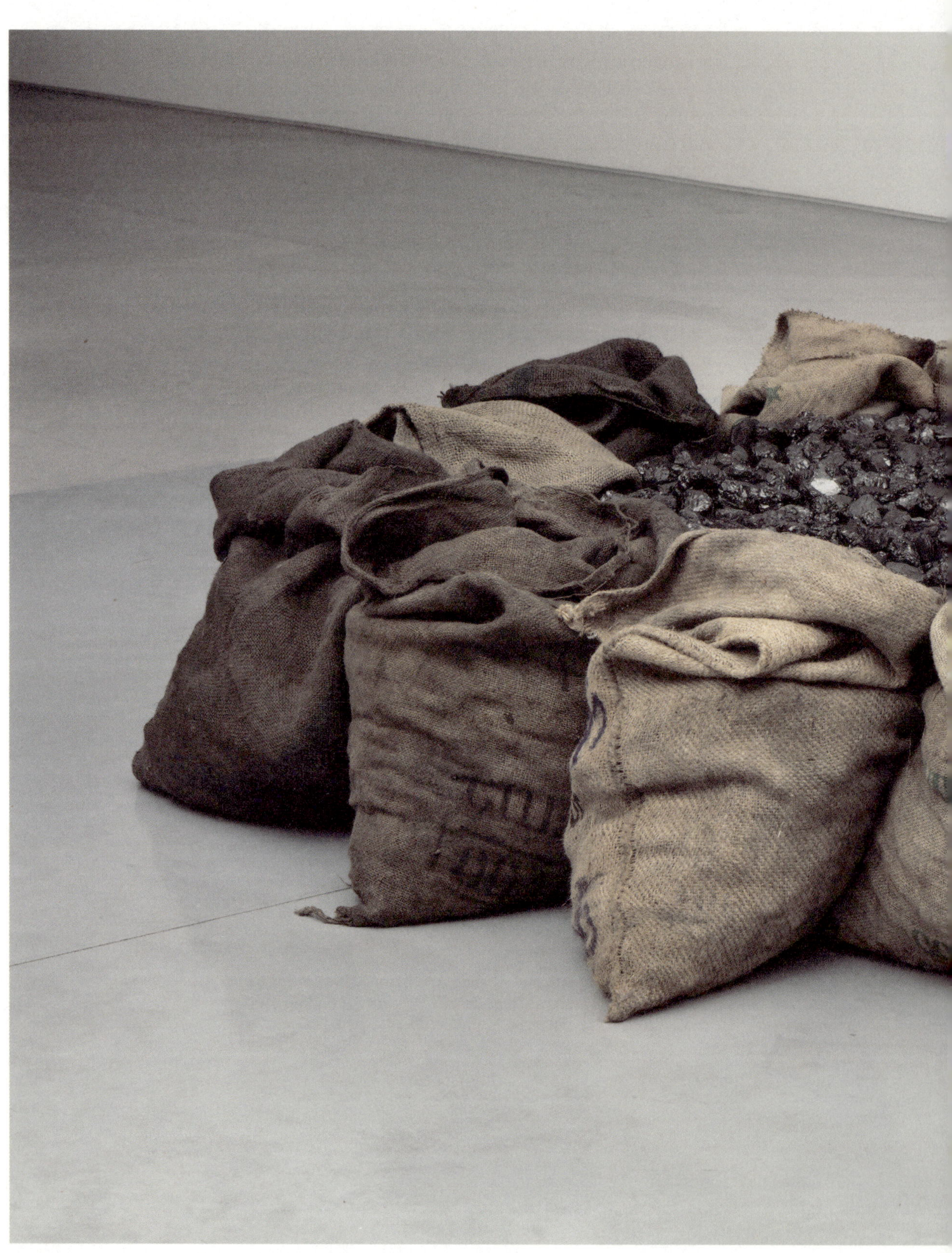

Jannis Kounellis, *Untitled*, 1968, jute bags, coal   cat. no. 28

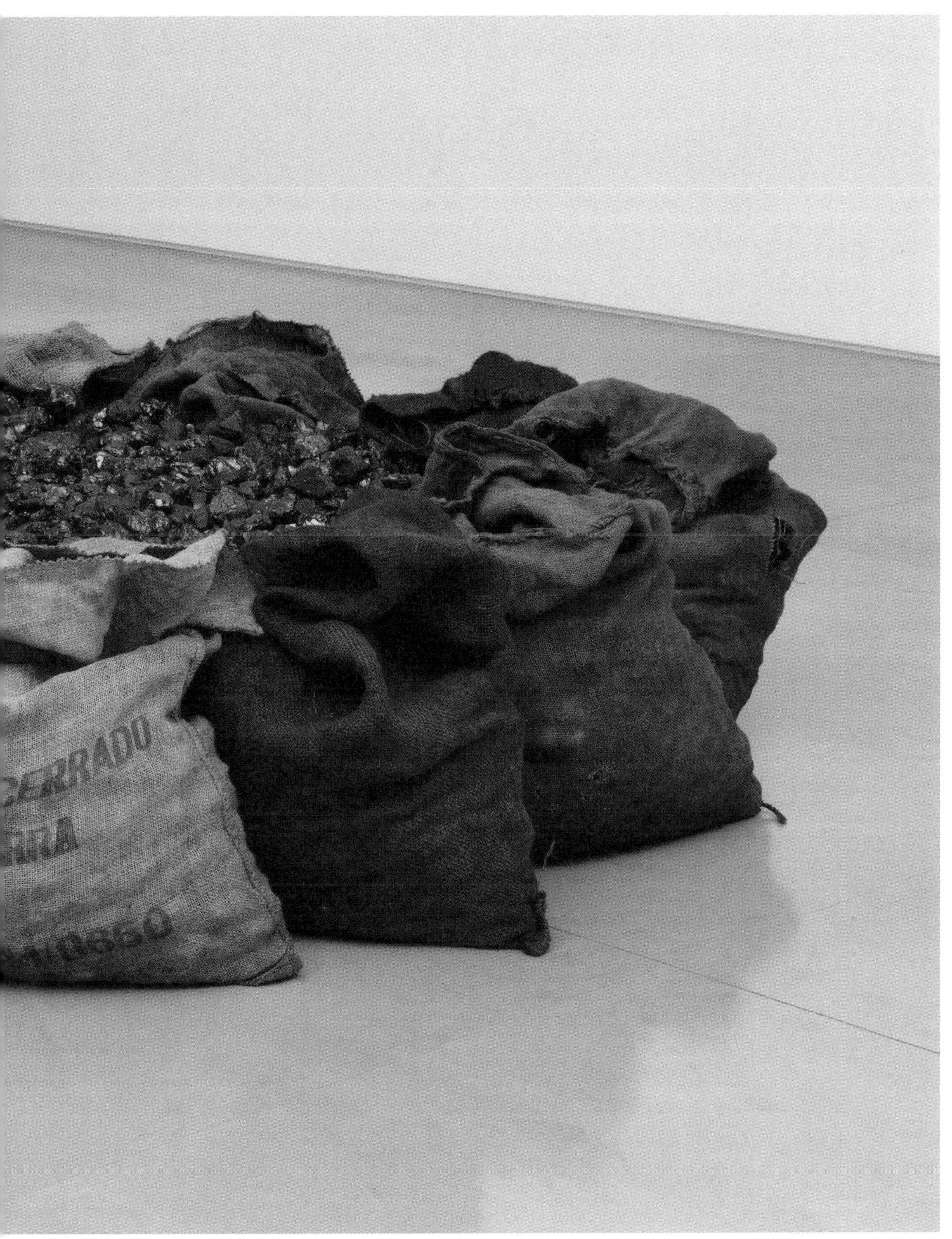
CERRADO
RRA
0860

GERMANO CELANT

ARTE POVERA

Originally published in Art Povera
(New York: Praeger Publishers, Inc., 1969), 225–30.

Animals, vegetables and minerals take part in the world of art. The artist feels attracted by their physical, chemical and biological possibilities, and he begins again to feel the need to make things of the world, not only as animated beings, but as a producer of magic and marvelous deeds. The artist-alchemist organizes living and vegetable matter into magic things, working to discover the root of things, in order to re-find them and extol them. His work, however, does include in its scope the use of the simplest material and natural elements (copper, zinc, earth, water, rivers, land, snow, fire, grass, air, stone, electricity, uranium, sky, weight, gravity, height, growth, etc.) for a description or representation of nature. What interests him instead is the discovery, the exposition, the insurrection of the magic and marvelous value of natural elements. Like an organism of simple structure, the artist mixes himself with the environment, camouflages himself, he enlarges his threshold of things. What the artist comes

in contact with is not re-elaborated; he does not express a judgment on it, he does not seek a moral or social judgment, he does not manipulate it. He leaves it uncovered and striking, he draws from the substance of the natural event—that of the growth of a plant, the chemical reaction of a mineral, the movement of a river, of snow, grass and land, the fall of a weight—he identifies with them in order to live the marvelous organization of living things.

Among living things he discovers also himself, his body, his memory, his gestures—all that which directly lives and thus begins again to carry out the sense of life and of nature, a sense that implies, according to Dewey, numerous subjects: the sensory, sensational, sensitive, impressionable and sensuous.

He has chosen to live within direct experience, no longer the representative—the source of pop artists—he aspires to live, not to see. He immerses himself in individuality because he feels the necessity of leaving intact the value of the existence of things, of plants or animals; he wants to take part in the oneness of every minute in order to possess above all the "autonomy" both of his own identity and the individuality of things. He wants to feel his vitality in order not to feel that he is a solitary vital individual.

Consequently, all of his work tends toward the dilation of the sphere of impression; it does not offer itself as an assertion, an indication of values, a model for behaviour, but as an experiment with contingent existence. His works are often without a title: almost a way to establish a physical memorial testimony, and not an analysis of the successive development of an experiment.

Life, as the events that make it up, in this way, turns out to be a moment of expectant anxiety, in which the objects accomplished do not present themselves under the form of inert things but as stimulating subject matter—a part of the world in an established and determinate moment—subjective actions that one leans upon in which animals, plants, minerals and men move themselves in an autonomous way.

It is clear, however, that as long as one considers the descriptive aspect, man, minerals and animals have little in common: even though all of these systems function in a similar way, tied as they are to a common process of transformation. For this reason the artist, as well as others from the ecologist to the scientist, is interested in the behaviour of that which is animate and inanimate. He does not accept description and representation of the exterior aspects of nature and life (also they are mass-media) and takes into consideration the special aspect—also those offered by micro-organisms (not very striking but very active). He is interested in placing in the right perspective the minor biomorphic and ecological facts, that can be compared with those that are bigger, more striking, but relatively inert; and with the apparent banality of natural and vital facts, he returns to the marvelous. Thus, he rediscovers the magic (of chemical composition and reaction), the inexorableness (of vegetable growth), the precariousness (of material), the falseness (of sense), the realness (of a natural desert, a forgotten lake, the sea, the snow, the forest)— the instability of a biophysical reaction—thus become discovered as an instrument of consciousness in relation to a larger comprehensive acquisition of nature.

At the same time he rediscovers his interest in himself. He abandons linguistic intervention in order to live hazardously in an uncertain space. He finds it insupportable to consider art as a threshold of anticipated values and he uses it for his self-discovery. He does not accept the role of the "prophet" because he does not trust cultural control (artistic, intellectual, etc.) that suggests slavishness (spectator, public, etc.) as a pattern of values. He comes from the closed spaces of the galleries and the museums (at times, notwithstanding all, he goes back there); he goes down to the public places, crosses forests, deserts, fields of snow, to appraise a participating intervention. He destroys his social "function" because he no longer believes in cultural goods. He denies the moralistic, fallaciousness of artistic production, the creators of the illusionistic dimension of life and reality. He believes only in his own personal experience, while his relationship with the world does not take place any more through analyzed and manipulated images (comic books, films, photographs, etc.) and the things used for discussion (material "for," gesture "for," action "for") but with the images of things. He identifies himself with them, to the point of making them a part of himself, and their biological offshoots. Thus his availability to all is total. He accumulates continuously desire and lack of desire, choice and lack of choice; that is he finds himself in a type of life that overcomes the formulation of thousands of experiences. Assuming for himself that unique instrument of questioning and stimulation, he inserts himself in order not to be assimilated, he makes a jump from "naturalness" and escapes continuously from acquisitive dimension.

He abolishes his role of being an artist, intellectual, painter or writer and learns again to perceive, to feel, to breathe, to walk, to understand, to make himself a man. Naturally, to learn to move oneself, and to re-find one's own existence does not mean to admire or to recite, to perform new movements, but to make up continuously mouldable material.

What follows is: impossibility to believe in discussion for imagery, in the communication of new explanatory and didactic information, in the structure that imposes regularity, behaviour, synthesis that leans upon a moralistic, industrial subject; estrangement, therefore, from the existing archetype and continuous renewal of himself; total aversion for discussion and aspiration towards continuity, towards aphasia, towards immobility, for a progressive identification of consciousness and praxis. The first discoveries of this dispossession are the finite and infinite moments of life; the work of art and the work that identifies itself with life; the dimension of life as lasting without end; immobility as a possibility of leaving contingent circumstances in order to plunge into time; the explosion of the individual dimension as an aesthetic and feeling communion with nature; unconsciousness as a method of consciousness of the world; the search of psycho-physical disturbances plurally sensitive and steadfast; the loss of identity with himself, for an abandonment of reassuring recognition that is continually imposed upon him by others and by the social system; the object-subject as physical presence continuously changing, as a trial of existence that becomes continuous, chaotic, spatial and differs temporally. "Art comes," states Cage, "from a kind of experimental condition in which one experiments with the living." To create art, then, one identifies with life and to exist takes on the meaning of re-inventing at every moment a new fantasy, pattern, of behaviour, aestheticism, etc. of one's own life. What is important is not to justify it or to reflect it in the work or in the product, but to live it as work, to be surprised in knowing the world, to be available to all of the facts of life (death, illogic, madness, casualness, nature, infinite, real, unreal, symbiosis). In fact, accepting the ideology of life one can exalt both its infiniteness and its contingency, one can live and kill life, reason about madness and go mad from reasoning. To think and to perceive, to fix figures and to present, to feel and to exhaust the sensation of an event, in a fact, an idea an action—everything can then become language and being, with its gestures, its actions, its body, its territory, its memory, its daily and fantastic reality. To communicate with persons and things means then to be in aesthetic and participating communion with the world, without posing the problem if the communication of values, of art, is a cosmic living.

Thus, art begins creating to place itself as a possibility in material (vegetable, animal, mineral and mental); its own dimension that identifies itself with knowledge and perception, becomes "living in art," that fantastic existence continually at variance with daily reality that opposes the building of art, that resulting from the place of art—from visual research to pop art, from minimal to funk art. A work of art—that of pop, op, minimal and funk artists—that is ready not for an intervention but for an interpretation of reality, a discussion on the images that tend towards a clarification and a criticism of the methods of communication (comic books, photographs, mass-media, technology produced objects, micro-perceptive structures, etc.). To create art as a critic of popular and optical images, that collaborate for the clarification of the social system, but block the crushing energy of life, nature, the world things and do away with the sensory significance of any kind of work; to create as an intervention that is carried out by means of the intellectual scheme of critical-historical literature, photographic advertising, imaginary, objective means, structurally psychological, perceptive, in order to domesticate in prefixed schemes the vitality of real daily life; to create art that moves itself within the linguistic systems in order to remain language, an act to live by means of continual isolation; to create art

as cultural kleptomania that
lives on the assumption of the
destructive charges of other
languages (politics, sociology
and technology); finally to create art as a separate language
that speculates on codes and on
instruments of communication in
order to live in a dimension of
exclusiveness and recognition
that makes it an aristocratic
and class question, an action
that scratches at the whole
of the superstructure without
blunting the natural structure
of the world.

On the other hand, the systematic procedure of life that
becomes contemporaneously, time,
experience, love, art, work,
politics, thought, action, science, daily living—poor in
choices and assumptions—if not
contingent and necessary; a life
as an expression of creative
existence, working, mental politics. There it creates work,
art, thought, life, politics and
complex living that lets itself
be used by the connections
of the system; here a living in
work, in art, in thought, in
politics deprived of recognizable, disoriented, infinite,
undiscussible constancy, given
the uncertainty of the evolu-
tionary cycle of daily reality. To live in work, in art, in
politics, in science as a free
design of itself, tying itself
to the rhythm of life for an
exhaustion, immediate and contingent of real life in action,
in facts and in thought.

In the first case, being,
living, working makes art and
politics "rich," interrupting
the chain of the casual in order
to maintain in life the manipulation of the world, an attempt
to conserve also "the man well
endowed when faced with nature;"
in the second case, life, work,
art, politics, behaviour,
thought "poveri," employed in
the inseparableness of experience and consciousness with the
political and mental event, with
contingency, with the infinite,
with the a historical, with the
chain of individual and social
motivation, with man, with environment, with space, with time,
with the social situation....
The declared intention of doing
away with every discussion,
misunderstanding and coherence
(coherence is in fact a characteristic of concatenation of
the system), the need of feeling
life continually going on, the
necessity, dictated by nature
itself, to advance at jumps,
without having to collect with
exactness the confines that gov-
ern modifications. Yesterday,
therefore, life, art, existence, manifestation of oneself,
manipulation, political beings,
involved because based on a
scientific and technological
imagination, on the highly spe-
cialized superstructure of communication, on marked moments;
a life, an art, a manifestation
in itself, a manipulation, cat-
egorical and class-conscious,
that—separating itself from the
real, as speculative actions—
isolates artistic, political
and behavioural art with the aim
of placing it in a competitive
position with life: a life, an
art, a policy, a manifestation

of itself, a metamorphic manipulation, that through agglom-
eration and collation, reduces
reality to fantasy; a life, an
art, a behaviour, a manipulation, frustrated—as a recep-
tacle of all of the real and
intellectual impotence of daily
life—a life, an art, a moralistic policy, in which judgment
is contradictory, imitating and
passing the real, to the real
itself, with a transgression of
the intellectual aspect in that
which is really needed. Today,
in life or art or politics one
finds in the anarchy and in
the continuousness of nomadic
behaviour, the greatest level of
liberty for a vital and fantastic expression; life or art or
politics, as a stimulus to ver-
ify continuously its own level
of mental and physical existence, as urgency of a presence
that eliminates the manipulation of life, in order to bring
about again the individuality of
every human and natural action;
an innocent art, or a marvel-
ousness of life, more political
spontaneity since it precedes
knowledge, reasoning, culture,
not justifying itself, but life
in the continuous enchantment
or horror of daily reality—a
daily reality that is more like
stupefying, horrible poetic
entity, like changing physical
presence, and never allusive to
alienation.

Thus, art life, politics
"poveri" are not apparent or
theoretical, they do not believe
in "putting themselves on
show," they do not abandon themselves in their definition, not
believing in art, life, politics "poveri," they do not have
as an objective the process of
the representation of life; they
want only to feel, know, perform
that which is real, understanding that what is important is
not life, work, action, but the
condition in which life, work
and action develop themselves.

It is a moment that tends
toward deculturization, regression, primitiveness and repression, towards the pre-logical
and pre-iconographic stage,
towards elementary and spontaneous politics, a tendency
towards the basic element in
nature (land, sea, snow, minerals, heat, animals) and in life
(body, memory, thought), and in
behaviour (family, spontaneous
action, class struggle, violence, environment).

The reality, in which one
participates every day, is in
its dull absurdity a political deed. It is more real than
any intellectually recognizable
element. Thus, art, politics
and life "poveri," as reality do
not send back or postpone, but
they offer themselves as self
representatives presenting themselves in the state of essence.

Dansaekhwa artist Kwon Young-Woo began to work exclusively with paper in the 1960s, unlike others in the movement who typically engaged the "canvas" of painting as a surface and a broader art historical framework for intervention. Kwon chose paper because of its specific Korean context, as the rice paper (*hanji*) was used primarily for calligraphy, the tradition of artistic writing (*Seoye*). Instead of relegating it as a surface to receive ink, information, and skilled mastery, he made the paper his subject. He enacts a method akin to obsessive compulsion, in which he tears, scratches, and cuts the paper, often using his fingernails as the tool. Implicit within this work is an assessment of the fragility of the material's core structure and its inherent vulnerability.

His approach treats the paper like skin, in which his actions produce wound-like consequences that cannot be healed. The final result is the aftermath of a violence that does not happen as single explosion, but rather a drawn-out process of small systematic punctures and incisions. To delineate the contrast within the body of work, sometimes the tears are surrounded by an abundance of untouched blank space. As art historian Joan Kee describes, "It is significant that Kwon refused to describe the untouched expanses as 'empty,' 'blank,' or 'void,' a move that leads us to consider blank space as the absence of touch."[1] The work poetically speaks to the fraught political condition of Korea in parallel to its creation, including the intrusion of the military rule of the 1970s that withheld individual liberty and autonomy, an assault that deteriorates the mind and binds society as much as the threat of physical brutality.

L.M.

1   Joan Kee, *Contemporary Korean Art: Tansaekhwa and The Urgency of Method* (Minneapolis: University of Minneapolis Press, 2013), 65.

Untitled, 1976, Korean paper   cat. no. 29

Maria Lai was originally from Sardinia, an Italian island with a rich legacy of weaving perpetuated by generations of women. The craft influenced her works that honored the tradition with radical and mindful disruptions of structure and process. For example, her series *Telai* from the 1970s features deconstructed looms that become a canvas for combines of materials the artist had on hand: thread, wood, paint, twine, hay, clothespins, cutlery, etc. The liberation of the loom from function to sculpture makes it unusable for its original intention, but through Lai's intervention the object illuminates its own condition as a receiver of the culture that directly surrounds it. Until recently, Lai's artworks were not thoroughly rooted in art criticism or assigned to a definitive movement like her Italian contemporaries in the *arte povera* movement. Her work exemplifies the approach of "poor" material explorations that were prevalent in other facets of art, craft, and design at the time, an ethos shared nationally in Italy and internationally beyond the fixed canon.

Also in the 1970s, Lai began to create books in which material served as the primary language rather than any legible text, privileging the poetics of the visual over the written. She created books with oven-baked bread dough, as well as a prolific series of embroidered books, an example of which is included in *Landlord Colors*. In the creation of these books, she used the sewing machine like a pen, mimicking writing with thread that she allowed to tangle or hang like wild overgrowth. Herein, the books become representations of knowledge beyond academia or linear history, a collective knowing that is inherited, shared, and expanded.

L.M.

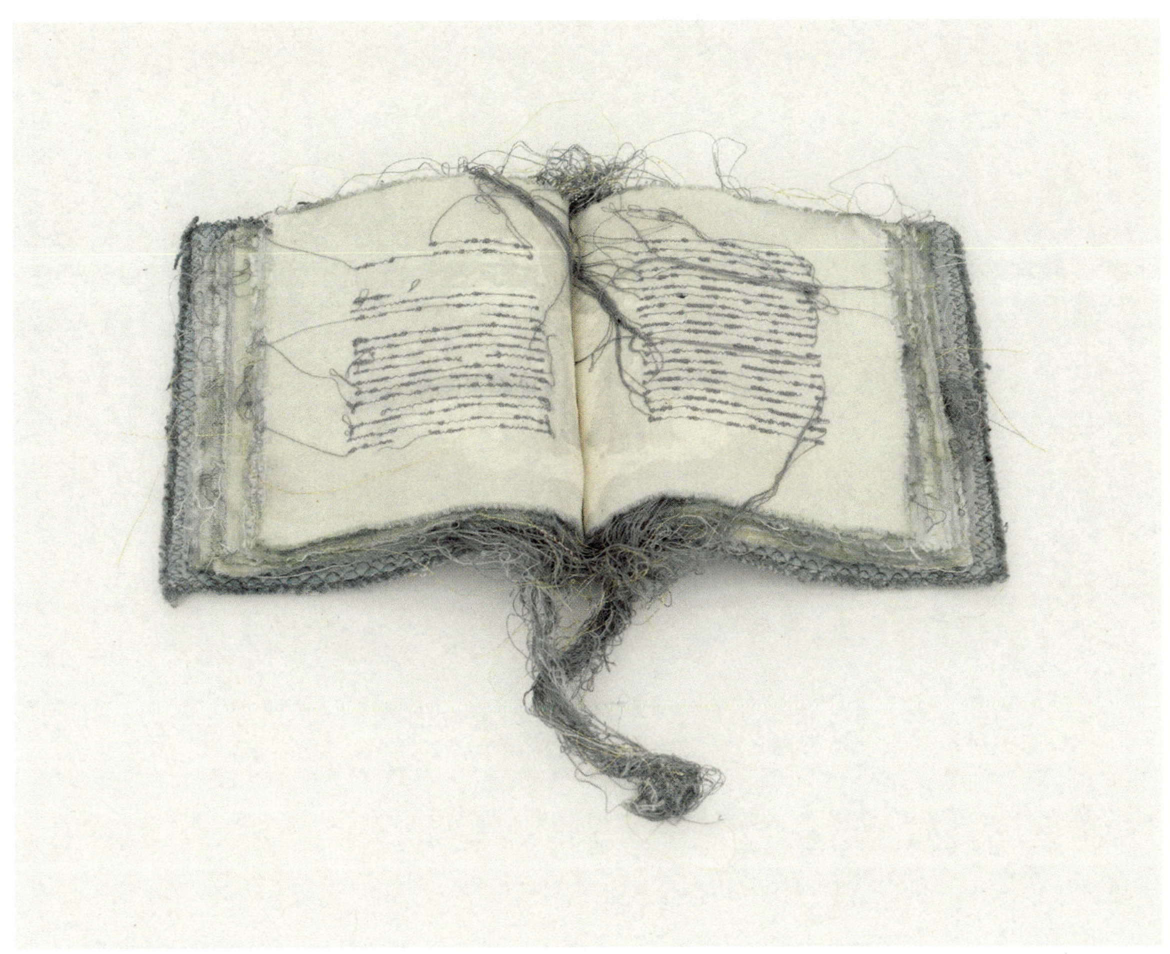

Book, 1984, fabric, thread   cat. no. 30

In a practice that includes ceramics, drawing, sculpture, and painting, Addie Langford's artistic methodology has origins in slow craft, which can be described as the patient undertaking of process and the mindful inquiry into the source of materials. She is an inquisitor interested in communicating with the material and extracting the poetic potential at its limits. For instance, a recent series of paintings originate from an everyday, tactile experience of Detroit car culture—the interior of the automobile. She stretched on canvas the manufactured material used inside of cars meant to withstand the punctures, weight, and pressure of the human body. Its industrial name is "composite hide" because it uses the leftover scraps of mass production from the leather industry—a combination of many animals. Composite hide is made of three layers: a top layer of synthetic rubber, a middle of cloth mesh, and bottom layer of actual leather detritus. At first, she painted on the top synthetic layer that paradoxically is cast to emulate the texture of real leather—it is what hands feel on a steering wheel. When paint is applied to the surface, it races down and dries suspended like water spots on a window.

For *Landlord Colors*, Langford initiated the *Verso Phthalo Series*, which used the underside of the composite hide—typically unseen—made of actual animal skin. This surface is prone to absorption, and mark-making instantly becomes permanent. As a complementary process, Langford walks across the surface with a thick brush and lets the natural weight of her arm sag—a body giving reverence to bodies. Langford is influenced by the Korean *dansaekhwa* painters who used found material canvases, such as Ha Chong-Hyun's use of agricultural hemp. To think about these material legacies in parallel, the surfaces directly relate to their respective economies, while their method of paint application is strategic and emotive.

L.M.

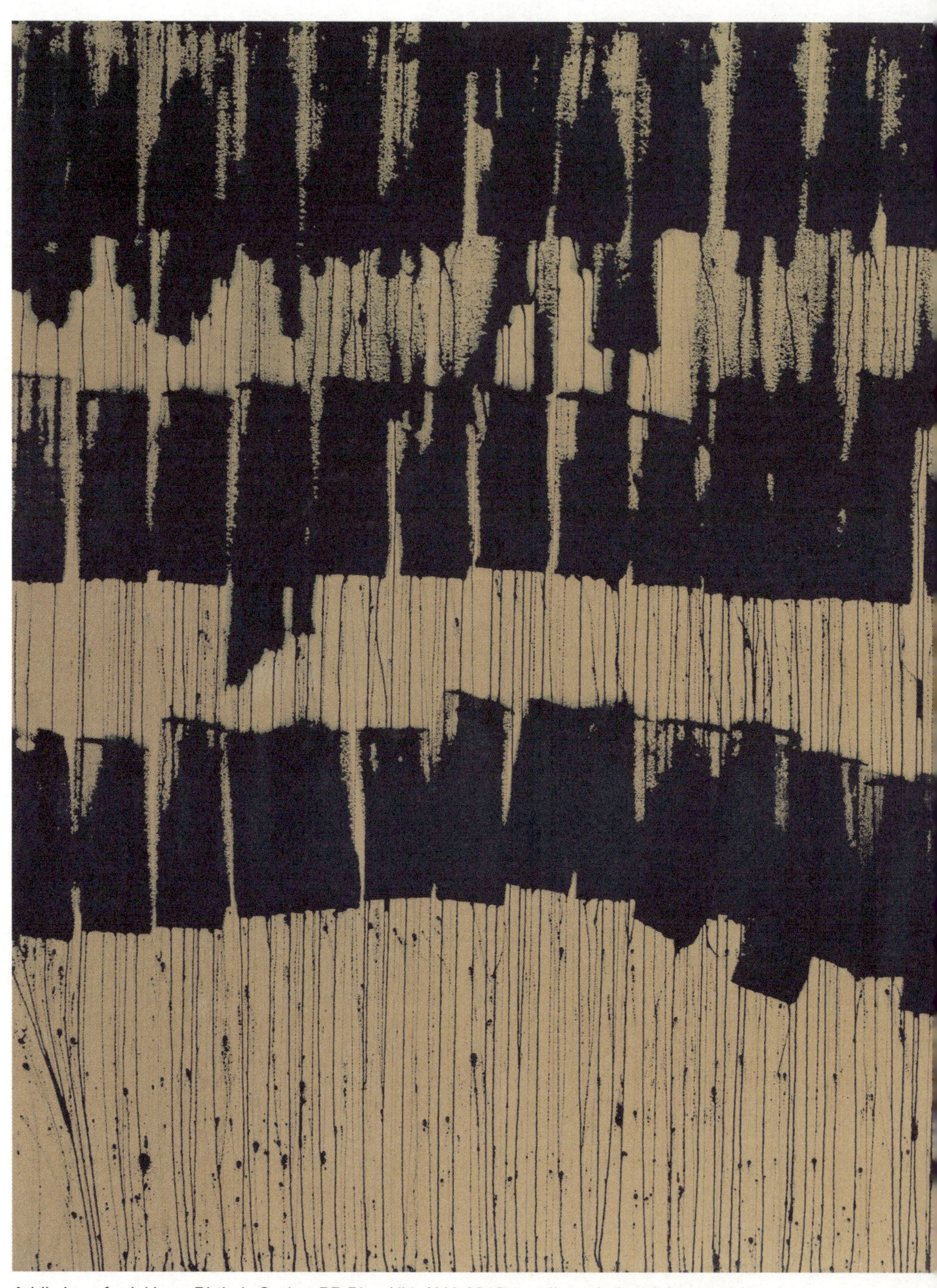

Addie Langford, *Verso Phthalo Series: BR Blue / #1 / LU*, 2018, acrylic on industrial composite hide, verso   cat. no. 31

Lee Ufan is an artist and writer whose career comprises significant contributions through his paintings to the Korean-born *dansaekhwa* and, through his sculptural experiments, Japanese *mono-ha* movements. Born in South Korea but largely based in Japan, he conducts a rigorous investigation of minimalism and the potential limits of gesture, material, and perception in his work. Lee is often credited as curating the first exhibition of Korean artwork that came to be known as *dansaekhwa* (monochrome painting) in Japan in the 1970s.

Lee's *Relatum* series began in the late 1960s, a material exploration that continued for more than fifty years. This version, initially conceived in 1971, is composed of stones resting on and pulling a thin sheet of rubber. In his sculptural works, the physical materials are presented in their unaltered form. Lee described the philosophical mediation between the materials as "encounters," and he regarded these interactions as a tension between opposition and acceptance. Curator Alexandra Monroe expands on his conceptual practice within the sociopolitical context of Japan and Korea: "Like others working around the world circa 1970, Lee was at the forefront of an international tide that detached Westernization from modernization, and modernization from ideological universalism.... [Lee] posited an emphatically material and durational relationship between viewer, object, and site. His language was more than a dialogue with neo-avant-garde concepts at this moment of rupture; it was a radical expansion of the possibilities for art in a world where colonialism and imperialism, 'otherness' and 'difference' had real-life implications."[1]

L.M., I.G.W.

1   Alexandra Munroe, "Stand Still a Moment," in *Lee Ufan: Marking Infinity* (New York: The Solomon R. Guggenheim Museum, 2011), 2.

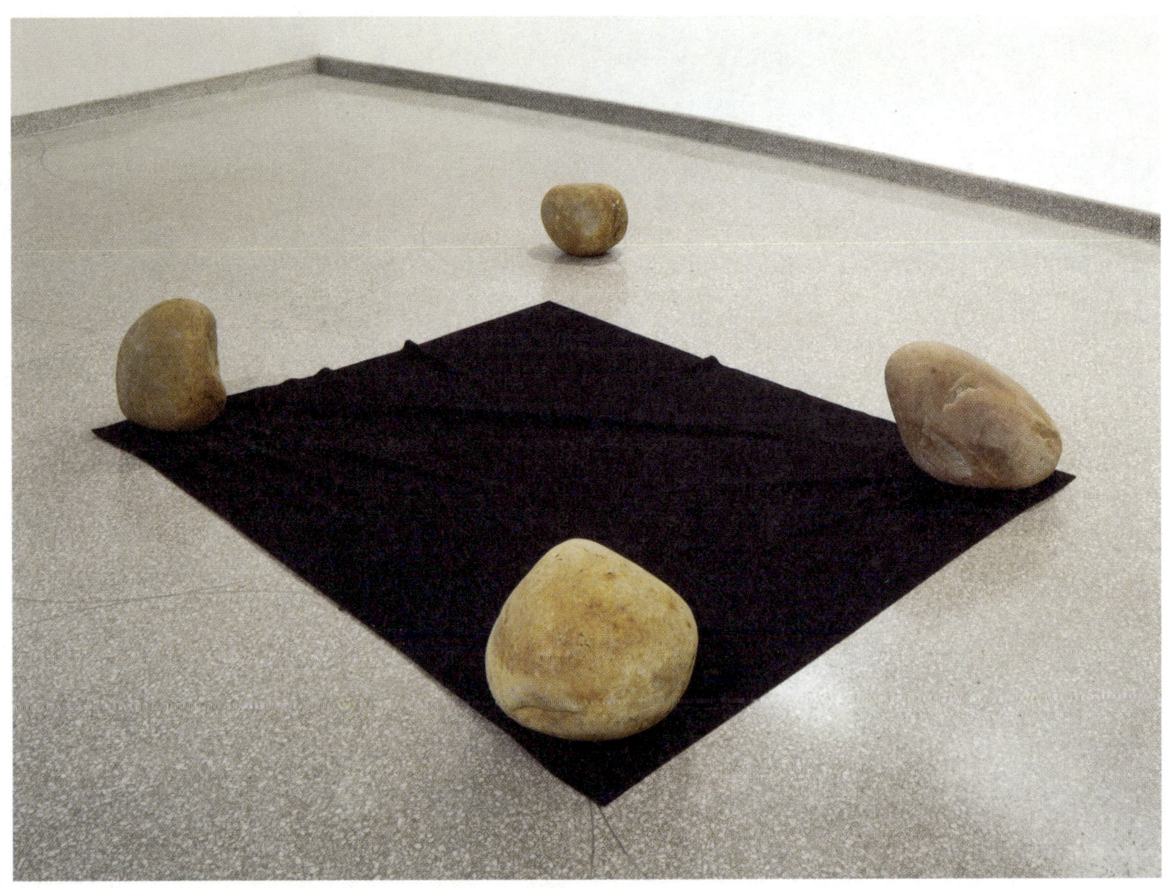

Relatum, 1971/2011, rubber, stones   cat. no. 32

THE POWER OF RESTRAINT AND INTEGRATION

Originally published in Dansaekhwa with Lee Ufan
(Seoul: Kukje Gallery, 2015), 20–25.

The following is a conversation between Lee Ufan and Yongwoo Lee as part of Lee Ufan's participation in the 56th Venice Biennale collateral event Dansaekhwa at the Palazzo Contarini-Polignac. In their conversation they discuss a wide range of subjects related to Dansaekhwa, including its significance in art history, its social and political background, and its aesthetic philosophy.

YONGWOO LEE (L) : Dansaekhwa is a Korean word that means "a single color." Translated for the Western reader it means "monochromatic painting." But while the monochrome in the West was based on rejection of color, which had dominated the tradition of painting, Dansaekhwa may be seen as being focused on the subjects of self-control and integration, and not, specifically, a rejection of color. In Dansaekhwa, color is a tool and a mode of expression that results in the artwork. That is to say, Dansaekhwa describes an expansive definition of paintings that, unlike monochrome, was premised on a prediction that painting's relevance would end. What is the meaning of color to you? I ask you this question because your use of color has been very limited since the 1960s up to now.

LEE UFAN (U) : First of all, the beginning of Korean Dansaekhwa is circumstantial. Paint was considered just a necessary material and it was not a matter of choosing a certain color. In the 1960s through the 1970s when the Dansaekhwa movement was founded, materials were rare and freedom of expression was limited due to poverty and military politics. Simply finding paint to use meant that artists made work using only the minimal actions. (Of course, it is probably true also that Koreans had their own monochromatic sensibility that was subconsciously in effect.) We can also say that there was at that time a distinct awareness of and commitment to resisting against society. This was coupled with artists' ongoing belief in the possibility that they could still make original paintings in the greater international art world. I also think this kind of Eastern or Korean methodology and color palette has matured gradually over time.

Whether it was due to local conditions or beliefs, there are similarities on the surface but there are differences as well. In my case, in the 1970s I primarily used the colors blue or orange made from pigment, and then also began to use black (also produced from stone pigment), and later gray. Recently I have begun to occasionally use blue or red acrylic. Regardless, I have always intentionally selected extremely limited colors. For me, color is a variable material. I feel that I had to choose a color that was conceptual, and that it should be from real life although it should also feel distant at the same time. In the East, there is the Buddhist philosophy of yin and yang that says that color (all phenomena) is emptiness, and emptiness is color. I think that the yin and yang of color played an important role in the way negative space in Oriental paintings is created with sumi ink. Ironically, in order to suggest a realm that transcends the concept of color, it is important to realize the variable materiality of color as a single and restrained medium.

L : You have described Dansaekhwa as an "art of humility." I believe you are

referring to the minimal expression, or the expressive restraint, in Dansaekhwa, and I feel that this idea is reflected in your own sculptures and paintings. Having more or less expression does not determine the aesthetic or the narrative of an artwork. Nevertheless, it is not easy to continue pursuing artistic restraint throughout one's entire career, so I believe this must be an inherent characteristic of the artist. Do you think that the restraint of expression found in Dansaekhwa was actually in response to the specific demands of this time period?

U : When I say Dansaekhwa is an "art of humility," I am referring to the aesthetics of yin and yang, of both showing and hiding the ego. Modernism signified an expression of the self, whereas contemporary art is an expression that relates the inner with the outer world. Dansaekhwa does not reveal an image or form of the self but, rather, is an expression that respects the reciprocal relationship of the simple materials of paint and canvas, and the neutral actions of creating. A story is created only through the harmony of paint or the actions taken on the canvas, and the artist does not set forth his own assertion. It is this approach that is viewed as being "shy." And the yin and yang of this approach has allowed for greater universality.

While all this could be related to tradition or an

artist's predisposition, one could also say that the given time period and cultural milieu allowed Dansaekhwa artists to achieve an aesthetic of self-control. In my case, I tried to limit and simplify concept, material, and actions when making both painting and sculpture, and focused on their relationship with the interior and exterior in an attempt to open up a bigger world. What restrains me is my ethics and my approach to manifesting this openness to a higher outer dimension.

L : The period of the 1960s and '70s out of which Dansaekhwa emerged was a profoundly complex time. Dansaekhwa took root during a repressive period of military dictatorship that followed a series of tragic historical events, including Japan's occupation of Korea, the Pacific War, the Korean War, and ultimately the division of Korea. There was a lot of hybridity in terms of social discourse and social values at the time. Despite this complexity, Dansaekhwa does not seem overly defined by the chaos. If we establish that art is a manifestation of social production, then there is not a purely aesthetic ideal, divorced from its context. Given this, what is the political and social stance of Dansaekhwa?

U : As I recall, it was difficult to speak out in Korea during the 1970s. It was also the age of monochrome, in which our freedom of expression was extremely limited. In my view, the stance of Dansaekhwa artists amid this oppression, chaos, and poverty was that of silent resistance, an approach based on the gesture of expression as nonexpression. During this time artists used radical approaches, using repetitive actions of painting and erasing, pushing paint through hemp from its verso and then pushing the paint back through the surface, repeatedly painting and scraping, or blackening newspapers, all as a method of destabilizing content. All of these actions were not a way to present a certain ideology but to express a silent but anarchistic resistance.

L : So would I be correct if I said that Dansaekhwa had its own method of struggle, which could be defined as silent resistance?

U : At the time, artists did not hold governmental or bureaucratic positions and they were unknown. Yet they kept a unique stance to resist against the established order and authorities. They were outsiders. However, as the GNP level of our country shot up and popular support for democratization increased, the artists in the 1980s who expressed social criticism more explicitly through their artwork criticized the artists of the seventies. Their criticism was based on their assertion that artists working in the seventies ignored society and history and made work based only on surface expression. It is understandable considering the circumstances at that time, but from a broader perspective, artists working in the seventies did engage in the methods that were possible at that time. The beginning of Dansaekhwa is actually the vestige of expressing resistance by not expressing. We cannot deny that Dansaekhwa has endured, both through its persistent resistance as well as having identified with international developments rather than seeking domestic recognition. I would like to add that I think Dansaekhwa's greatest importance was that it denied modernism, which emphasized a kind of image or form, and opened up the possibility of expression through the mutual interchange of disparate elements. Just as Arte Povera, Supports/Surfaces, Anti-Form, and Mono-ha were the manifestation of new artistic and political science, Dansaekhwa embodied the politics of its time.

L : There is an abundance of qi in your work. And each viewer will see a different expression depending on how they perceive that energy. People of the East call it "restrained energy" and Westerners call it "integrated strength." When you combine the two, you have "restrained and integrated energy." I think if your works were descriptive and prosaic, we would have seen a completely different aesthetic depiction. I believe that restrained and integrated energies are at the core of your

art. In other words, it's like the "hidden power" when one wants to speak out but turns away in silence instead. Art delves deeper as it ripens; it is similar to the growth of hidden power and technique.

U : You have a good understanding of the characteristic of my work as "restrained and integrated energy." What's interesting is that it's difficult to evoke this "restrained and integrated energy" without a physical association. This means that the artist's trained body, focus, and rhythm is critical in the work. In order for the work to increase tension and density by releasing contradictory aspects and to radiate energy, extreme focus and extraordinary physical discipline is required. This is a poetic and transcendental act. It's close to a miracle. This is possible because the body, while being my own physical form, is at the same time a part of nature and can be considered to be debris in space. The body is not my tool but, rather, a living engine that absorbs its surrounding energy and then releases it. This says everything. I hope for the artwork to also be a living body. Its composition and structure is important, but it's difficult to move the audience if it cannot evoke vitality. When energy of restraint and integration is visually activated it causes the canvas to vibrate, activating the surrounding space and the audience.

L : The phrase "the compromise of Oriental spirituality and Western form" is often used in setting the context for modern art of the 1960s and '70s such as Dansaekhwa or Mono-ha. At first it sounds like a rational explanation, but for me it's really a dangerous statement because it equates the Oriental world with spirituality and the Western world with objectivity and materialism. Of course the formal influence of Western art on Korean or Japanese art in the 1960s is significant. But at the same time, in order to view these influences as equal, further explanation is needed.

U : The problem arises from the way one interprets context. I question relating the Oriental and Western world through a simple binary equation. You could think of it in terms of mixing ideas freely without any boundaries then reediting from there, or you can pick and choose depending on specific examples and ignore the context accumulated from previous experiences and knowledge. In this day and age, it's difficult to track down a single rationale or point of origin because of the distribution and speed of information; although there is always a regressive minority that argues for the rediscovery of the modern and primacy of originality.

From my experience, no matter how secular one claims to be, he cannot deny that his DNA or experiences from the past seep into his work. Maybe that's why I think of the universe of the future as my origin, and from time to time it feels as if I'm traveling through the past. As the ideals of capitalism began to erode in places such as Europe, America, and Japan in the late sixties and seventies, an air of reconstruction began to take hold. While recently critics have started to view Mono-ha in a positive light, it was actually heavily criticized in the beginning because it seemed to deny the importance of cultural style. At the same time, because deconstruction was its starting point, Mono-ha could not take its form through solving a set of questions—a stance that ensured it was a movement based around formally inconclusive gestures. This is the foundation of the essence of Mono-ha.

L : The physical gesture becomes an important aspect when explaining Dansaekhwa. The gesture on the canvas becomes one of its defining aspects, and each artist has different methods or approaches to working on the canvas. How would you explain your physical process?

U : When I saw Barnett Newman's exhibition at the Museum of Modern Art in New York in the early seventies I felt a new enthusiasm for painting. Unlike Newman's focus on spatial development, I began to explore temporal aspects of painting, using the body as a parameter. With paintings by artists such as Newman or Sol LeWitt, it's entirely possible to create the same expression using machinery or an assistant, as long as there is an organizing concept. But I wanted to attempt a method of expression based on experiencing important moments in life through my own body. I created works in which I dipped the brush in paint, held my breath and repeatedly placed dots on the surface. At first the painted mark was saturated with pigment, but eventually it thinned then disappeared, a series of gestures that revealed the passing of time. The repetition of such gestures was extremely mechanistic, but at the same time it was a technique in which I could feel a type of breathing and rhythm that became the structural surface.

For my gesture to become realized, there needed to be a concept of physiological order or an objective structure that I could follow. In the case of this work, I needed to train my breathing so that the act could be carried out. That became my attitude and method for expression. Maybe it is in response to this gesture that many have commented on feeling the "performance" in my work. Recently in my painting, spatial concerns are becoming more important than time, but despite the strict symbolic structure of "the stroke," you can still feel the hidden gesture.

L : In your sculptures, the use of materials is very limited. It is solely stone and steel. Stone represents natural material and steel symbolizes the industrial material that built modern civilization. Even the expression of the two relationships is restrained in the extreme, and association is implied through the series title *Relatum*. What is this relationship? Is it nature and civilization, or does it suggest some sociopolitical associations as well?

U : From the late 1960s to the mid-1970s I used diverse materials from both industry and nature. As I continued, it eventually converged to stone and steel (though there are exceptions), or, depending on the situation, one or the other. The reason my primary materials were simplified to stone and steel is that stone is a representative element of nature while steel represents industrial society. At the same time they're originally the same medium. It's as if I am engaging in a dialogue between nature and industry.

Just as in my paintings, my sculptures are based on my continuously simplifying and restraining. In order to critique mass production and mass consumption I rely on working with less, and, with materials that cannot be reproduced, I think I've finally arrived at a mode of minimal expression. Although I use simple and neutral materials, in drawing attention to their relationship with each other as well as the surrounding space, I aim to create a more open mode of expression.

It's not a way of depicting an image but, rather, it's

a method to draw out the res-
onance of a space by forming a
relationship between the materials. In an exhibition they
are set up so that they're in an
equal relationship instead of a
dependent one. Showing various
relationships by having the two
materials face each other, laying them down or standing them
up, having them touch or keeping
them apart, suggests abstraction
on a higher level. Such scenes
are quite obviously critical and
will evoke a political dynamic.

L : I believe the traditional
use of ink painting (sumi) carries the most weight in Asian
art. I'm not advocating the
revival of ink-and-wash painting, but the foundation of art
supported by the enormous imaginative potential of the ink
block and the invention of paper
brings about a confidence in
history. Sumi painting is calligraphy yet also painting, a
philosophy but at the same time
a methodology. When I look at
your series *From Point*, *From
Line*, and *From Winds*, I can feel
the influence of the sumi ink
sensibility. This is in contrast
to contemporary work that is so
heavily influenced by digital
technology. Can we also explain
Korean Dansaekhwa in context of
the tradition of ink painting?

U : I was influenced by traditional ink painting but I've
never considered the possibilities of it. The fragility of traditional paper, the
issues of spontaneous expression, ink bleeding into the

paper without any constraints,
all evoke the harmony of agrarian or communal society, and
it's difficult to repeat the
tradition of sumi ink painting under today's constantly
mobile, urban, hybridized, and
confrontational conditions. At
the same time, concepts such as
the universal idea at the root
of traditional ink painting that
life and spirit are contained
in one brushstroke, or blank
space, suggest a new aspect of
painting for me. But it seems
too simplistic to connect the
Dansaekhwa artists with traditional ink painting. It's difficult to feel the power of a
brushstroke or the emptiness of
space from their surfaces. Going
forward, Dansaekhwa must establish its own context.

Whether it is painting or
sculpture, I try to transcend
the object itself so that you're
able to experience another level
of space through the work rather
than simply looking at it. This
subverts the meaning of art in
all traditions. It may seem to
be a naive or a futile attempt.
But consider this: In this day
and age when all formative
beliefs have been overturned and
there's a limitless universe,
how can my artistic attempt be
considered to be vain? Just
as space reverberates when a
bell tolls, my work will reveal
temporal spatial dimensions.

Julio Llópiz-Casal navigates the complicated spaces of archive, memory, and art history across twentieth-century Cuba. Cuba is a place where notions of a local avant-garde are a contentious subject in a country that heavily self-edits its own history, particularly with regard to the United States.

Archivo I and *Archivo II* consist of two floppy disks that claim to contain personal letters by Félix González-Torres (1957–96) and Ana Mendieta (1948–85), two American artists of Cuban origin who came to prominence in the contemporary art world during their respective lifetimes, but whose careers were tragically cut short. The floppy disk assigned to González-Torres purports to be documentation of letters the artist had written to his family in Camagüey in central Cuba, while the other disk contains letters that Mendieta sent to the United Nations with the subject line: "Cuba." Both are speculative correspondences; no proof exists to confirm them. The lack of clarity around what constitutes factual information, propaganda, and urban myth is a pervasive condition throughout Cuba.

The selection of the floppy disks is purposeful, as this was the format used by the Cuban security agency to store such information. Llópiz-Casal's archives assert that more than data is obtained under espionage. Personal and cultural memory is also captured and rendered inaccessible to the island's everyday citizens. Furthermore, the disks act as a metaphor for a country trapped by obsolescence—both materially and ideologically.

A.G.F.

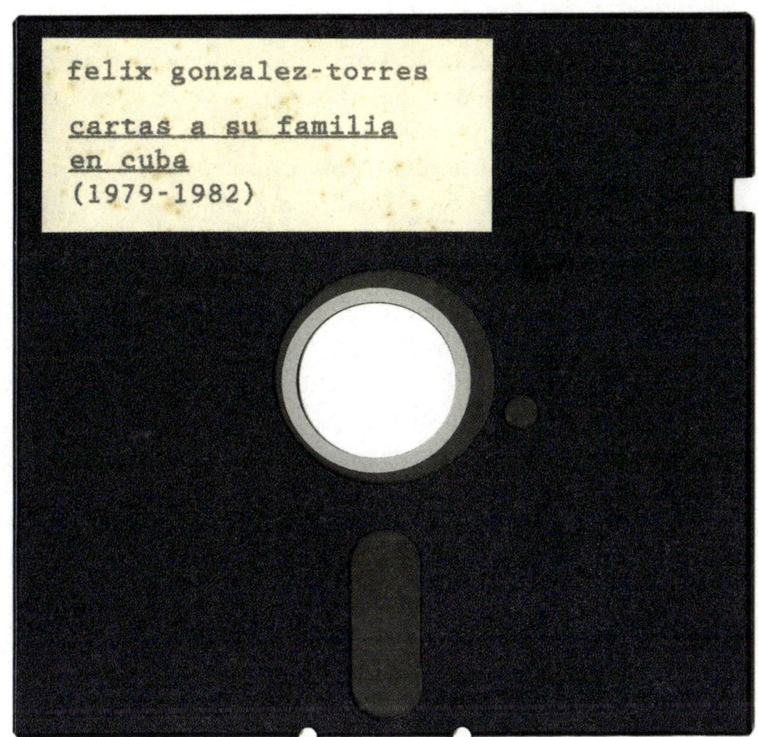

Archivo I, 2014, paper label, magnetized floppy disk   cat. no. 33

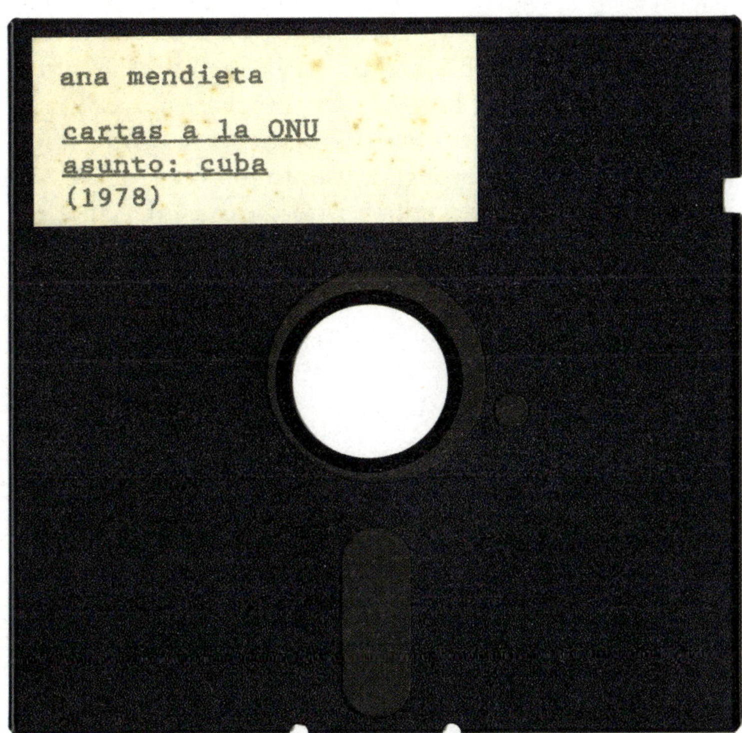

Archivo II, 2014, paper label, magnetized floppy disk   cat. no. 34

Detroit writer Morgan Mies astutely observed, "The art of Kylie Lockwood…resonates with ancient history. Many of the art objects she has created over the years look like they might have been discovered during an archaeological dig, or stolen from a museum of antiquities in some little-known Mediterranean town."[1] This transhistorical connection to the history of making also extends to the regional and familial. As a Detroit native and graduate of the Center for Creative Studies, Lockwood's dexterity and competency with materials are often notable attributes of the artists raised in the city, a facet of its industrious past. The specific inheritance of craftsmanship in porcelain, however, came from Lockwood's grandmother, a doll maker, who passed on the skill during the artist's childhood.

In the creation of *Porcelain Legs in the Posture of David*, Lockwood asks: "What was Michelangelo thinking about when he made the statue of David? Stability? Beauty? Optimism?" She conflates the two—auteur and subject—by casting her own body to mimic David's *contrapposto*. The term describes the naturalistic stance of Italian Renaissance sculptures in which a human figure stands with weight shifted to one foot and with a slight twist of the torso, maximizing the body's desirability—the red carpet pose of its time. The process is a performance by proxy: the artist's body stands in his position, his flesh morphs into her flesh. She casts her legs in porcelain; once dried, she knocks the legs down, leaving only the lower fragments. Placed on a pedestal of unfired clay, Lockwood then carefully applied polish to each toenail. Sanctity is sacrificed for relevance; the monumental sculpture comes into the twenty-first-century ethos—radical, feminized, impermanent.

L.M.

1   Morgan Mies, "Kylie Lockwood," *Essay'd*, March 2018, https://essayd.org/?p=2152.

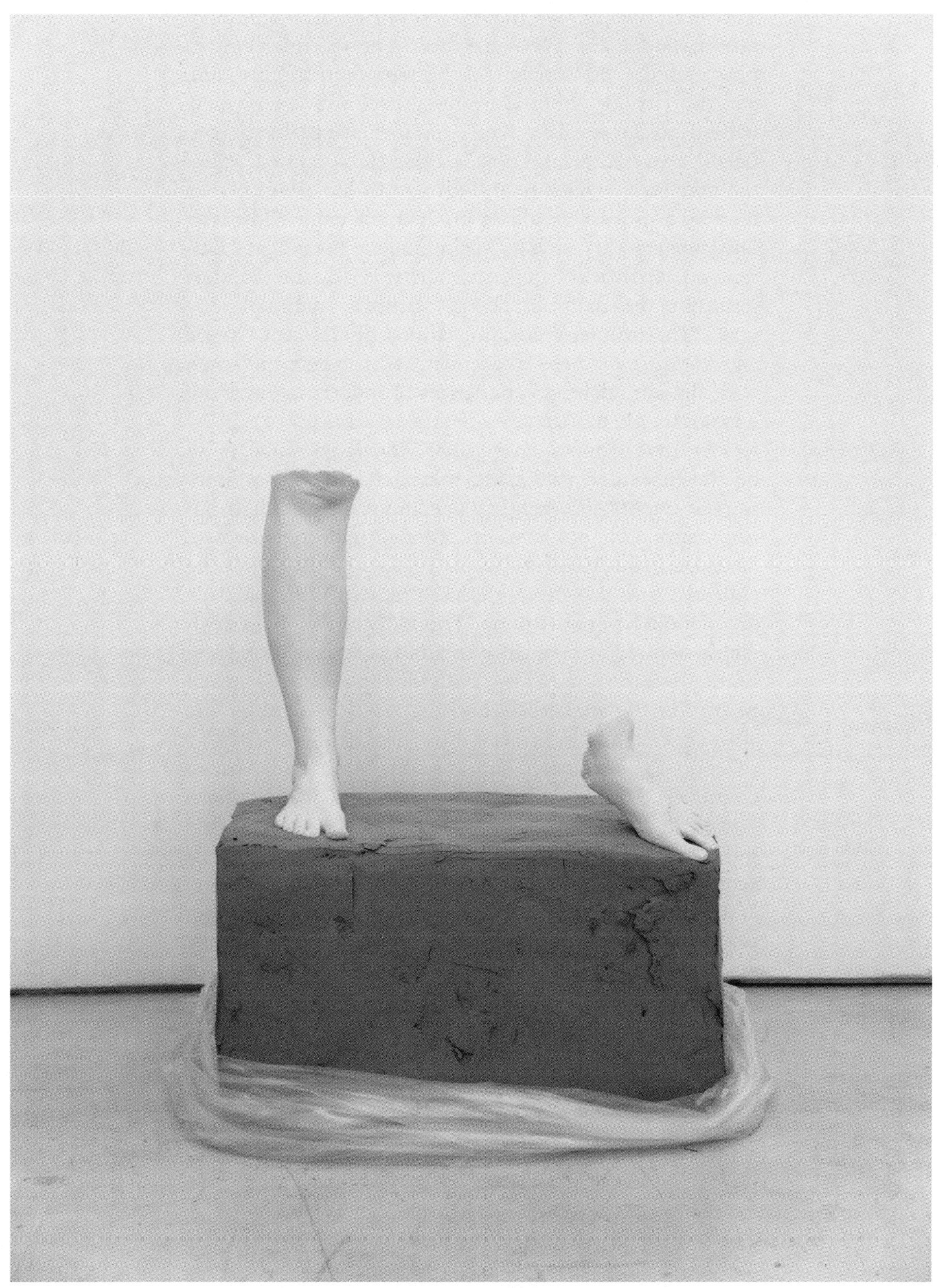

Porcelain Legs in the Posture of David, 2016, pigmented porcelain, unfired clay, nail polish, plastic bag
cat. no. 35

The narrative arc of material interests in contemporary art since the 1960s has been one of expansion; it now includes the intangible, the temporal, the cerebral, and the virtual—from Giovanni Anselmo's use of magnetism to James Lee Byar's performative mysticism. Greek artist Andreas Lolis, a classically trained sculptor, connects us back to antiquity with his use of carved marble, a process as old as civilization itself. However, Lolis enacts this archaic technique to investigate current sociopolitical concerns. Writer Damiano Femfert positions the material choice within a national context: "The immense cultural burden of classical Greece and the intrinsic need to deconstruct it in order to go on with life are relentless challenges of modern Greece and a major theme in its contemporary art world."[1]

At first glance, *Permanent Residence* appears to be the discarded packaging materials that are ubiquitous in twenty-first-century consumer life and distribution: cardboard, polystyrene, wooden pallets. However, on close inspection, the items reveal themselves to be skillfully and deceptively crafted marble with exacting and detailed imperfections. This deft use of hyperrealism is applied strategically to address Greece's ongoing humanitarian crisis, as the individual pieces are stacked to mimic the makeshift housing used by immigrants who seek refuge in Greece, now a prominent gateway to enter the European Union from Asian and African countries. The material adds significant weight, both physically and conceptually, to a harsh reality often hidden or ignored. Marble is the medium used to craft sculptures of icons, to ornament grandiose architecture, and to preserve civic heroes in refined poses. Through the conversion of the transient to the permanent, the discarded to the prominent, Lolis asks us to confront the true legacy of our humanity.

L.M.

1   Damiano Femfert, "Andreas Lolis," *The Breeder*, http://thebreedersystem.com/artists/andreas-lolis/.

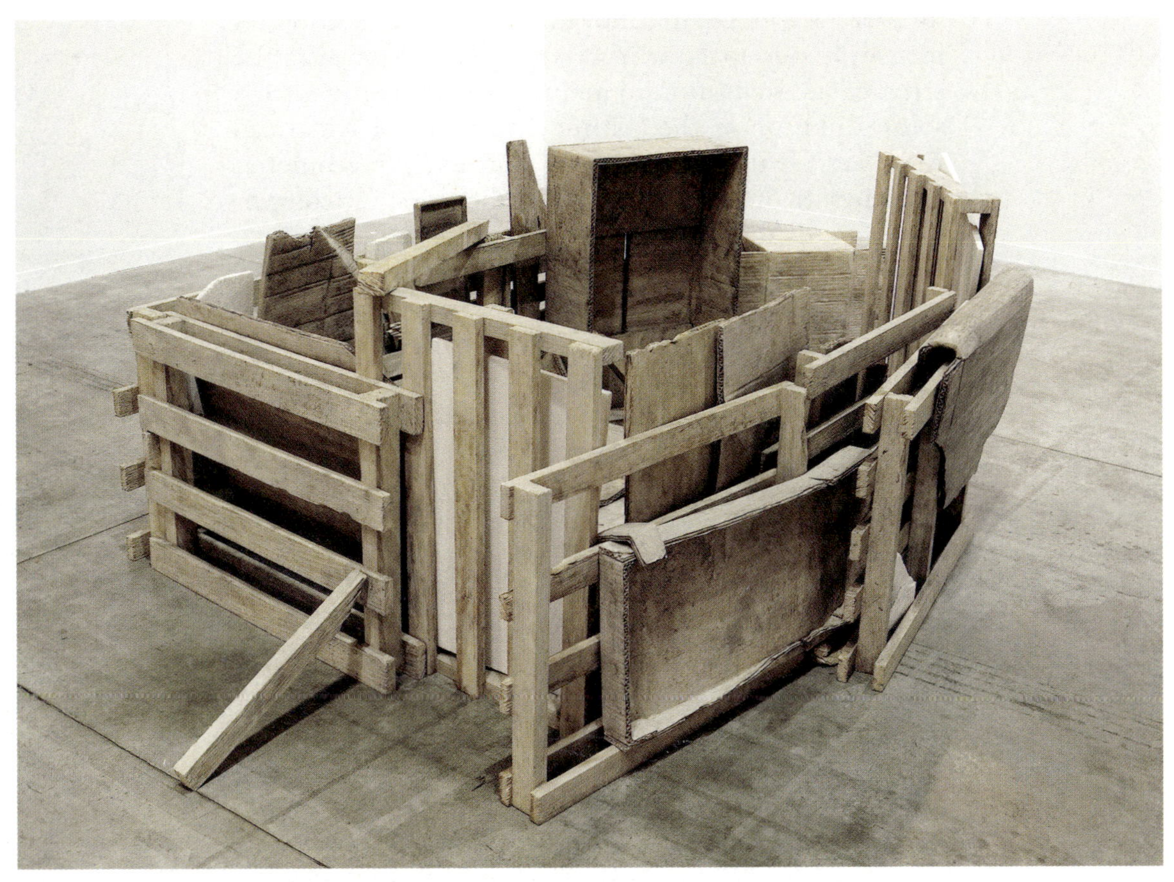

Permanent Residence, installation view at Biennale de Lyon, 2015, marble

In 1968, Alvin Loving moved from his hometown of metro Detroit to New York City. The next year, the artist catapulted into the mainstream art world with a solo exhibition at the Whitney Museum of American Art that featured a series of hard edged geometric paintings. Soon after, the artist made a dramatic departure towards the creation of materially abstract compositions. While Loving was often inspired by the social, political, and personal stimuli around him, he came to the sewn and dyed pieces not intentionally, but through "accidents and incidents."[1]

In an interview with James Little in 1985, Loving shared an anecdote behind the sewn compositions. In 1973, his daughter was in his studio and spilled something on one of the geometric paintings he had made for an upcoming show. Loving told her to "wash that off," and afterwards he found himself drawn to the color and saturation that this happenstance had produced. The next morning, the artist cut up sixty paintings into smaller pieces and sewed them back together.[2] The dyed cloth works of the 1970s yielded a creative liberation for Loving. Like many of the constructions from this period, *Untitled* (1973) communicates the freedom of rejecting the rigidity of the two-dimensional canvas coupled with the sculptural sensibility of its looser, irregular form. Furthermore, Loving's defiant act against hard-edge forms was made possible through the deconstruction of unrestrained fibers, making more palpable his experience of black life in the years before and after the 1967 Detroit Rebellion.

T.R.A.

1   Katy Siegel, "Self-Made Painting," *Al Loving: Torn Canvas* (New York: Gary Snyder Gallery, 2012), 6.
2   James Little, "Al Loving: Painter," *Artist and Influence* 4 (1986), 59–68.

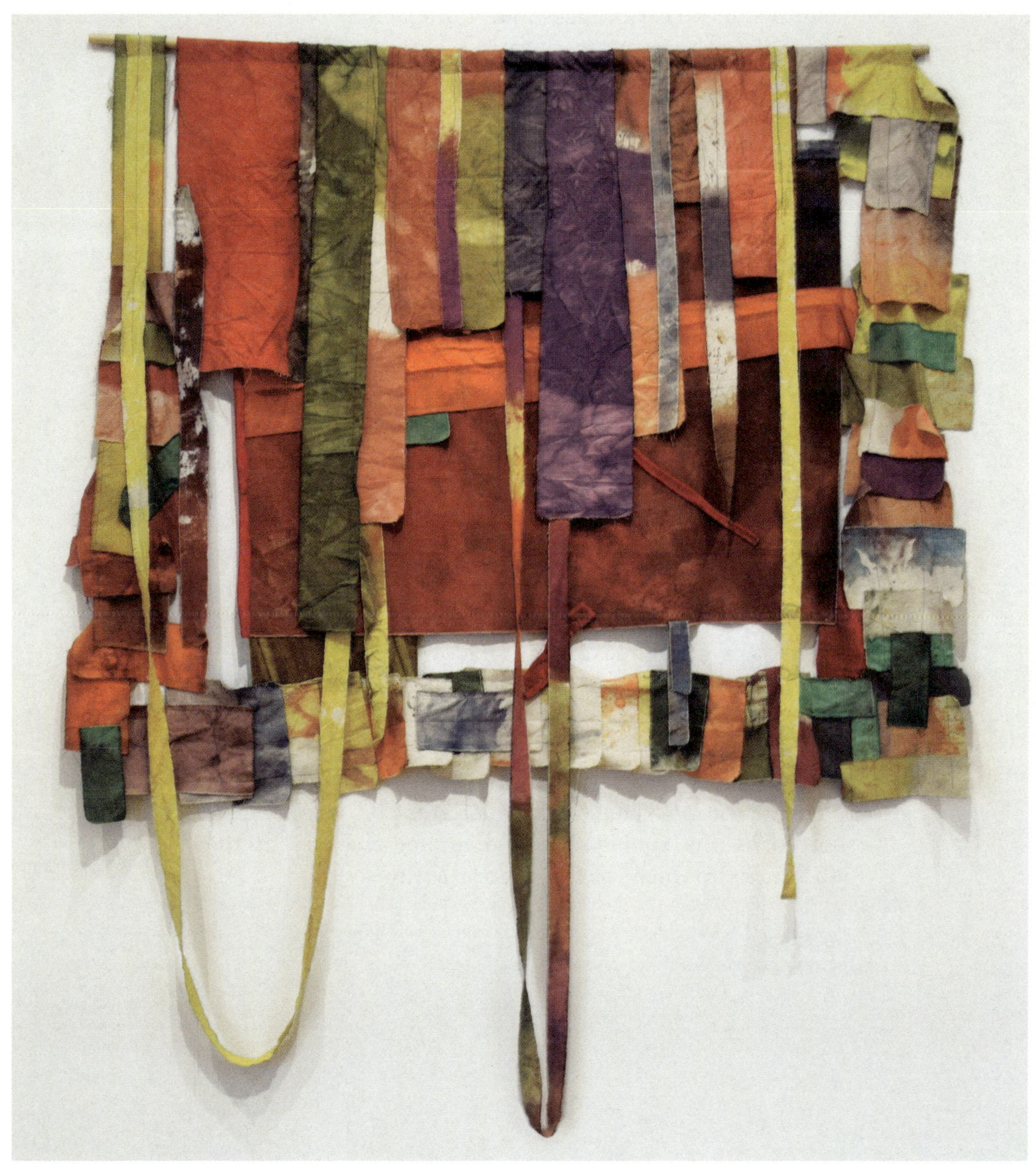

Untitled, 1973, acrylic on canvas   cat. no. 41

Notions of precariousness and vulnerability were prevalent themes among many of the Cass Corridor artists during the postindustrial decline of Detroit in the 1960s and 1970s. Michael Luchs is one of the most revered yet reclusive members of the movement. Recurring throughout decades of his work is the silhouette of a rabbit, also an evasive creature, which has become the central icon throughout his oeuvre. As exemplified in *Untitled* (1976), the animal and its distinct pose remain consistent throughout each work; it is portrayed in the crouched position, one it instinctually holds in stillness when being hunted. Paradoxically, the retreat of Detroit's human population since the mid-twentieth century has led nature to reclaim portions of the landscape, where rabbits roam among their natural predators, such as foxes and coyotes.

Luchs often shifts his material approach in rendering these rabbit figures, and his various experiments with found, industrial material are shared by his Cass Corridor peers. In this depiction of the rabbit, Luchs has presented a near shadow image of the animal, whose outline is seen through jagged lacerations of worn fringed fabric that is bound to cardboard and wood. Luchs evocatively emulates an aesthetic of precarity, and here one viscerally experiences his violent act of creation. The work illustrates the anxiety produced by the subjugation and unpredictability of the urban environment of Detroit at the time.

T.R.A.

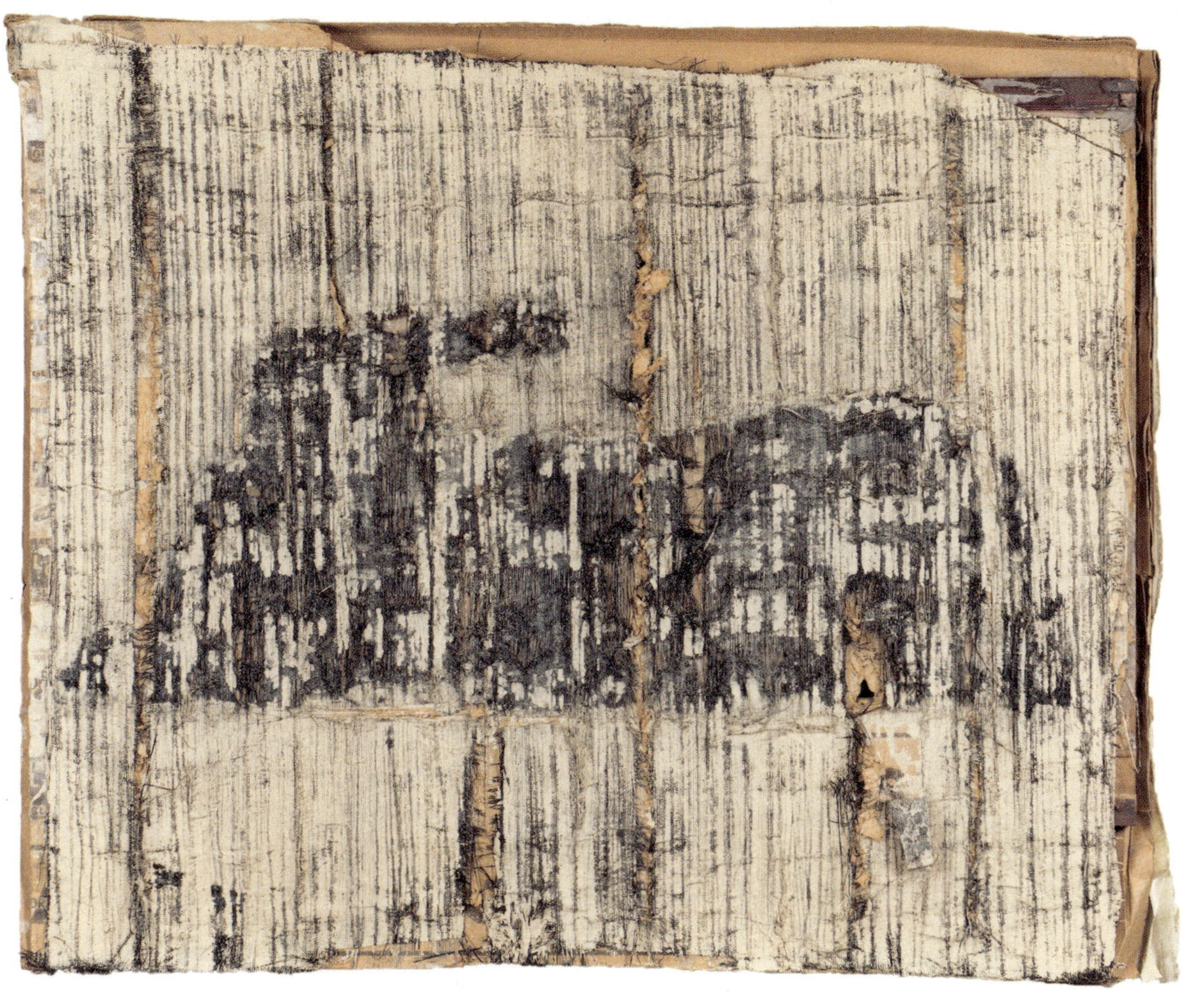

Untitled, 1976, synthetic fiber, paint, cardboard   cat. no. 42

Interdisciplinary artist Tiff Massey is immersed in discourses regarding America's most reprehensible institution—chattel slavery—which in 1860 enslaved nearly four million men, women, and children according to census records. The textile industry was one of many that perpetuated the transatlantic slave trade system through the cultivation of cotton on America's southern plantations, its export to England and other countries for textile manufacturing, and its use as barter in the acquisition of slaves in Africa. Fabrics were also imported from the East to the colonial United States to clothe Americans and their slaves. Calico, osnaburg, and gingham were some of the most popular fabrics. Massey engages with both the history and visual language of these textiles in her *White Out* series, as she explains, "[gingham was] made from cotton manufactured with slave labor and then used to create uniforms or markers for slaves on plantations."

Gingham is distinguished by its contrasting pattern composed of vibrantly dyed fibers and white fibers woven together to create its distinctive checkered design. Enslaved women were known to wear the pattern as a turban, or tignon, to cover their heads while they carried out forced domestic labor. This style of dress became an iconic trope of the "mammy" caricature in popular American culture. As a form of social commentary, Massey has removed the perpendicular pattern of the cloth by hand and created parallel lines. Through this undoing, Massey produces a revisionist fabrication as a way of reimagining histories under her control—a metaphorical erasure of colonialism and its legacy of forced labor.

T.R.A.

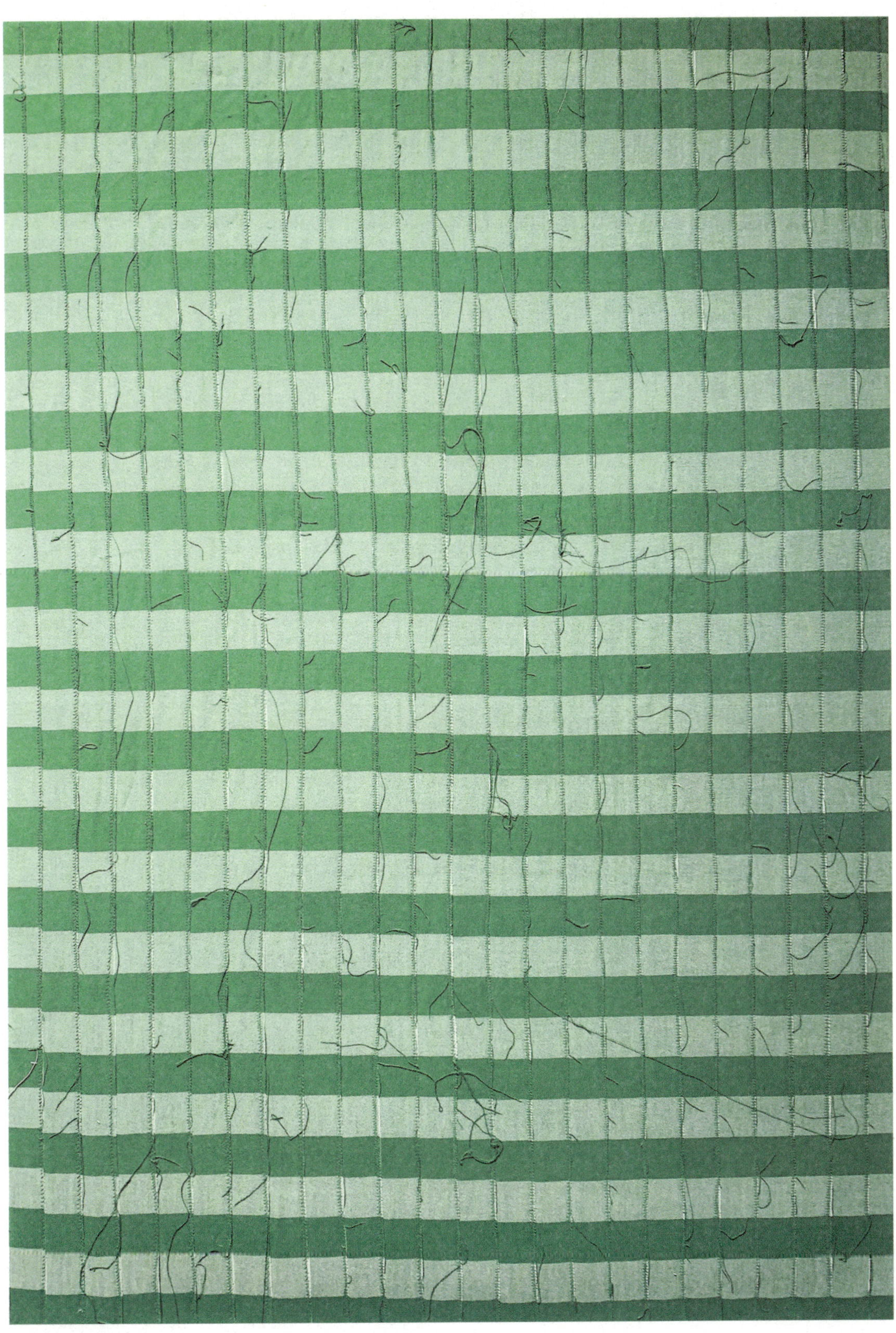

White Out (Green), 2018, cotton fiber   cat. no. 45

157

Throughout his prolific career, Detroit artist Charles McGee has sought to distill the energy of life that connects humans to the natural world. He has stated that his creativity is born from this persistent question: "What does nature give us, to make reason out of why we are who we are?" McGee believes the unrelenting state of change—whether entropy, metamorphosis, or deterioration—is part of a larger force that art helps us understand.

Throughout nearly eight decades, McGee's artworks typically maintain a joyous, rhythmic energy in the form of paintings, assemblages, and fabricated sculptures. The *Urban Extract* series, however, represents a deviation in his oeuvre in which there is less evidence of his own hand; the works instead foregrounds found objects and materials extracted from Detroit's urban environment. Composed primarily of wood and plaster, the series could be construed as architectural artifacts of a struggling city in the decade following the Detroit Rebellion of 1967. However, perhaps one can view this series in a broader and more positive sense: nature makes its mark on even the most seemingly stable of human-built structures, but it is the self-determination of the artist that allows for a constant state of creation, in both art and community.

This idea of collecting his surroundings extended to his impact on the creative community. McGee ran the artist collective Gallery 7 from 1969 to 1978 and founded the Charles McGee School of Art. In 1979, the same year he constructed the *Urban Extract* series, he co-founded the Contemporary Art Institute of Detroit (CAID), showcasing the latest art by and for the community. CAID lasted decades beyond its inception.

R.M.

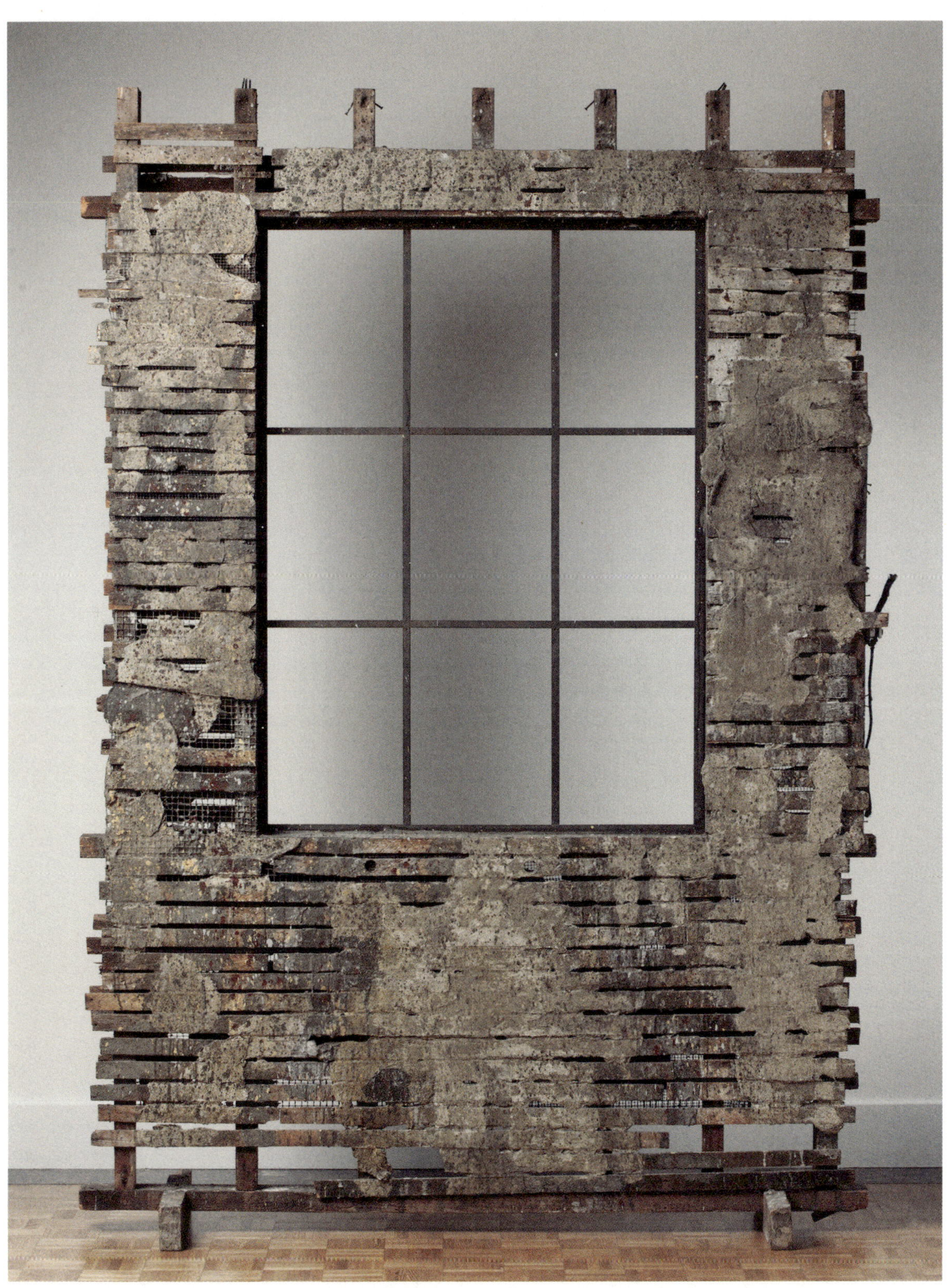

Urban Extract II, 1979, mixed media, wood, plaster

MATERIAL DETROIT:
Encounters, Accidents, and Intuitions

"…Materials alert us to the textures of black life that are often flattened by logics of visibility alone, and in so doing open up corporeality and materiality as crucial archives of black radical aesthetics."
—Sampada Aranke, *Material Matters: Black Radical Aesthetics and the Limits of Visibility*

"Matter doesn't disappear, it transforms. Energy is the same way. The Earth is layer upon layer of all that has existed, remembered by the dirt."
—Adrienne Maree Brown, *Emergent Strategy: Shaping Change, Changing Worlds*

In the early twentieth century, Detroit was regarded as an idyllic destination for black Southerners because of the promised wealth of opportunity generated by the Fordian automobile industry. Detroit's black population increased 611.3 percent—from 5,741 in 1910 to 40,838 in 1920—the most rapid growth for any large city in America.[1] The Great Migration was not only about increased access to jobs, but also the opportunity for flight, an escape from the racial violence of the Jim Crow American South. These acts of migration were made by Southern blacks to ensure stability and safety for themselves. They were also acts of prospective investment, a move towards a future they had never been allowed to imagine.

In her book *In the Wake: On Blackness and Being*, Christina Sharpe gives us *anagrammatical blackness*, a term that describes a technology of black being, one "that exists at the index of viability and potentiality."[2] Anagrammatical blackness defines black ontology as a constant practice of rearranging, making itself anew and atemporal.[3] Because black Americans perpetually occupy this liminal space between "viability and potentiality," they have developed a certain level of agility in their mundane ways of being. Blackness and its agents then become amorphous, a form that evades a specific place or time. It is all place, all time.

For the artists I discuss in this essay, their respective backgrounds are directly influenced by the exodus from the American South—the Great Migration—and its routes, hopes, and fugitiveness. However, I wish to attend to the permeability of histories that *preceded* the Great Migration the speculative futures that prompted and followed the exodus. Artists Charles McGee, Allie McGhee, Gilda Snowden, and Carole Harris are products and conduits of the migration and speculation, and they make the anagrammatical tangible through their encounters, accidents, and intuitions with material. For these artists, materials such as iron, wood, clay, and fiber have become symbolic prosthetic apparatuses, bridges between economic bleakness and economic efficacy. Furthermore, these prosthetic apparatuses ultimately become tools that aid in the speculation and building of liberated futures.

W.E.B. Du Bois states that the black worker "is a founding stone of a new economic system in the nineteenth century and for the modern world."[4] He continues:

> "Black labor became a foundation stone not only of the Southern social structure, but of Northern manufacture and commerce, of the English factory system, of European commerce, of buying and selling on a world-wide scale; new cities were built on the results of black labor, and a new labor problem involving all white labor, arose both in Europe and America."[5]

Cedric Robinson continues by noting that the black worker was introduced to the modern world "not as slaves that one could come to an understanding of the significance that these

Black men, women, and children had for American development. It was as labor."[6] It is, however, Huey Copeland's reading of Fred Moten's theoretical recognition of black bodies and their history of forced labor that is most useful in this analysis:

> Moten's writing instances a critical orientation toward the sensible rooted in the historical production of black flesh—suspended between sexes and genders, animate and inanimate, person and thing, animal and machine, agent and material—that underlines the porousness of ontological categories as well as the brittleness of Western culture's epistemological foundations, which time and again place the black body as limit and exemplar, whether captives in the slave-ship hold, specimens on the examining table, or magnetized targets of state violence in the streets.[7]

If we understand these artistic black hands (and bodies) in this sense—as materials evading violence, materials subject to forensic exploration, as both agents that use commodity and commodities that have been used by agents to create more commodities—we are able to complicate the dynamics between materials and such hands. How then has this relation between black hands and material been altered throughout the afterlife of slavery in the twentieth-century industrial expansion? How do black hands and black bodies reclaim themselves through labors in ways that are self-gratifying? What do we make of these hands, backs, arms, legs, and minds that came out of such origins? How might these bodies labor with materials to speculate about or produce futures of self-sovereignty through art-making?

In the year 1979, Europe's first female prime minister was elected in England. Margaret Thatcher and US President Ronald Reagan are often thought of as collaborators who were responsible for the collapse of communism and the Soviet Union in 1989. Their most significant impact, however, was their revolutionary partnership in implementing conservative free-market policies. Many believe their strategic deregulation policies were to blame for industrial irresponsibility in the latter half of the twentieth century, which ultimately led to the 2008 financial crisis. In 1979, before the recession of the 1980s, many automotive plants closed in the city of Detroit and elsewhere in Michigan, spawning mass layoffs and increased unemployment.[8]

In 1979, the artist Charles McGee began foraging decayed and discarded materials from Detroit's built environment as the city started to reflect the beginnings of economic decline. This decline would reach its height over thirty years later during the city's bankruptcy. The materials of wood, wiring, and iron window sills that McGee collected were gathered in Detroit's Eastern Market neighborhood from a building that was then a ruin—formerly his old barber shop in the once-historic Black Bottom neighborhood where many African Americans settled during the Great Migration after leaving the American South. McGee took the materials back to his studio and constructed an amalgamation of the narrow wooden slabs placed horizontally, one situated on top of the other. An overlay of plaster and resin saturated the surface of the wooden panels, and gridded wire sheets were placed sporadically throughout the structure's surface, creating cohesion between a variety of objects. The result is a fixed structure that stands eight feet high and six feet wide. The metal mullions that make up the glassless window frame are fixed firmly in the center. A lone wire hangs from the right side of the piece, knotted tightly at the base of the entire structure.

The work *Urban Extract II* (p. 159) is an indicator of McGee's prophetic impulse that is embedded within his eighty-year-old creative practice. McGee and his haptic encounters with material run parallel to transgressions that are associated with black reclamations of (labor) power in the twentieth century. He came to Detroit in 1934 from South Carolina after spending the first decade of his life carrying out agricultural labors on his family's land. He often recalls the pleasures he found in repairing broken axes that were used for cutting wood. The tactility of repair through matter was a site of gratification for the young child. McGee moved to Detroit at age ten and was raised in the city's Black Bottom area. The neighborhood eventually was razed during the mid-twentieth century to accommodate the installation of Interstate 75, a highway adjacent to the Eastern Market area where McGee scavenged materials in the 1970s.

In his ninety-five years on Earth, most of which have been spent in Detroit, McGee has witnessed the perpetual cycle of "viability and potentiality," deconstruction and reconstruction, and decline and recovery. This mirrors Detroit's motto *Speramus Meliora; Resurgent Cineribus*, or "We hope for better things; it shall arise from the ashes." *Urban Extract II* punctuates the burgeoning economic anxiety of 1979 and captures the environment of the city—then and now—after the economic decline fully reached its peak. Through the use of the debilitated wiring, glassless window, and plastered wood that reference one site but also gesture toward events that would follow, one could think of McGee's way of working as one informed by unconscious prescience. Instead of peering through a voyeuristic lens and romanticizing a loss of structure, McGee utilizes materials from discarded ruins to create "a remnant of, and portal into, the past," a "fragment with a future."[9] The altered extraction is evidence of the anagrammatical, proving that the discarded can be made formidable again and perhaps even sustain in moments to come. McGee as artist becomes ethnographer, archaeologist, and conjurer. The making of *Urban Extract II* is making anew. The appropriation of

memory matters because it comments on the liminal space that occupies the past, present, and future and becomes an act of (self) possession, a way of seeing the materiality of self and of community that occupy each of these areas throughout time.

Urban Extract II was created after McGee spent several decades in Detroit, where he observed local, national, and global transformations, from the atomic bomb in Nagasaki to the cryptic nature and extreme loss that surrounded the Vietnam War. Transgression was paramount. During the 1960s and early 1970s, the United States witnessed a prolific era of black textual production and art-making that was sited, in part, in the city of Detroit as well. Such efforts sought to resolve and call attention to issues of invisibility, violence against black lives, and economic disparity within marginalized communities. Broadside Press (founded by the poet and archivist Dudley Randall) in addition to other independent black-run publications, such as *Inner City Voice*, *The South End*, and *Solid Ground*, marks a particularly significant space and time within Detroit's African American community that was intent on producing text ephemera in addition to organizing around racial and economic disparity.

Simultaneously, there was a proliferation of independent black-owned galleries and artists' collectives, such as Gallery 7 led by Charles McGee, Extended Arts Groupe led by artist and scholar Dr. Cledie Taylor, Contemporary Studio led by artists

Ernest Alston and Henri King, and the still-active National Conference of Artists led by scholar Edsel Reid and artist Shirley Woodson Reid. The practice of forming communities and the establishment of cooperative economies enabled a zeitgeist of black visual and textual production during an era of much political and economic peril.

"[W]hat's the difference between flight and fatality? What are the politics of being ready to die and what have they to do with the scandal of enjoyment."
—Stephano Harney and Fred Moten, *The Undercommons: Fugitive Planning & Black Study*

During the 1960s and 1970s, the painter and Gallery 7 member Allie McGhee responded explicitly to the perilous racial environment that surrounded him in Detroit. As he was coming of age in the city, he made works that reflected the precarious moment, illustrating black plight and fugitiveness during and after the post-Civil Rights Movement. As a salve for the social unrest at the time, he found solace by engaging with themes and subjects beyond what was tangible and immediate. In *Sacred Music*, 1979 (fig. 1) McGhee rendered abstracted figures under an overlay of a chalky off-white color palette. Throughout the composition there is a textured linear pathway of crushed pumpkin seeds. "It was a time when I was still really impressed with African Art; the pumpkin seeds were an association

with the cowrie shell. I was eating millions of pumpkin seeds in the studio and I would put a layer of paint on and I would pour the pumpkin seeds on there," said McGhee of his experimentation.[10] McGhee repetitively applied and scraped an edible substance to obscurity as it became simply texture on the canvas. The cowrie shell derives from snail-like animals often found in tropical waters near the Indian Ocean. The shell itself has been known to hold

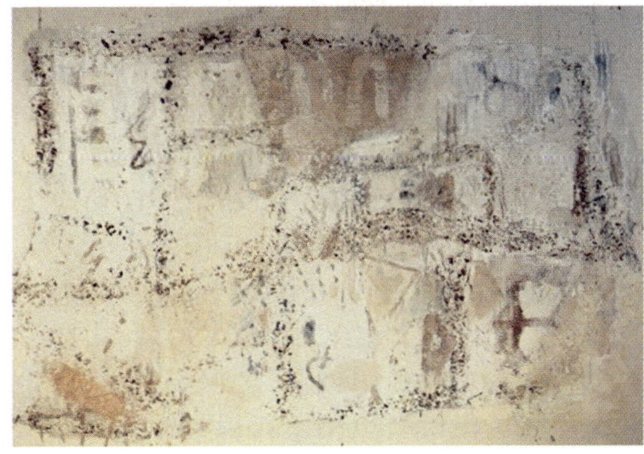

FIGURE 1

Allie McGhee, *Sacred Music*, 1979, acrylic paint and seeds on canvas

a breadth of spiritual and economic value throughout history, specifically within African and South Asian cultures. During the expansion of the slave trade in Europe, cowries were exchanged in coastal West Africa for groups of slaves. Perhaps McGhee was interested in tapping into this historical significance of the cowrie, yet instead of incorporating the actual shell, he employed pumpkin seeds, the most readily available material that is somewhat tantamount in form. The effect of the seeds plastered over

165

paint, which was then scraped off with a sharp metal tool, resembles a scene of small oceanic shells that have been brought ashore with forceful waves and buried slightly beneath the sand. The surface of the painting is jagged and looks as though the piece has taken shape through a caustic erosion process.

McGhee's ability to take a material and abstract it indicates his desire to subvert and complicate, but he also inserts play and trickery. Kevin Young describes the "hiding tradition"[11] of African American culture in which he references Robert Harris Jr.'s citation of the familiar saying "got one mind for me, and one for the master to see."[12] He observes that the "black imagination involves much that is hidden, squirreled away, stored. Hiding was a tradition not just of the body but of the mind."[13] McGhee's work gestures within such a tradition, relying on material and symbolic marks to decode and recode his imaginings and his own language.

Carole Harris takes a similar approach to her constructions made from a variety of elements. Harris, a black female Detroit-based artist, worked at the monumental flagship J.L. Hudson department store shortly after the 1967 Rebellion as one of its first black interior designers. After several decades of employment as a designer for major corporations and later independently, she pivoted from the commercial world into an artistic practice wherein she makes soft sculpture constructions. Similar to Charles McGee, Harris spent a great deal of

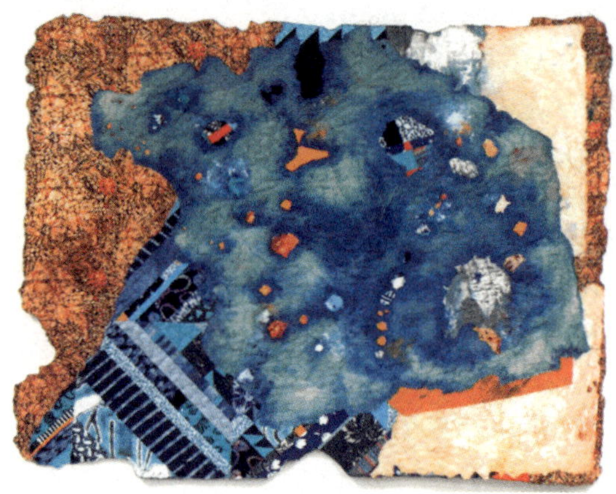

FIGURE 2

Carole Harris, *Wall Series: Athens*, 2013, fiber

time exploring Detroit's urban environment, and she developed an interest in the layers of dress and redress that are visible during a building's construction or demolition. Her work seeks to emulate what is revealed and what is concealed in the process of disrepair. Harris's art involves the black tradition of quilting—sewing fabric pieces together to collage a hidden narrative. In addition to providing comfort, the quilt in black American heritage is often used to communicate lore and coded information. Harris invokes this "hidden tradition;" however, the narrative is driven from the material itself rather than an orchestrated pattern.

In a recent series of works called *Mapping Time and Place*, Harris celebrates the aesthetics of deterioration. She believes that the scars on a structure, object, or even a person disclose the beauty of time and lived experience. To mimic this effect in fiber, Harris employs a technique of rusting objects over cloth or subjecting the work to natural elements. The outcome is a rusted, indelible mark-making, sometimes to the point of corrosion. In the work *Wall Series: Athens* (fig. 2), Harris utilizes found, solid-colored, and patterned fabrics that have been rusted and burned. The blue fabric that is central in the piece contains holes throughout its mass, revealing a vibrant orange layer and patterned pieces underneath. The edges of the work are unrefined and look as though burning has compromised the once perfectly rectangular form.

Artistic impulses relating to an assemblage tradition were also present

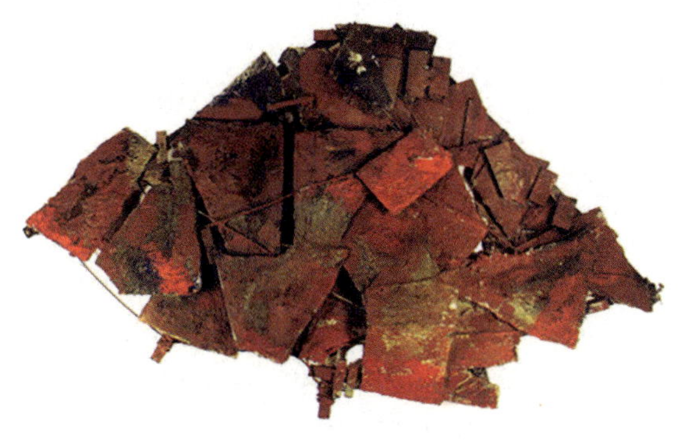

FIGURE 3

Gilda Snowden, *John T*, 1988,
wood, paint, encaustic, rope on Masonite

in the work of another black female artist, Gilda Snowden. While growing up on Detroit's Northwest side near LaSalle and Inverness Streets, Snowden was given a microscope by her father.[14] Together they collected swabs of saliva from their mouths, dabbed them on glass, and slid them underneath the microscope. Snowden

was enamored with the movement of tiny organisms in her saliva. This desire to investigate informs her practice as an artist. An amalgamation of experiences culminated in a series of assemblage works in which the artist addressed time, materiality, and familial admiration through making art. From 1985 to 1988, Snowden made the *Album* series that included several pieces of assemblage work with appropriated images of her family. In 1987 her parents died within six months of each other. Through this loss, Snowden became motivated to dig deeper into the material of self. "I felt free to tap into my own history and genealogy. I became interested in where I came from. Before that, painting was schoolwork. The kind of migration that my parents made was what a lot of African Americans were making in the early twentieth century."[15]

John T, 1988 (fig. 3) is a sculpture of painted constructions made by Snowden that is a monument to and metaphorical portrait of her father. Wood slabs have been mounted on a wooden base that is not clearly visible to the viewer. Rope covered in red brick-colored paint is arbitrarily woven in, out, and around slabs of wood that are also covered in the red encaustic pigment. The sculpture is approximately seven feet wide and five feet long and is positioned as a wall relief, not viewable in the round. The assemblage of wooden planks, which are oriented seemingly at random, create a triangular shape. Where some wooden planks do not meet, there are gaps that provide insight into the work's base, inciting curiosity around its production. It is difficult to identify the order in which objects were added, when they were painted, and how the construction even began. The elements in this work were found and rendered in a way that echoes the poetics and precariousness of foraging for art materials.

By the 1990s Snowden had moved to oil on canvas to develop one of her best-known signature series, *Tornadoes*. Her hand is evident in these works as she often applied brisk curvilinear marks that visualized kinetic energy. The hurried lines reflect the anxiety Snowden felt around tornadoes, mirroring their force and unpredictability. She shared that while she had a deep admiration for her mother, she also feared the possibility of inheriting her mother's mental illness.[16] *Tornadoes* became the transfer of restless energy from the inanimate and psychological to the material and tangible. A repetitious and sometimes mundane movement of the hand provided opportunities for personal recovery and contentment.

All four of these artists investigate their subject matter and material explorations in a manner that is somewhat stealthy. The use of abstracted, often found, materials allows for a constant rearranging of self and subjectivity in their art-making. These artists encourage one to consider the ways in which the history of black labor relations in America, and more specifically in Detroit, may impact their respective practices. They engage with conventional and unconventional materials that are made by hands that reclaim and are liberated, hands that are informed by methods of making anew, and by notions of atemporality provided by black cultural lineages. The ways in which Charles McGee, Allie McGhee, Carole Harris, and the late Gilda Snowden tend toward anagrammatical blackness— the method of referencing one time and all time, the ability to make new through collaboration with material— is inherently a form of what Adrienne Maree Brown describes as "emergent strategy," a concept of "intentionally chang[ing] in ways that grow our capacity to embody the just and liberated worlds we long for."[17] To be a product of the Great Migration is to be inherently emergent, subject to and willing to change. Whether it is through working with coded language, engaging with hidden traditions, or prophetically engaging with both the past and future through material, these artists create works that enact a liberated labor.

1   Beth Tompkins Bates, *The Making of Black Detroit in the Age of Henry Ford* (Chapel Hill, NC: The University of North Carolina Press, 2012), 16.

2   Christina Sharpe, *In the Wake: On Blackness and Being* (Durham: Duke University Press, 2016), 75–6.

3   Sharpe, 76.

4   W.E.B. Du Bois, *Black Reconstruction* (New York: The Free Press, 1935), 15.

5   Du Bois, 15.

6   Cedric Robinson, *Black Marxism: The Making of the Black Radical Tradition* (Chapel Hill, NC: University of North Carolina Press, 2005), 199

7   Copeland, Huey. "Tending Toward Blackness." *October* 156 (2016): 143.

8   Doron P. Levin, "Grim Outlook of Early 1980s is Back for U.S. Auto Makers," *New York Times*, December 7, 1989, https://www.nytimes.com/1989/12/07/business/grim-outlook-of-early-1980-s-is-back-for-us-auto-makers.html.

9   Brian Dillon, "Introduction: A Short History of Decay," in *Ruins*, ed. Brian Dillon (London: Whitechapel Gallery, 2011), 10–19.

10   Interview with Allie McGhee, November 17, 2017, recorded by author.

11   Kevin Young, *The Grey Album: On the Blackness of Blackness* (Minneapolis: Greywolf Press, 2012), 23.

12   Robert Harris Jr., *African American Review* 29, no. 3 (Fall 1995).

13   Young, *The Grey Album*, 23.

14   Gilda Snowden and Dick Goody, *Album: A Retrospective, 1977–2010* (Rochester, MI: Oakland University Art Gallery, 2013).

15   Snowden and Goody, 12.

16   Gilda Snowden, interview by Sean Marshall for the Cass Corridor Documentation Project, Detroit, Michigan, April 13, 2011.

17   Adrienne Maree Brown, *Emergent Strategy: Shaping Change, Changing Worlds* (Chico, CA: AK Press, 2017), 3.

The year 1967 marked an epoch in Detroit history in which racial tension crescendoed in the form of a rebellion by the city's black citizens that lasted for several days. It caused damage still evident more than fifty years later. Painter Allie McGhee responded to the devastation that many black Americans felt at that time through a series of representational works. However, McGhee realized such scenes of emotional bleakness were anything but catharsis. As he worked with his black peers to activate Gallery 7, an artists' cooperative, he encountered traditional African sculpture through private collections and traveling auctions. McGhee began to view these sculptures, and pan-Africanism more broadly, as a source of inspiration, and it opened his practice to new forms of experimental symbolism. He added a layer of satire, notably through the use of the recurring "banana-moon-horn" shape, which offers complex readings ranging from nature, humor, and the earliest forms of visual language.

In 1969, McGhee found a discarded cone-shaped piece of cloth on a street in Detroit. He took the cloth back to his studio, later realizing that it was an icing cone used for cake adornment. Yet to his eyes, the cone resembled a Ku Klux Klan hood, a headpiece often worn by members of the white supremacist organization who are known to inflict violence upon black Americans. McGhee marked up the tattered hood with concentrated masses of black pigment and action-filled curvilinear lines. Dirt and rust marks are visible along the edges of the triangular-shaped cloth. McGhee pairs the work with a petrified banana that is now blackened with deep fine lines on the outer skin, creating a beautiful texture despite its perished state. The expired fruit paired with the Klan hood indicate a slow-fading vitality made possible through domestic terror. Titled *Ku Klux Klown*, McGhee inserts a humorous element to the work while referencing the deeply tragic racist history of America.

T.R.A.

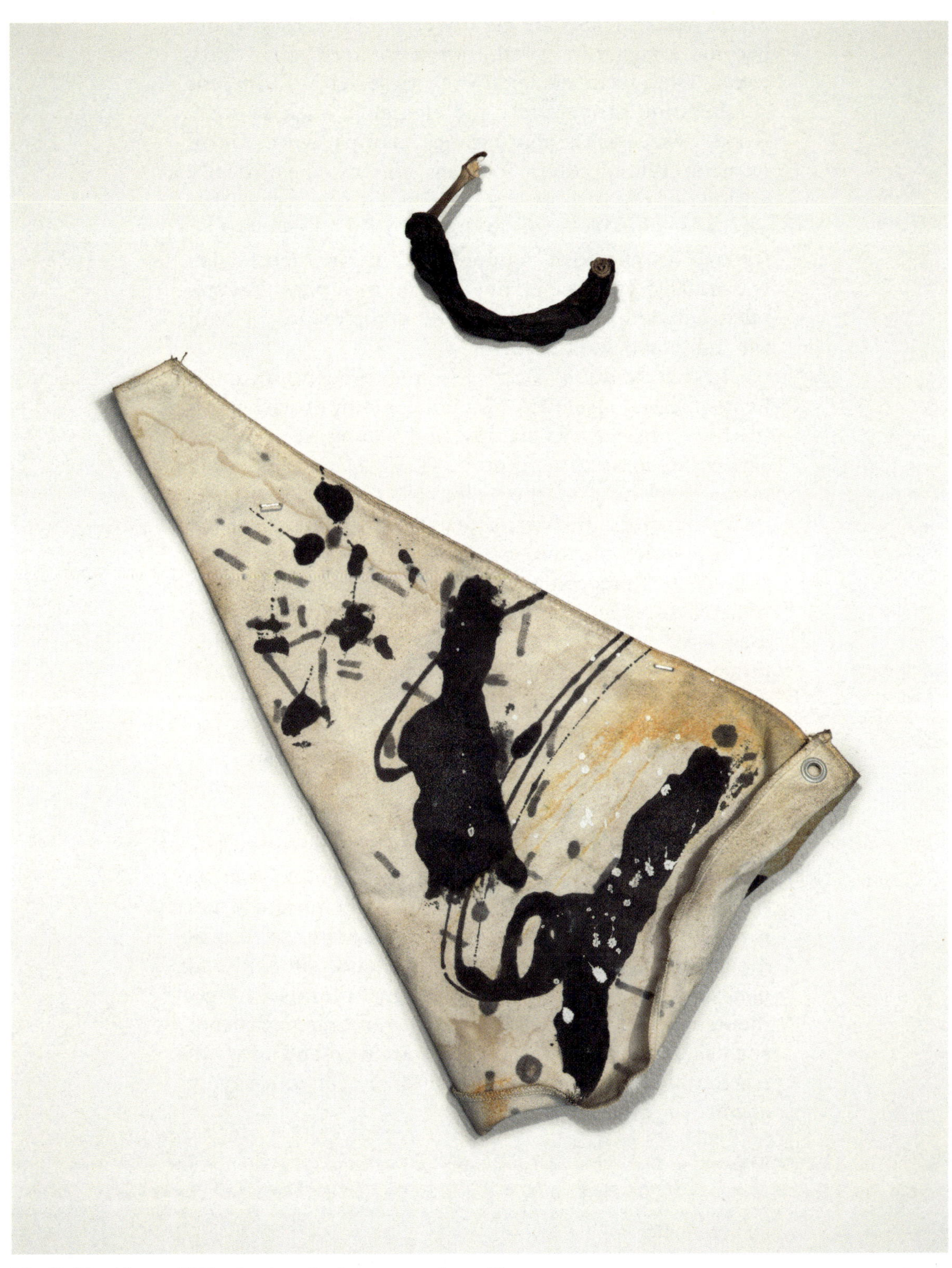

The Ku Klux Klown, 1969, mixed media, banana   cat. no. 47

Mario Merz's igloos are an archetypal form that would become a signature for the artist for more than forty years. They were rendered each time with a different combination of materials and elements, such as steel, wood, wax, glass, clay, stone, clamps, wire mesh, or neon tubing. Merz, perhaps the most politically attuned of the *arte povera* artists, did not accept that art needed to be overt in its political aims. Rather, through his choice of materials and forms, Merz's igloo was imbued with social and cultural meanings that spiraled outward, encompassing the complexities of both the individual and the social.

In this iteration, Merz uses steel tubes to form the hemispherical structure, attaching a skin of wire mesh to these ribs with C-clamps, and adding neon tubing across the dome to spell out "1 + 1 = 2." The equation is the beginning of the Fibonacci sequence, another recurring motif in Merz's oeuvre. The Fibonacci, an infinite series of numbers in which each digit is the sum of the preceding two numbers, creates branching structures and spiraling forms that have long been associated with growth patterns in nature and divine proportions such as the golden section. Read through a social lens, however, this simple equation contains the seeds of the single individual, who with the addition of one other, sets into perpetual motion an ever-increasing collective number—from one to infinity. Metaphorically, the scaffolding effect of the numerical sequence—whereby each numeral (or worker) is dependent on its predecessors in the system—can be read as an exploration of alternative systems and structures within the context of contemporaneous movements in Italy, such as *Autonomia* (autonomism) and *Operaismo* (workerism). These post-Marxist movements rejected traditional strategies of organized labor such as unions in favor of nonhierarchical and anti-representative forces acting autonomously yet collectively against the system.

A.B.

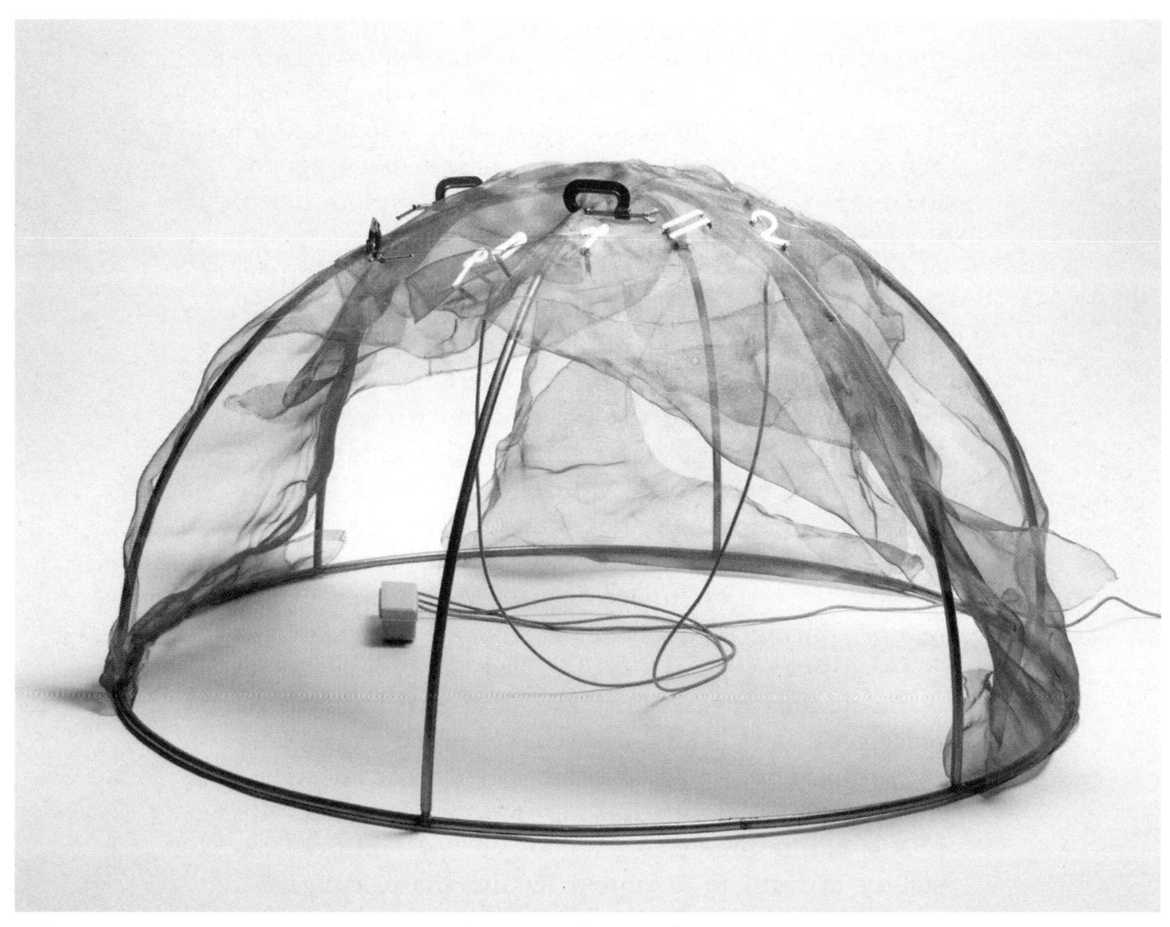

Igloo, 1971, steel tubes, neon tubing, wire mesh, transformer, C-clamps   cat. no. 49

Marisa Merz is an integral figure of the *arte povera* movement and, significantly, the only woman to be attributed to its canon. Historically overlooked relative to her peers, she has recently been recognized for her strategy in conflating material and meaning: the lived and the performative object. Her exploration of the organic form as it is iterated in mundane or "poor" materials is elevated through an interest in the vernacular or craft-based techniques and methods. Her work resides in the liminal divide between the domestic and the formal, as she attests: "There has never been any division between my life and my work."[1] *Living Sculpture* is part of a larger immersive environment made out of aluminum, which Merz installed in the home she shared with her husband Mario Merz and daughter Bea.

Merz grew up under Benito Mussolini's fascist regime, during which women were directed towards self-sacrifice in childbearing and subordination to domestic life. In her work, objects of consumption are redeployed as radically changed, yet deceptively familiar forms. Here, the chair is fabricated from folded and rolled panels of industrial aluminum. The material's pliable nature produces generous curves, and this sensuality of form is disrupted by the sharp, dangerous edges of the strips of metal. Merz enacts a method by which we might better understand our experience of daily life; she makes the familiar alien and, thus, somehow exposes the underlying peculiarity and menace of the familiar.

L.M., I.G.W.

1 *Zero to Infinity: Arte Povera 1962–1972*, exhibition guide, (London: Tate Modern, 2001).

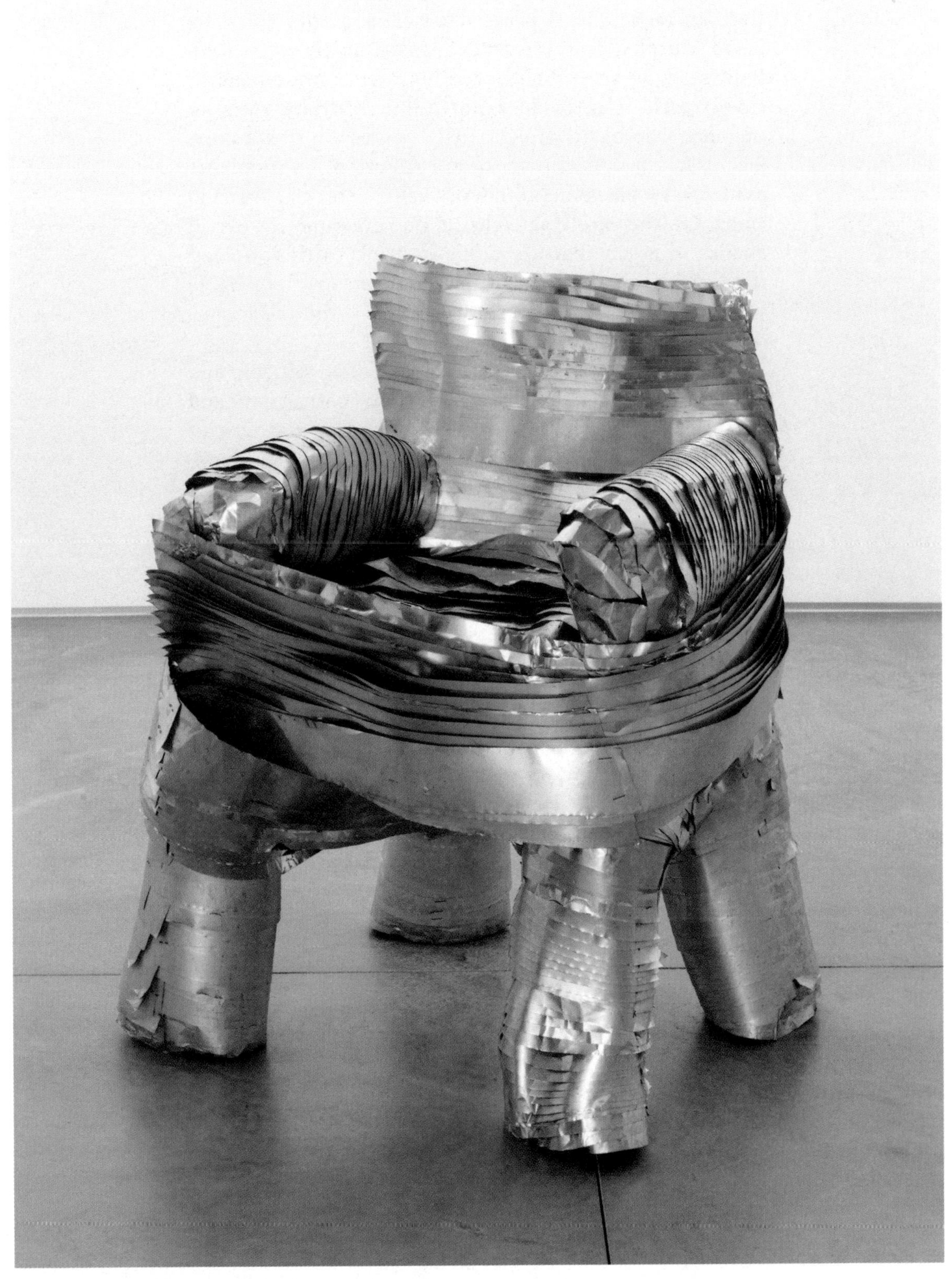

Living Sculpture, 1966, wood, aluminum   cat. no. 50

Landlord Colors came to be the title of this exhibition through a 2015 press release for a solo show by Jason Murphy, who referenced this term by artist John Baldessari as an influence for his own comprehensive investigations into color narration. Murphy runs an ongoing web-based project titled www.colortaxonomy.world. In a purposeful act of misdirection, he supplants evidentiary classification with self-referential attributions. On the scrolling website, one encounters several shades of green that are referents back to this project: *landlord* (a sickly, beige-diluted green); *arte povera* (a yellowed, aged green); and *cranbrook pitch* (a boisterous, clover green).

Murphy's father was a Detroit police officer, and the oppressively neutral hues of civic institutions and hospital waiting rooms were a commanding aesthetic of his childhood. His taxonomy is a conceptually driven, episodic rebellion against the mundane—almost like daily affirmations—and this position against conformity extends to the way he defines himself as a painter. A new work created for *Landlord Colors*, *Superman II* is an example from his series of "dip paintings" that function like material tests on a monumental scale. The receptors for the paint here are two large industrial rubber sheets that have been dipped in an off-green—one of the more unpopular colors in the realm of tasteful or desirable art according to his research. Clamps hold the rubber canvases to the makeshift "stretcher" consisting of a rebar frame held up by wood and concrete blocks. The rubber was left to drip-dry, and this takes much longer on an impermeable surface. In this regard, *Superman II* can be understood as a metaphor for Detroit in recent decades, a hero against all odds, holding on by the skin of its teeth.

L.M.

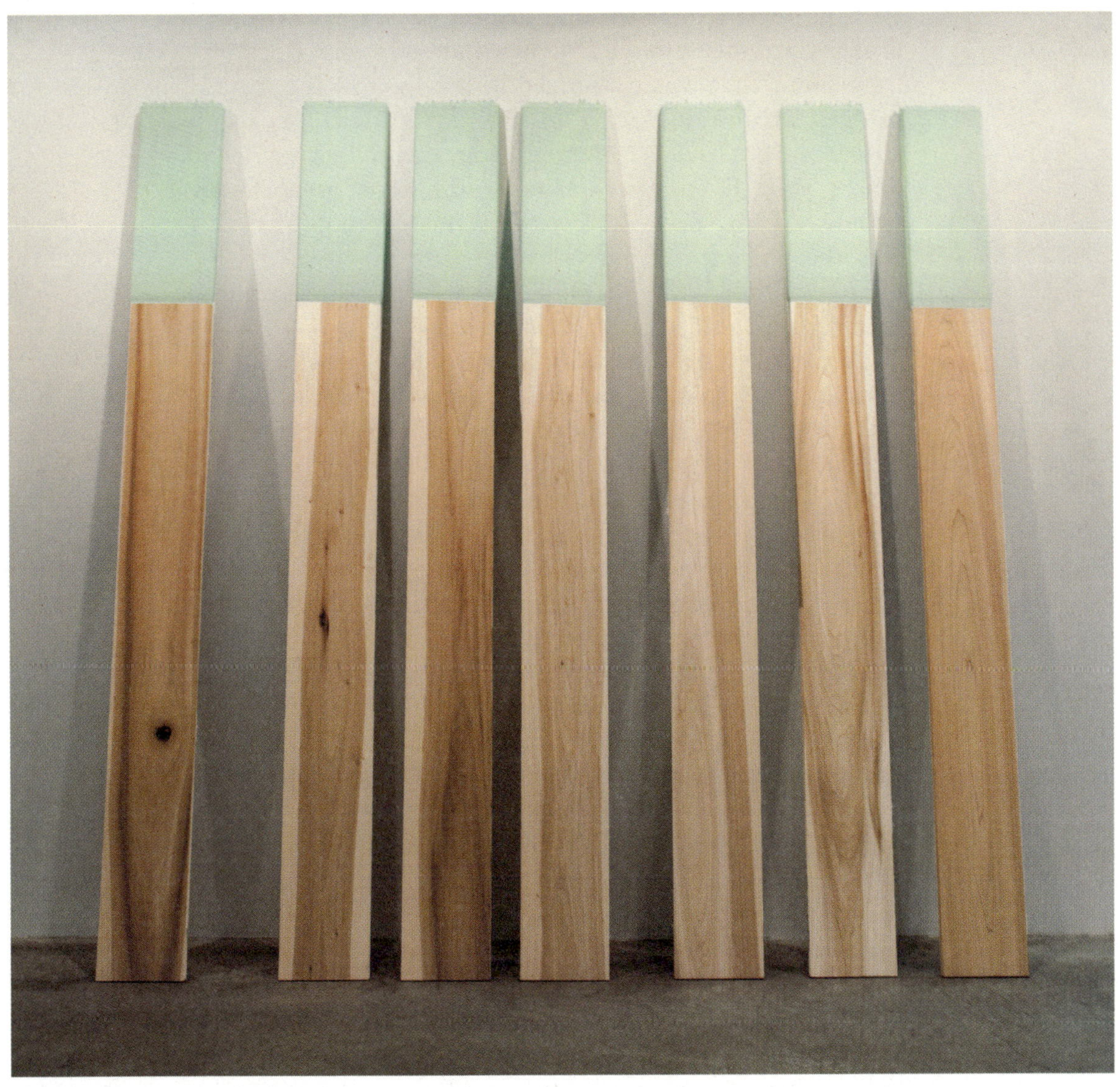

Litmus Test, 2014, poplar, paint

Perhaps regarded as the quintessential Cass Corridor artist, Gordon Newton is a key figure in the Detroit movement that was canonized in the Detroit Institute of Arts' exhibition *Kick Out the Jams: Detroit's Cass Corridor, 1963–1977*. Named after the neighborhood where they lived, the artists of the movement had widely varying styles. However, one common thread was the presence of aggressive artistic processes that often paralleled the turmoil of the city—precarious materials in action for precarious times.

Newton's *Diamond Follow* exemplifies this performative force through his use of industrial tools upon the surface—a power saw and an auto-body grinder. The sense of physicality and immediacy of impact on the viewer are central to his sculptural works, and the reverberation of the artwork's creation still emanates from the torn wooden surface. While Cass Corridor artists were engaged with the industrial landscape of Detroit, many were simultaneously negotiating its counterpart in nature. Newton explains: "I begin each of my projects as a geometric shape and then alter it. I can see this process being like nature taking over and changing the original form, or like man altering nature. I've been heavily influenced by the environment of Michigan—the pine trees, the Great Lakes, the cycles of nature that I see. I hope to suggest these cycles and the passage or even freezing of time in my works."[1] In this respect, *Diamond Follow* is another addition to mankind's epic allegories on the ongoing battle of man versus nature and man versus himself—Detroit has dedicated chapters in both. As perhaps an antidote to the chaos, on the verso of the artwork Newton attached a John Deere seed spreader, a form of human innovation that promotes the continuation of nature's growth.

L.M.

1   Julie Myers, *Subverting Modernism: Cass Corridor Revisited* (Lansing: Eastern Michigan University Gallery of Art, 2013), 57.

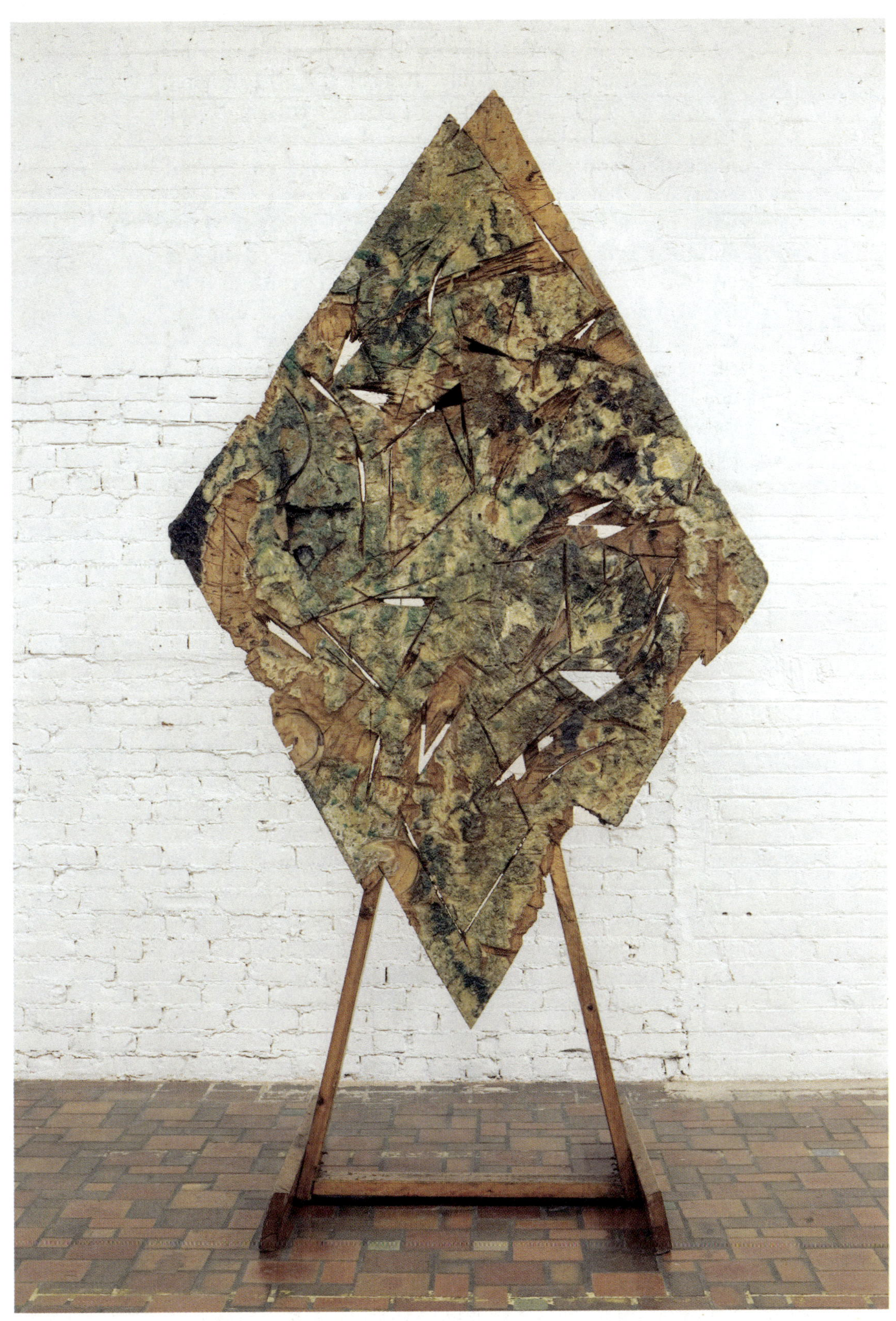

Diamond Follow, 1975, canvas, paint, polymer resin, synthetic fabric on wood   cat. no. 52

Reynier Leyva Novo is from a generation of artists who were born well after the Cuban Revolution, but as children and young adults had an acute experience of scarcity and uncertainty in the aftermath of the 1989 collapse of the Soviet Union, the country's former ideological and economic partner. Through conceptual strategies that mine political history, Novo contends with our subjectivity at moments of epochal shifts and their consequences. In an ongoing series titled *The Weight of History*, Novo utilizes an algorithm from INk 1.0 software to calculate the amount of printing ink used to compose official documents that directed the course of Cuban and international history—penal codes, immigration laws, foreign relation sanctions, etc. Based on the algorithm, Novo paints solid black rectangles with the measured ink; devoid of language, they convey what is repressed instead of communicated in such decrees—an exercise in emotive minimalism.

For *Landlord Colors*, Novo creates a new work that continues this act of transference between sociopolitical history and material abstraction. A common object inside many Cuban houses is a type of welcome rug made from recycled and secondhand clothes woven with plastic bags. Such rugs typify the kind of everyday innovation intrinsic to Cuban life. In the case of *Untitled (Immigrants)*, a 16-square-foot textile is made from the clothes of Cuban immigrants. The clothing was collected in Little Havana in Miami, sent back to Cuba to be torn and woven by paid workers, and then returned to the United States to be exhibited at Cranbrook Art Museum. The voyage across the sea, between the two countries, is integral to its production. It is the passage every immigrant must make, and the personal items once worn on their bodies now act as a surrogate. Psychologically, the woven textile speaks to the inherent fragmentation of the subject who emigrates. Moreover, Novo's process mimics the distance traversed between resources, labor, fabrication, and consumer in our global economic marketplace, which is often informed by complex trade agreements instead of logic and proximity.

L.M.

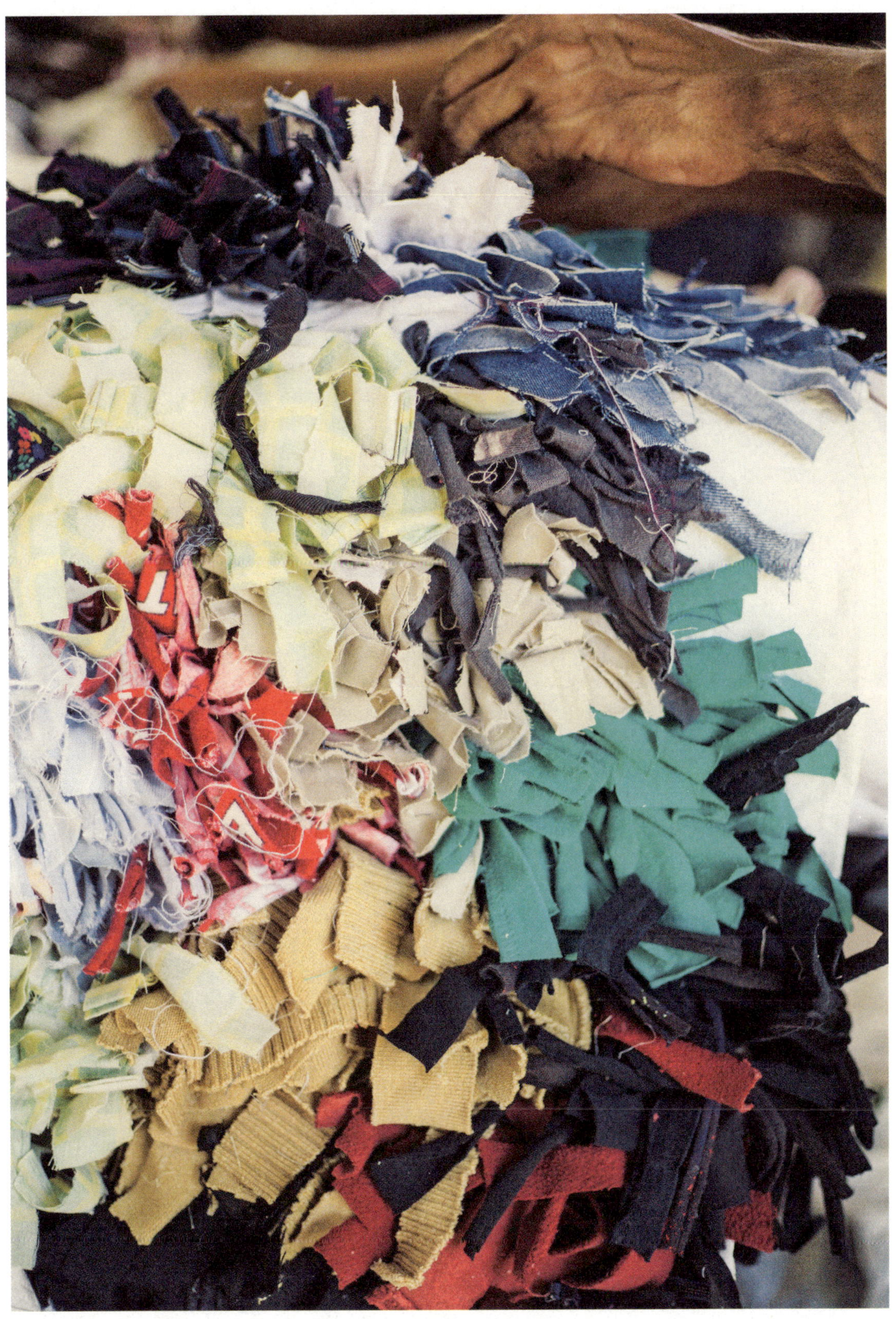

Untitled (Immigrants) (detail), 2019, clothing   cat. no. 53

GIULIO PAOLINI

Giulio Paolini is distinguished among the *arte povera* artists for a highly conceptual practice, including his approach to material and art history. An example of the latter is his incorporation of casts of classical Greco-Roman sculpture in *L'altra figura* (*The Other Figure*), a strategy employed by several artists in the movement including Michelangelo Pistoletto and Jannis Kounellis. Much of the world experiences the originals or casts in encyclopedic museums; however, they are present in the everyday streetscape of the artist's environ of Turin, the same city of *arte povera*'s inception. The use of the sculptures expands on the notions of "the everyday;" herein, the daily confrontation of Italian art history is a vernacular language experienced by the populous and mined from this context.

L'altra figura has six different versions that were created between 1980 and 1986. This particular version is of Eros, the mischievous god of love who meddles in the affairs of gods and mortals to incite drama. Two identical plaster busts of Eros are arranged facing one another as if mirrored, looming over the shattered remains of their triplet. This form of mimesis is a theme throughout Paolini's practice, and his conceptual leanings extend to the nature of the casting process. Paolini explains: "The plaster cast and the photograph are equivalents for me because they represent two techniques which reproduce models of imagin[ation]. Even though they are different materials, they have the same function—to produce a simulacrum.... Yet plaster is also a material you can touch and therefore when it breaks it is revealed for what it is. It becomes an image of not what it recounts but what it truly is."[1]

The series was created during the final years of Italy's Years of Lead, a period of domestic terrorism and bombings that were ongoing from the late 1960s to the mid-1980s. Within this cultural context, it is interesting to imagine how contemporaneous viewers might interpret the poetics mimicking reality: a country reflecting on itself and its own self-destruction.

L.M.

1   Giulio Paolini, "Conversation Piece with Susan Taylor, 1984," in *Carolyn Christov-Barkargiev, Arte Povera* (London: Phaidon, 1999), 259.

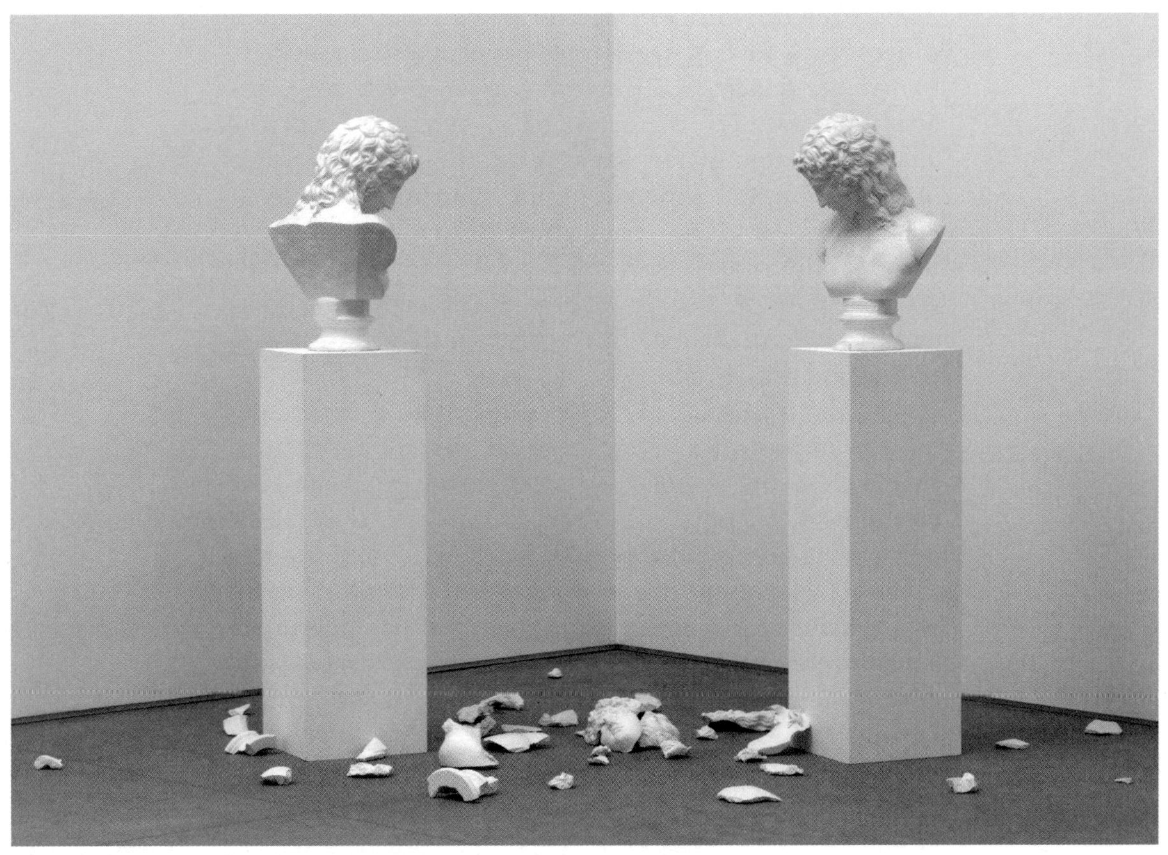

L'altra figura (*The Other Figure*), 1984, plaster, two plinths   cat. no. 54

After studying and working in Vienna for more than a decade, Greek artist Panos Papadopoulos returned to Athens during the financial crisis. From the window of his studio, the artist had a direct view of the antique Temple of Hephaestus on the northwest side of the Agora of Athens. In his painting *Temple of Hephaestus*, a visual focal point of his daily creative life functions as a sort of compass for the artist's attempt to map the dissonant voices swirling across and throughout Athens in the aftermath of recent economic and social upheaval.

In the summer of 2013, Greece was experiencing the impact of a series of fiscal austerity measures that were being imposed as a consequence of the government-debt crisis that had dominated the Greek political and economic landscape since 2009. As the financial autonomy of the middle and working classes was systematically hollowed out, the streets of Athens became a primary stage upon which frustrated and disenfranchised citizens articulated their grievances against the Greek state. These street protests were manifested visually as graffiti, as individual tags and textual admonishments. Papadopoulos started *Temple of Hephaestus* that summer, appropriating the aggressive scrawl from the real-time debates emerging on the streets of Athens and in the artist's own thoughts. Through the multiplicity of authors, words shift in and out of focus on a muted gray ground and emerge from a border of raw canvas and marginalia scribbled in English, German, and Greek. The work is as much an internal debate as it is a reproach of political failure—a rhetorical investigation of art's potential, if any, as a panacea to the city's and nation's ailment.

I.G.W.

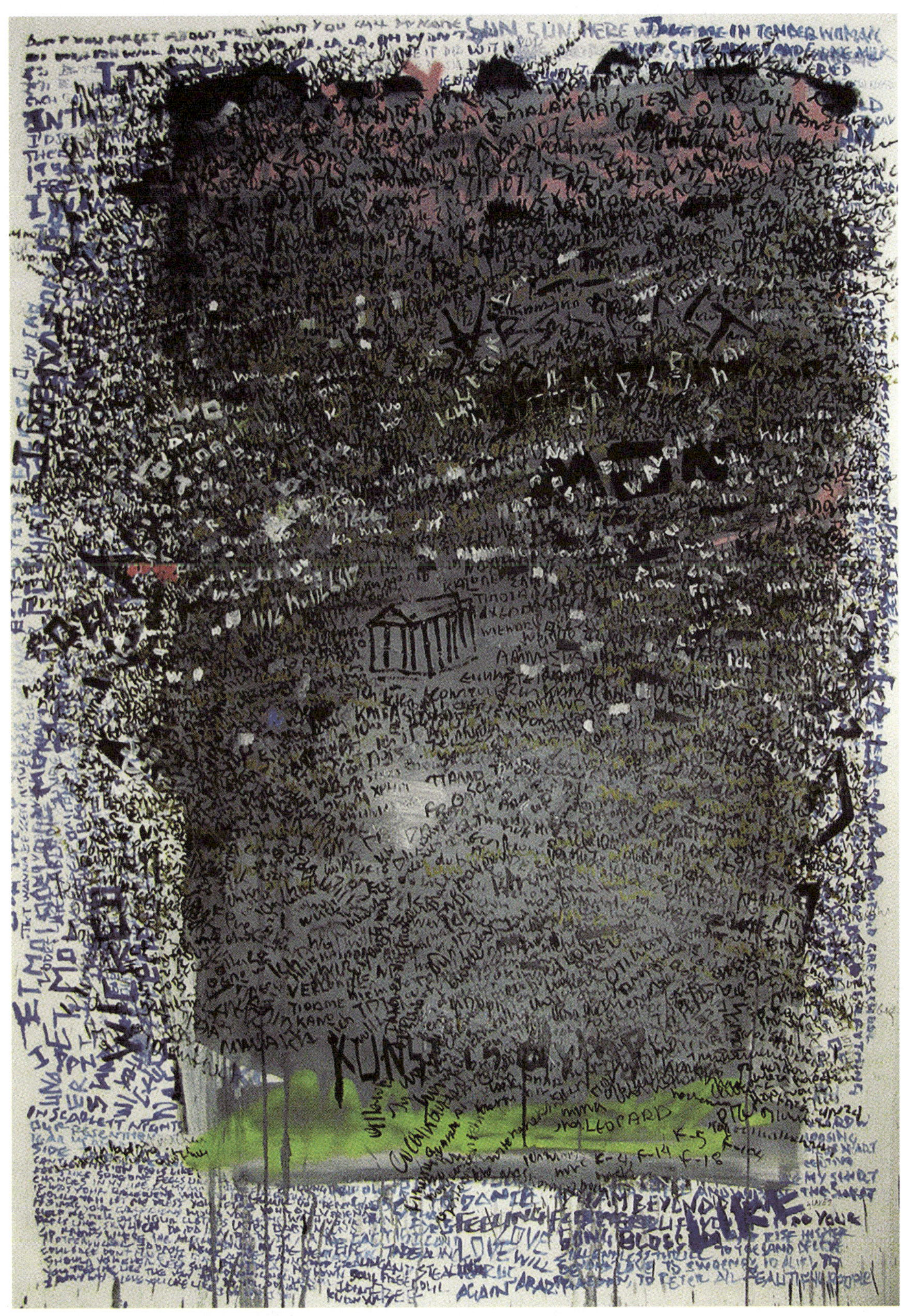

Temple of Hephaestus, 2013–14, oil and marker on canvas   cat. no. 55

PARK HYUN-KI

Park Hyun-Ki was a pioneer of video art in the Korean art scene starting in the late 1970s, which extended internationally when he was included in the São Paulo Biennial in 1979. In that exhibition, he exhibited *Stone Tower*, a sculpture of piled stones with a television monitor inserted between them, displaying an image of two stones, thereby continuing the cairn: the physical body and the mediated body. The conception of this video work occurred in the direct aftermath of the rapid modernization of South Korea during the Yushin era of the 1970s, in which the government prioritized economic growth over the human rights of its people. These years of oppression came after a succession of wars with consequences that still deeply affect the national psyche. Like all Koreans born in the first half of the twentieth century, Park experienced oppressive colonial rule by Japan, where his family was displaced before returning to their homeland.

From the same series as *Stone Tower*, the work *Untitled* (1984) is an important evolution of an aesthetic strategy in which Park created a malleable metal seesaw to balance a real stone and a monitor with footage of another stone—the TV hovering inches above the floor. Today, we experience the real stone in the present and a document of its equivalent from thirty-five years ago, an immobile but still time-based transmission. The stone remains relevant, perhaps immortal, while the passage of time is deduced by the obsolescent technology of the television, an artifact from the recent past. Park uniquely approaches the medium of video from the perspective of Eastern philosophy with a reverence for the natural world; here, this belief is weighed against a Western-initiated materialism. Park asks us to meditate on this tenuous balance—an imperative, as technology now pervades all aspects of contemporary life. There is no antiquation of this dilemma moving forward.

L.M.

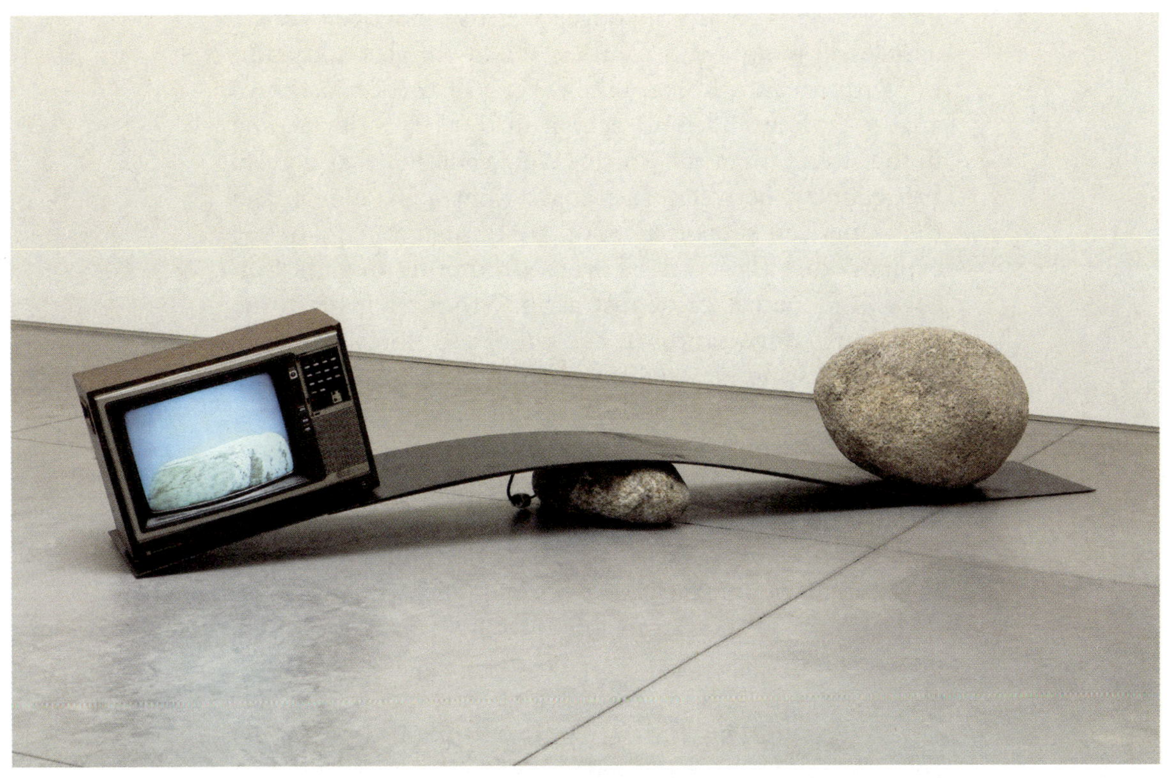

Untitled, 1984, video installation, single-channel video, color, silent; monitor, stone, steel   cat. no. 56

Park Seo-Bo is an artist whose extensive practice over six decades in many ways parallels the arc of abstract painting within South Korea. Like several of the *dansaekhwa* artists, Park attended art school in the 1950s during and in the aftermath of the Korean War, a conflict that divided the country between the Soviet-supported North and the American-supported South. Art historian Joan Kee explains that these artists were attempting to gain "fluency in the language of abstraction" to participate in the global art conversation of the time, yet Korean abstraction has distinctive qualities due, in part, to the government's imposed limitations on material, information, freedom of expression, and ability to travel.[1] Like many of his colleagues, Park would depend on a resourcefulness throughout the decades with aesthetic consequences, as seen in his early works in which he used discarded tents as canvas or hemp stretched over metal debris.

In 1973, Park began his prolific series of works on canvas titled *Écriture (Writing)*—his compositions are performed acts of inscription. Already in his forties at the start of the series, the artist had generated an in-depth practice influenced by both the meditative techniques of Buddhism and the intellectual strategy of abstract action painters, such as Jackson Pollock. The canvases of *Écriture* contain scratches on the surface into which the paint was pushed with a writing tool. However, the results are not a legible written language. Rather, his circular waves impact the surface without pause and convey a sense of personal anxiety, as well as the universality of the human condition under duress. "Noncommunication" as a method to communicate was the approach of many of the *dansaekhwa* artists, who found expression within monochromaticism and abstraction. Park explained in the early 1970s: "I painted nothing, my work had no form, no emphasis, and no ins-and-outs, except for the pure vibration coming out of not doing anything—an action through nonaction."[2] Conceptually, his intentions of nonaction parallel the political context of censorship that surrounded the work, in which artists living through the Yushin regime were often coded and quiet in their expression of resistance.

L.M.

1   Joan Kee, *Contemporary Korean Art: Tansaekhwa and the Urgency of Method* (Minneapolis: University of Minnesota Press, 2013), 8.
2 . Park Seo-Bo, artist statement of solo exhibition at Tokyo Gallery, June 1973.

Écriture No. 65–75, 1975, oil and pencil on canvas   cat. no. 57

FROM MY NOTEBOOK
OF FRAGMENTARY THOUGHTS

Originally published in Space, *no. 125,*
November 1977, 46.

I gave up expressing images not because of the bankruptcy of modernism, the end of humanism, or an acute realization that the fulfillment of modern life was nothing but a conceptual illusion. Rather, it was because my greatest interest is in living through natural and pure deeds.

It is all too clear that the expression of images amounts only to a sort of illusionism. There, instead of saying that I seek a world free from expression, I suggest that the act of expressing images lacks purity because it is imbued with intentionality. I emphasize an escape from images and expression because I want to live in the actions themselves through the absence of intentionality, and I wish to taste the tremendous sense of freedom that comes from natural and pure deeds.

A long time has passed since I became fed up with the deception of words such as *the arts, expression, distinctive, creative.* In fact, I would like to be uncreative and indistinctive.

I seek to go beyond the reality or image of a thing in order to draw out its structural foundation. That is also the reason why I denounce intentionality and endeavor to live in nature and anonymity through aimless deeds.

I repeat over and over again the absurd practice of leaving traces of actions and then erasing them. Between the two, I gain nothing and give nothing. If anything, there is only an impartial structure that shakes me loose and empties me.

Just because there are those who say that contemporary art endlessly repeats the same things does not mean that repetitive things are necessarily contemporary art. There are many misunderstandings regarding this point. People may think that contemporary art takes the same forms and duplicates them stylistically, but that is not the case. As one memorizes incantations or practices Zen Buddhism, incessant repetition represents a stage of escaping the self. It is not just form that is repeated but also the emptying of myself. As a result, I occasionally see by chance those who imitate their own style and mistakenly view such an unfortunate situation as the fate of contemporary art.

I am not an opponent of color. However, I nonetheless renounce painting with many colors. As an expression of my concern with colors, such a rejection arises not from a comparatively anti-color attitude but from an interest in painting that goes beyond questions of color.

When I ask myself why I paint white paintings, I cannot help but reply that it is because of my simple concept of nature. Even if a color does not draw attention to its own distinctiveness, it adds to the disruptiveness of nature. Moreover, it is not suitable for a color

to bring out its distinctiveness in an imageless structural expression.

If one wrote calligraphy using various colors, people would perceive the distinctiveness of the colors before they saw the characters themselves. To give another example, if one took the calligraphy of [the prominent Chosŏn scholar, calligrapher, and artist] Kim Chŏng-hŭi (1786–1856), made an exact replica using tracing paper, and then took a photograph of the original and the imitation, it would be very difficult to distinguish the real from the forgery just by looking at the photograph. This is because we would look only at the form. But if we looked at the two in the flesh, anyone could tell the difference. This is likely because we can sense the spirit underlying the works.

According to Greek mythology, the creation of the world's first spider came about as an act of omnipotent retribution by the gods upon a human woman named Arachne (hence, the words arachnid and arachnophobia). A highly gifted weaver, Arachne boasted her mastery of the craft was superior to that of Athena, the goddess of many things, including handicraft, the arts, and skill. Ultimately, her story is about pride and human limitation, an eternal misfortune that continues to be problematic and relevant in the contemporary moment. Often, the gods were an ancient society's attempt to negotiate with nature, whose perilous effects today are exacerbated by careless industry and misguided attempts to ignore its unconquerable power.

As a present-day practitioner from this rich lineage, Zoë Paul's weavings are intentional acts of mediation between several intertwined social histories, natural processes, and technological advancements. Paul uses as her structural base decaying refrigerator grills taken from the scrapyards of industrial mines surrounding the Greek islands—a handmade production composed upon the indifferent remnants of industry. The history of refrigeration is also an active agent in the meaning of the work, as its invention radically changed the social structures of warmer climates, including that of Greece. Until the early twentieth century, food was shared collectively, but progress in domestic life was geared towards individualized consumption; this led to food being wastefully packed, produced, and discarded. Now into the twenty-first century, the new version of progress addresses the communal through technology and media, yet the same threat of isolation is at stake.

For *Landlord Colors*, Paul will create a large site-specific painting that references ancient Greek human renderings, yet use her distinctive stylistic hand. Throughout the wall mural, Paul will install her weavings that are carefully crafted reminders of past errors that are still urgently present.

L.M.

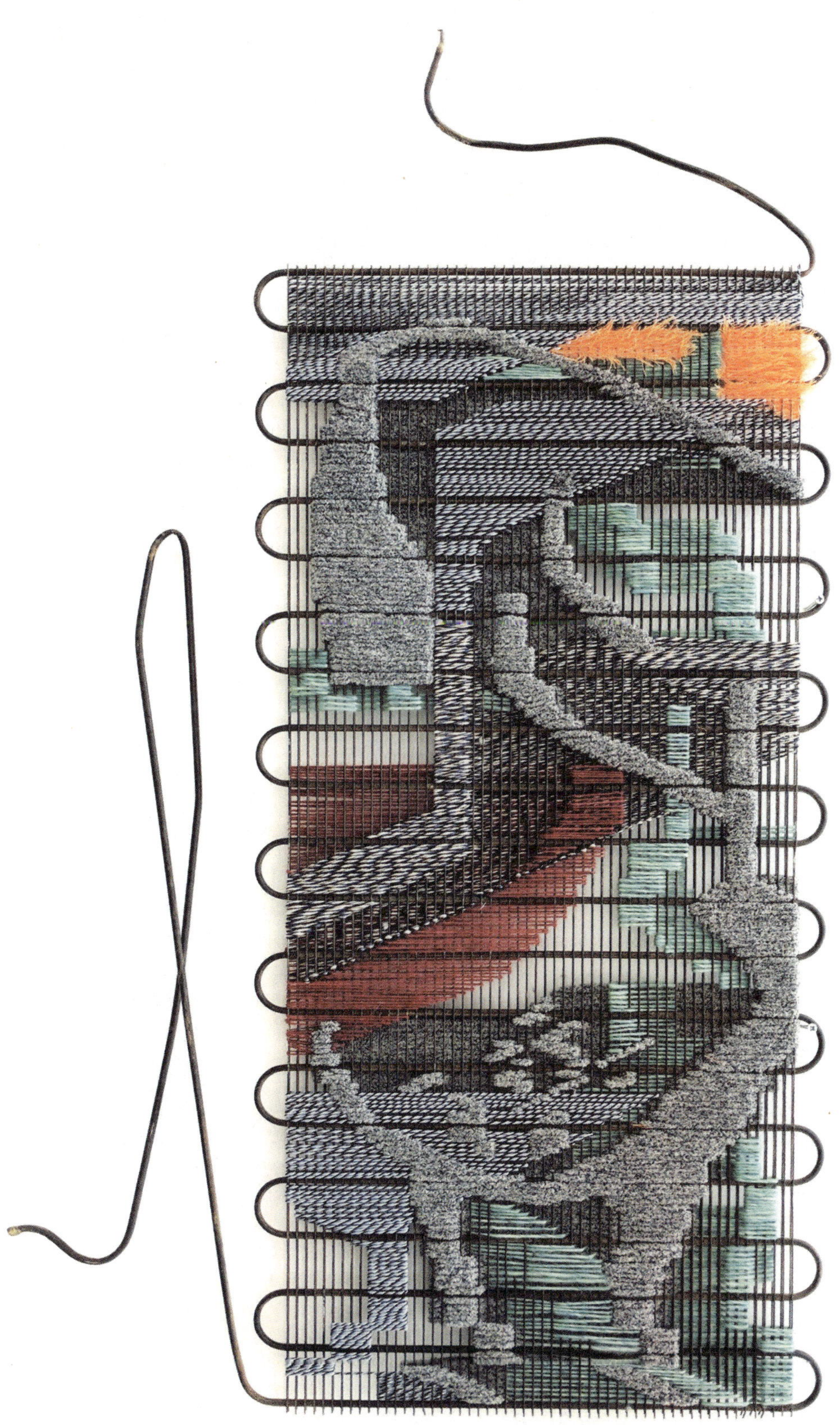

Untitled, 2017, wood, thread, refrigerator grill   cat. no. 58

195

As a signature figure of the *arte povera* movement, Michelangelo Pistoletto has remained dedicated to the theoretical experiment of intersecting art and life for more than six decades. In both form and concept, the dynamic of this pairing is evident in his expansive practice that includes sculpture, performance, public intervention, and his seminal "mirror paintings," in which scenes of everyday life are affixed to a reflective surface, making the audience an equal visual presence. He has been continuously invested in the potential of the collective; for instance, his inclusion in the 34th Venice Biennale was an overture to invite anyone as a collaborator. In his 1994 manifesto *Progetto Arte*, he wrote: "Art is the most sensitive and complete expression of human thought, and the time has come for artists to take on the responsibility of establishing ties among all other human activities, from economics to politics, science to religion, education to behavior—in a word, everything that makes up the fabric of society." In 1998, he founded an organization based on this ethos titled Cittadellarte, which is an experimental laboratory made up of researchers, and experts who address the maelstrom of contemporary life.

In *Metamorfosi* (*Metamorphosis*), a large double-mirror divides a mixture of rags and used clothes: one side multicolored, the other completely white. Depending on the vantage point, the clothes from either side appear to form a complete mountain, when in fact the two different halves are truly the whole. The crumpled and piled clothes are essentially shells without bodies, and the mirror, which is typically used for one's own personal reflection, is given over to the plural. Away from its 1970s Italian origin, the work invites a colloquial metaphor of a racially charged and divided America installed in the context of metropolitan Detroit in 2019. Herein lies the power of artworks that are salient triggers despite context and time; they remain eternally urgent to the human condition.

L.M.

(see *Landlord Colors: Material Detroit*, p. 249)

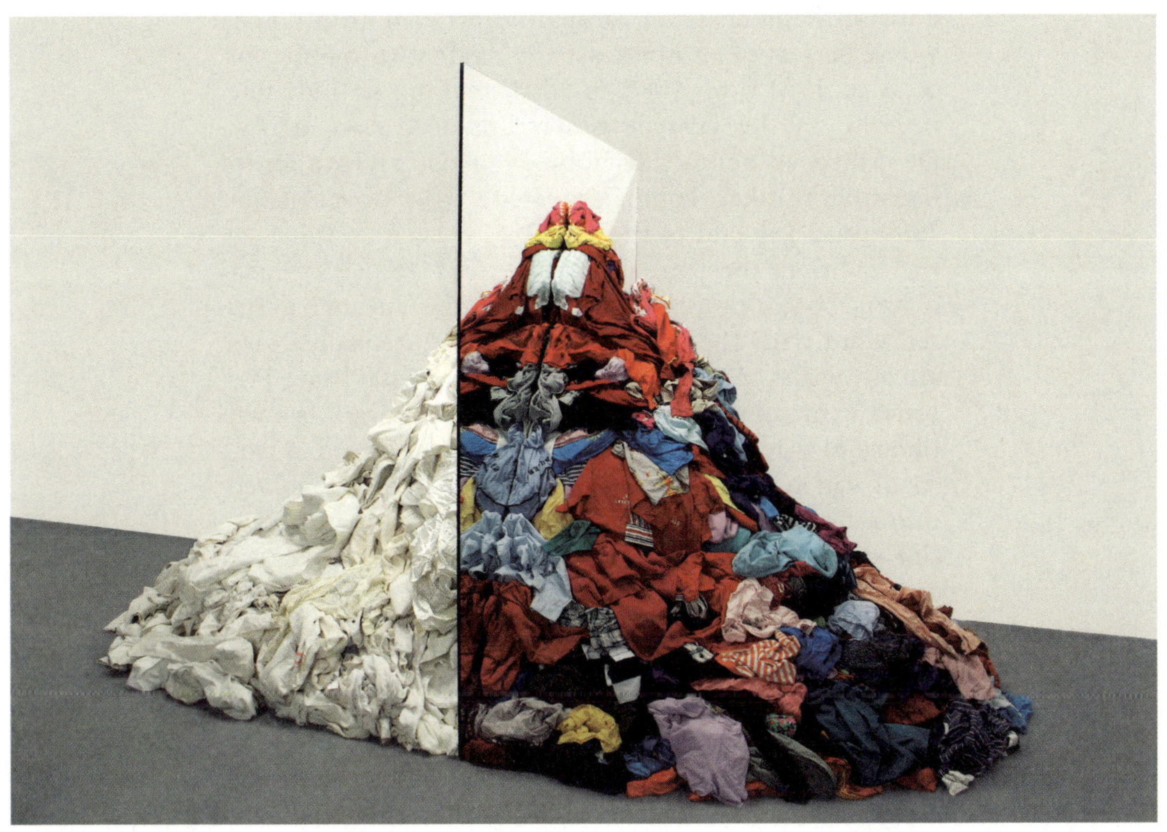

Metamorfosi, 1976/2019, mirror, rags　cat. no. 63

EDUARDO PONJUÁN

Eduardo Ponjuán is an influential artist within Cuba, where he served as a professor at the Instituto Superior de Arte (ISA) from 1987 to 2003, making an indelible imprint on the current generation of Cuban artists. Described as a multidisciplinary artist and an inexhaustible thinker, Ponjuán created "artist books" from 1989 until the end of the 1990s. However, contrary to the tradition, these are perhaps better regarded as book objects or sculptures that supplant the author's written word with the artist's own poetic intentions—we are left with the original title as a conceptual base. The series came about from the artist organizing his own library to think about what was of value to read, a personal version of literary criticism. The series evolved into sculptural masks—the corporeal head to our interior one—and therein, each book denotes a face or a door that is the metaphorical entry for knowledge. Ponjuán now regards each book as a self-portrait of the different aspects of his own identity.

In the 1990s, the series also became a library of recycled products in Cuba—material portraits of everyday life. The Special Period (a euphemism to name Cuba's profound economic crisis of the time) created a context of poverty that had an effect on all artistic creation. Ponjuán's books can be seen as a response to this condition by turning the acquired national patrimony (the library) into a piece of art, thereby becoming an exertion of freedom for knowledge.

A.G.F.

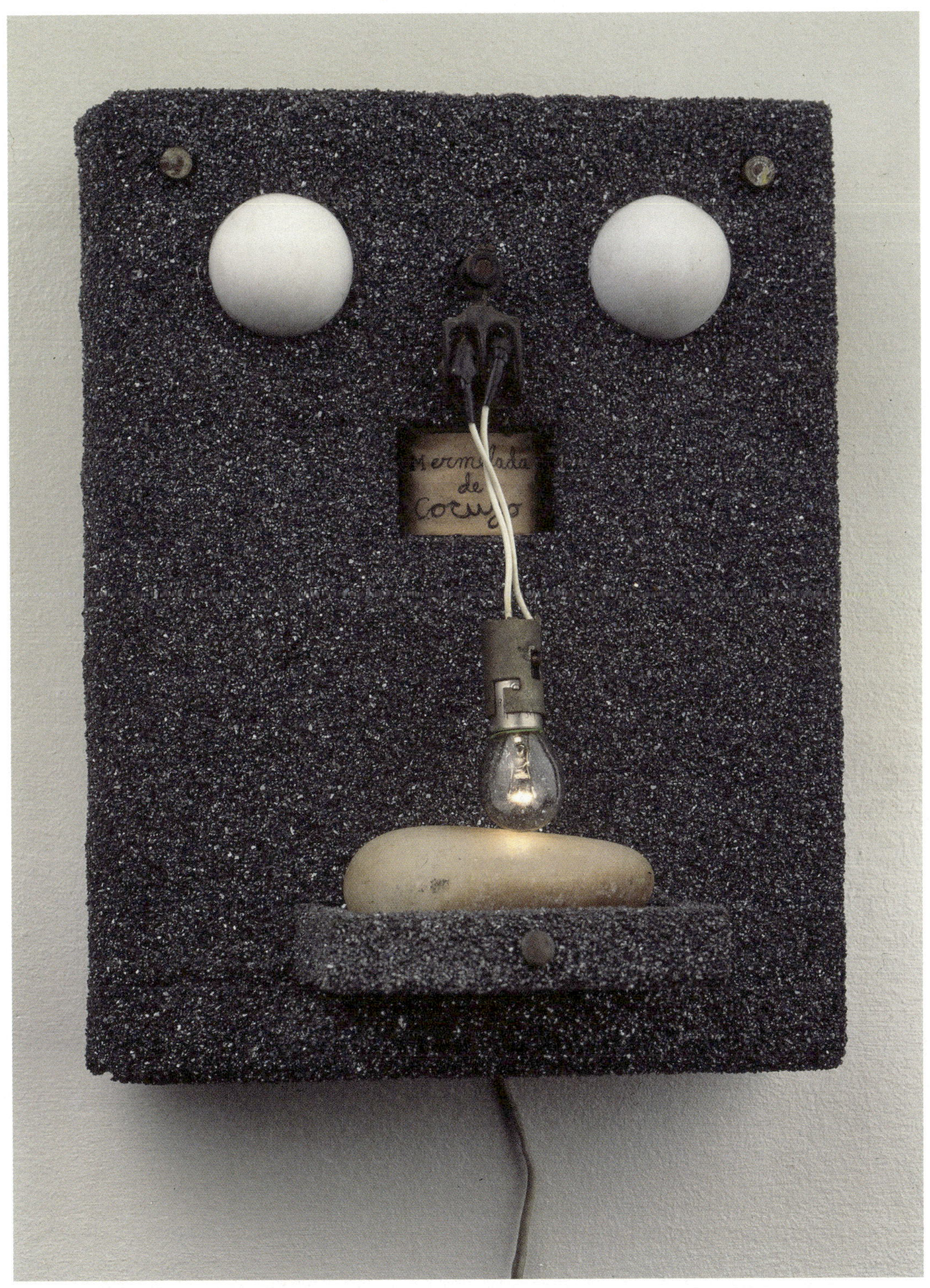

Monument to Columbus I, 1997, book, lamp, alabaster, kaolin stones, carborundum   cat. no. 64

EUGENIO VALDÉS FIGUEROA

TRAJECTORIES OF A RUMOR:
Cuban Art
in the Postwar Period

Originally published in Art Cuba
(New York: Harry N. Abrams, Inc., 2001), 16–23.

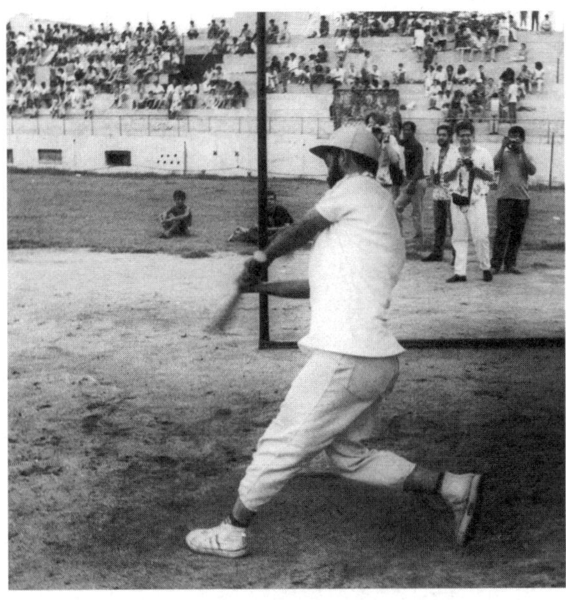

FIGURE 1

José A. Figueroa, *Cuban Art is Dedicated to Baseball*, 1989, photograph

*To find the absolute truth—
if such a thing existed—
resolves nothing; what is
important here is to decide
on our point of view, to
discover where we are standing, to know how to link the
things in the world around
us, and from there, with
all our will, impose our
reality.
—Edmundo Desnoes, Memorias
del subdesarrollo (Memories
of Underdevelopment, 1962),
cited in the editorial note
of Memoria de la postguerra
(November 1993)*

Rigorous state control of the
mass media has caused relations
between the public and private
spheres in Cuba to atrophy.
In reaction to this restric-
tion of information, rumor has
become an alternative mode of
discourse in Cuba. Rumor cir-
culates within Cuba using the
same hidden, illegal methods by
which products are distributed
in the underground economy, acting as a receptor and as a voice
for an underground culture. It
is fed by oral sources and uses
these same sources to propagate itself, side stepping the
official means of communication
and transgressing institutional
authority; rumor has created a

relatively independent domestic lexicon. Thus, to a certain degree, autonomous, extraofficial rumor ends up subverting and contaminating official information.

By the end of 1989, artistic expression began to take on many of the characteristics of rumor, as art retreated from its public, political position. The collective art of the streets moved inside and became more individual and personal. The tension between public and private, official and extraofficial, became identified with the contrasts between exterior and interior, society and art, and society and the individual.

Any dialogue between artists and the state was inevitably cut off by the vertiginous rush of politically provocative events that took place in the art world between 1989 and 1990. In early 1989 a series of exhibitions of contemporary art held at the Castillo de la Real Fuerza, approved by the Visual Arts Council of the Ministry of Culture, was closed after five days. Among the artworks deemed offensive were René Francisco Rodríguez and Eduardo Ponjuan's portraits of Castro. Depictions of Castro were legal but not encouraged, and the images included in the show were at best ambiguous in meaning. Marcia Leiseca, the Vice Minister of Culture who had overseen the "Cuban Renaissance" of the 1980s, was removed from her job.

The famously ironic and irreverent response to the closing of the show was the event *Cuban Art Is Dedicated to Baseball*, performed by artists, critics, professors, and students in Havana's José A. Echeverría Stadium—legal permission is required for a gathering, but not for a ballgame. But when the group Paideia issued a manifesto calling into question the "subordination of the intellectual to hegemonic structure," it was immediately forced to disband. The protests culminated during the 1990 exhibition *El objeto esculturado* (*The Sculpted Object*) at Centro de Desarrollo de las Artes Visuales (Center for the Development of the Visual Arts) in Havana. Angel Delgado's spontaneous and transgressive performance—in which he defecated on a copy of the newspaper *Granma*—quite explicitly controverted the "alliance with the institutions" advocated in the exhibition's catalogue.[1]

Even before the official announcement in 1990 of the so-called "Special Period," survival was all that was talked about in Cuba. The sophistry that characterized political rhetoric was dwarfed by the deepest and most pervasive crisis ever experienced by Cubans born after 1959. It is now common to acknowledge the impact of this whole crisis on the readjustment of the sociocultural dynamic.

The 1990s ushered in a period marked by austerity. The strict regimentation of all aspects of public life did not allow for private pleasures, desires, tastes, spontaneity, and escapes; instead, these were all drawn toward territory that evaded institutional control, in order to confront—at least through fiction—their own impossibility.

During the early 1990s, many of the most interesting art events happened at the margins of actual art institutions; one might be tempted to say that they happened on the periphery of society, except that the great majority were conceived as essentially sociological gestures. This withdrawal from the art scene had to do not only with a kind of "cultural secrecy" but also with an attendant process of alienation. This resulted in self-reflection, a critical self consciousness that directed the locus of art away from the street and toward the studio; from public space toward private space; from the inconsistencies of the fabric and structures of a world in crisis, and the straitjackets imposed by social discipline toward a utopian extraterritoriality found in the precarious security of rumor and metaphor.

The schools did not escape from this difficult period unharmed, suffering from material limitations and the absence of open debate. Lupe Álvarez, a professor at the Instituto Superior de Arte (ISA), discussed the "restoration of the aesthetic paradigm"—i.e., a return to traditional material, object-based art. This transition was both a response to the crackdown on public, political art and to the opening of collectors' markets abroad. In the political climate of the early 1990s, artists shied away from more radical art forms; and in a time of economic hardship, art that could be purchased by international collectors promised survival.

But art can exist at the margins and still be socially involved. One approach that emerged at this time was a new concept of teaching. Lupe Álvarez herself would become one of the defenders, indeed instigators, of unconventional teaching methods that went beyond the classroom and involved the conditions and intimacies of social life. Another ISA professor, Rene Francisco Rodríguez, began an ongoing project with students at the school, called Galería DUPP (which stands for *desde una pragmática pedagógica*, "from a practical pedagogy"). According to Rene Francisco, academic practice must be deconstructed through feedback and dialogue, and by merging living space with the pedagogic arena. The emphasis on art with a social purpose was intended to offer a context for the exercise of new demands, new themes, and also new commitments. The idea was that teaching itself should protect and exercise the romantic impulse and spirit of solidarity that seemed condemned to disappear.

In 1990, DUPP (which at the time included Abel Barroso, Fernando Rodríguez, Ibrahim Miranda Ramos, Dagoberto Rodríguez Sánchez, and Alexandre

Arrechea Zambrano) became involved with an event titled *La casa nacional* (*The National House*), which took place in a Havana apartment building. They went knocking on doors, asking the occupants if they could help them to restore or decorate their homes. Some tenants asked the students to paint the walls yellow (in traditional Yoruba culture, yellow alludes to the Caridad del Cobre, Cuba's patron saint) or blue (for the sea, Yemayá—or perhaps simply because the color went well with the furniture); others preferred more practical repairs on the plumbing, carpentry, or stonework. In every case the inhabitants agreed to share their living space and domestic life for several days with the young artists. Gradually, the building was dressed in symbolic clothing, in which references from Cuban vernacular tradition mixed with the personal tastes of each individual in the building.[2]

DUPP was just one of the new approaches to art making. Other artists, more cynical than romantic, converted the street into a laboratory. At the start of the 1990s, Carlos Garaicoa decided to mark a site in the city with a number "6." With this gesture, he inserted himself into the tracery of urban "writing," without any apparent intention other than the desire to experience that "magic instant, in which I [place] the unsuspecting viewer in my own game, based on the presence of the image."

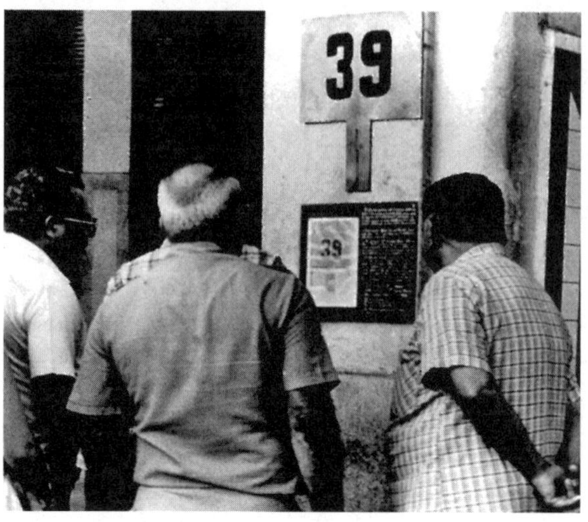

FIGURE 2

Carlos Garaicoa, *39*, Havana, 1991, photograph

The works *6*, *39*, and *Suceso en el 609* (*Event in the 609*)—all done in 1990 and 1991—appeared to indicate no more than the tracks left by Garaicoa in his transit through the city. These were not works made for the usual gallery-going public; rather they were a kind of "noise," lending a fictitious narrative to the chosen site. Garaicoa's markings on the city gained symbolic power over time, altering the rituals of daily life and producing new ones. They functioned like a street rumor: passersby experienced surprise and even suspicion, and they came up with their own stories of the numbers' genesis. The sequence of provocations and "contaminations" became events with their own mythologies.

The markings stimulated an obsession with their vacuous presence, as though the materialization of nothing could shake the general indifference of that time. Speaking of these actions years later, Garaicoa explained how loss of faith and lack of belief in the nation's project of social liberation filtered back through his work in the form of societal "interventions" whose only true intent was commentary, and whose success was highly ironic:

> Even as students at the ISA, we made jokes about that legacy of the generation that came before us, and we'd say with nostalgia, but also sarcasm, that ours was a generation born riddled with reversals and contradictions—we were the 1960s reeled backward, and so were condemned to suffer through everything from an inverted perspective; we were like the "hippies light" of the 1990s. After a few years of scandal between 1989 and 1991, there came a period of silence. The city was hushed, the double exile was evident.... There was an almost absolute emptiness, an existential void.... For everyone the apathy and absence of debate created an unease as harmful as the absence of the major [cultural] figures from earlier times.

Tania Bruguera's newspaper/artwork *Memoria de la postguerra* (*Post-war Memory*) was a fleeting attempt to fill that space for encounter, debate, and coherence—an attempt to recharge a dynamic that had been extinguished in the Cuban art world. It gathered writings by Cubans at home and abroad and was published secretly; after two issues, it was banned by the state. But Bruguera, a performance artist, had never been very interested in objects and their permanence; her work developed as the indelible trace of a gesture, as the echoes of an attitude felt more in time than in space. Process—its marks and trajectories—have constituted not only the raw materials of Bruguera's art but also its structure and finality.

And so, following the path of rumor, between 1993 and 1994 copies of the only two issues of this newspaper passed from hand to hand. With a limited print run and independent system of production and distribution, *Memoria de la postguerra* might have remained a rumor like any other; instead, it became a testament and definition of its epoch. The editorial note to the inaugural issue (November 1993) elucidated the paper's name and its central concept: "Post-war," for its resemblance to the physical condition of the city, the interior state of the people, the social nature of art."[3]

Memoria de la postguerra reminds me of the impact made thirty years earlier by the tabloid *Lunes de Revolución* (*Revolutionary Mondays*). Bearing in mind the contrasts and temporal distance that separate these papers, we can also note some important connections. Both newspapers ended up becoming the ephemeral action that brought some hope to a vanguard group of intellectuals and stimulated cultural debate; both had their genesis in periods of intense contradiction and profound uncertainty; and in both cases the printed product, the artistic gesture, and the cultural responsibility of the collaborators were accompanied by a rumor that later was harvested as a legend, as the mythology of a tangible event.

Yet *Memoria* differed from *Lunes* in that it was conceived as a simulacrum of a newspaper. *Memoria de la postguerra* was a collaborative work of art, appropriating journalistic structure and functions in order to challenge the muteness and immobility engendered by censorship. It was a performative, participatory work, but not a performance; it was engagé, but oriented toward ideological intervention rather than defined actions; it brought together a group of writers and artists, emphasizing personal testimony and with the explicit intention of reconstructing a social landscape out of disparate fragments. But it never became a collective action.

Unlike *Lunes*—which was launched in the romantic decade of the Revolution as a cultural supplement to a mass-circulation official organ—*Memoria de la postguerra* was born on the margins as a reaction to the fear, disillusionment, and skepticism of the 1990s. Yet these papers are linked by an important historical phenomenon: after the dissolution of Lunes and the collapse of intellectual debate

that came later in the 1960s, an exodus of intellectuals took place that was no less significant than the one of 1989–93, which directly preceded the first issue of *Memoria*. Tania Bruguera sought out not only artists who had stayed in Cuba but those who had decided to emigrate, as well as emerging creators still viewed with suspicion by state institutions. *Memoria* drew parallels between the internal and external "exiles" of Cuban artists. Luis Camnitzer rightly affirmed in 1994:

> What is noteworthy is the fact that at a time of unprecedented economic crisis in which distances have grown almost ad *infinitum* due to the lack of transport and the international dispersion of artists, *Memoria* has not only assembled ideas but has helped maintain a sense of coherence. [It is] a primary vehicle of communication.[4]

In 1994 two extraordinarily important cultural events took place: the founding of the art space Espacio Aglutinador by the artists Sandra Ceballos and Ezequiel Suárez and the Fifth Havana Biennial. These two events presented very different approaches to the issues of artistic freedom. How does one make art in a country where artists are continually censored? What, in fact, *is* the role of art?

In March of 1994, Ezequiel Suárez was prohibited from

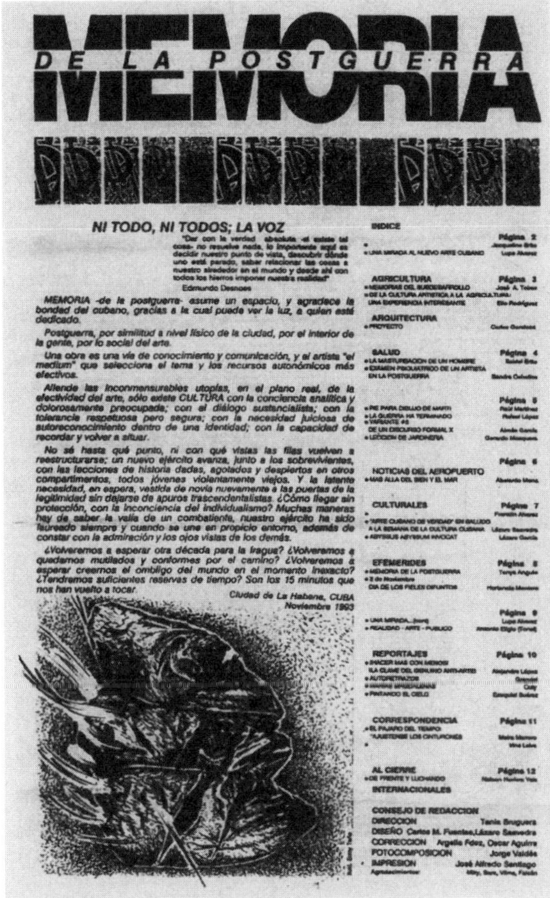

FIGURE 3

Tania Bruguera, *Memoria de la postguerra (Post-war Memory)*, front page, first issue, November 1993, newspaper

opening his solo exhibition, *El frente Bauhaus* (*The Bauhaus Front*), at Galería 23 y 12 in Havana. The poetic constructist figures of his oil paintings on canvas were seasoned with the prickly declaration "the institutions are shit." Dredging up the scatological memories of *El objeto esculturado* did not exactly secure his welcome with the administration of Galería 23 y 12. His paintings were immediately taken down and the show was canceled without public explanation only hours before it was to open. Days later, Suárez and Ceballos decided to exhibit the works in the small space they share for living and working in the Vedado district of Havana. The show was accompanied by a sort of manifesto, which stated the attitude and principles that still define Espacio Aglutinador:

AGLUTINADOR (art space) intends to exhibit and distribute the work of Cuban artists of all "sects"—alive or dead, residing within or without Cuba, young or old, known or unknown, promoted or nearly forgotten, modest or pedantic—as long as they are of indisputable quality and, above all, have that necessary dose of honesty and anxiety concerning the creation of veritable art. AGLUTINADOR is a cultural space, not a boutique. It does not intend to be elitist or avant-garde or populist or backward-looking: it wants to be (or become) just. Its only commitment is to art. It is not a "project." It is not a lovely idea put to paper by a highly organized mind. AGLUTINADOR is an event; it is happening quickly, naturally. . . . The possibilities for error are infinite.

If there is anything that AGLUTINADOR avoids like the plague it is coherence, that boring and nauseating "goodness" of the conscience.

Charles Baudelaire said:
"Art is long." AGLUTINADOR
(art space) says: "What a
lucid man!" Beuys used to
say: Every man is an artist.
To this we would add:
Every house is a gallery.

Aglutinador became a zone of
tolerance, embracing diver-
sity and refusing to obey limits
and norms. The pages of *Memoria
de la postguerra* had provided
a space to challenge institutional paralysis; the walls of
Aglutinador offered a place.
For Ceballos and Suárez only
work that was incoherent,
hybrid, undefined, chaotic, and
all but accidental could ade-
quately represent, or respond
to, a world of similar characteristics: "We had stopped
believing," Ceballos has told
me, "and Aglutinador was born
of that skepticism. The manifesto was a kind of tantrum in
the face of institutional dis-
crimination against forgotten, unknown, excluded, or self
excluded artists.... We have no
vocation for humbling ourselves
or for accepting taboos...that
is the very reason we created the space, not only as an
escape, but also to give free
reign to an unconscious spontaneity, without renouncing the
contradictions, the anguish,
or even the apathy in which we
are enmeshed—both as individuals and as artists."[5] To this
day, Aglutinador has been a way
to bring art to "real life,"
to transform an extra-institu-
tional site into a gallery of
attitudes.

Aglutinador calls into
question the notion of representation, appeals to unusual
methodologies, and proposes
strategies less concentrated
on the aesthetic of the objects
than on situations and gestures.
In a performance entitled *Cada
artista que se va es un frag-
mento que se pierde* (*Every
Artist Who Leaves Is a Fragment
that Is Lost*), which was part
of the exhibition *Inside Havana*
(1995), Suárez climbed up on a
scaffolding and with a steel
blade began to destroy the ceiling of his house. Exhibited at
the same time as Suárez's performance—during which spectators
were ducking falling pieces of
concrete Carlos Garaicoa's *Roze
... La casa de las mejoras* (*The
House of Improvements*) combined
distorted projections of images
of urban ruin with drawings of
fantastic obelisk-shaped buildings. All the while, the conta-
gious rhythm of *Chaonda*, a hit
musical of the 1960s, played in
the background.

Many of the exhibitions at
Espacio Aglutinador have emphasized the interior/exterior
relationship, whose conceptual
and spatial connotations extend
to other dichotomies—art and
society, individual space
and social space, art and the
individual, public space and
private space, official history
and extra official gossip,
art and politics, history and
mythology—but without los-
ing sight of the fact that
Aglutinador is first a domestic
space and secondarily a place
where art is made and shown.

In a society where everything is designed to feed paranoia, "nosing around" and "rumor-mongering" become part of everyday life. Voyeurism—practiced by the state and by society—has been one of the most interesting metaphors employed by Aglutinador, in works and performances where the line between those who "act" and those who "watch" is blurred. Anyone who crosses the threshold at Aglutinador must be prepared for disruption born of conflicting parallel situations or shrewdly elliptical cycles; visitors, artists, and the art exhibited are caught up in shifting boundaries as well as interchangeable spaces and roles.[6]

Several months after the creation of Espacio Aglutinador, the Fifth Havana Biennial opened. Without a doubt, the Biennial has been one of the few state-run events to confront the issue of silence. For over a decade, this event has constituted the most important part of the Cuban art scene. Its prestige is due not only to the Biennial's careful, astute selection of works and artists or the fact that it has opened the door to a successful career for many of its participants. The Biennial has injected our environment with a vaccine against provincialism, defending at all cost and against all difficulties the inclusion of contemporary art from Asia, Africa, and Latin America. By bringing art from outside Cuba to Cuba, the Biennial adds a global perspective to Cuban theoretical reflection.

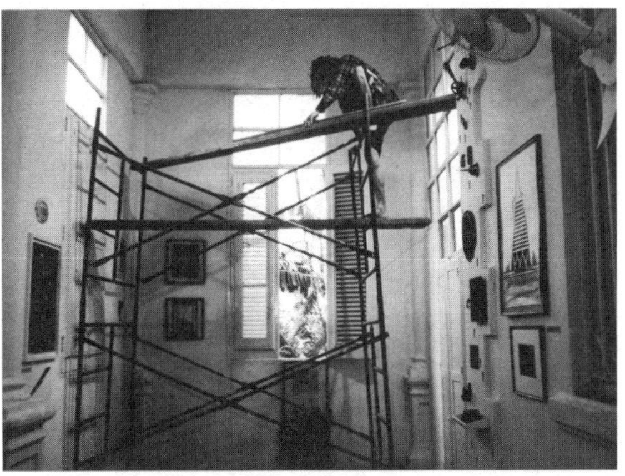

FIGURE 4

Ezequiel O. Suárez, performance at the opening of Carlos Garaicoa's exhibition *Inside Havana*, Espacio Aglutinador, 1995, photograph

But our main debt to the Havana Biennial is that since its founding in 1984, it has promoted the most interesting contemporary Cuban artists—from José Bedia, Tomás Sánchez, Ricardo Rodríguez Brey, Tomás Esson, Gory, and Tonel to Kcho, Luis Gómez, Manuel Piña, Tania Bruguera, Carlos Garaicoa, and Los Carpinteros, among many others whose talent has been recognized internationally.[7]

The Fifth Havana Biennial presented a body of work by Cuban artists that was quite different in tone from the works exhibited at Aglutinador. Art critics from outside the country were surprised by the ambiguous rhetoric of the Cuban art at the Biennial, which masked its themes and messages. The art was extremely metaphorical, examining the reception of art and public expectation and employing the signs and symbols of social rituals.

In fact, the Cuban presence at the 1994 Biennial represented a new strategy in art creation, perhaps best explained through the description of one of the artworks exhibited. The trio Los Carpinteros presented a group of works that they stated were done on commission to decorate the home of a (fictitious) Cuban-American collector. Most of the works in this series, called *Interior Habanero* (*Havana Interior*), were self-portraits. In *Marquilla Cigarrera Cubana* (*Cuban Cigar Label*), two of the artists appear nude, strolling confidently through the rooms of a museum. Below this image, like a footnote, one reads: "Sir, we've lost the whole game." "The whole game?" "All but one thing." "What!" "The desire to play again."

At Espacio Aglutinador, art resisted integration, declaring its reluctance to be discovered, whereas Los Carpinteros feigned integration, disguising suspicion with transparency. In one case, the artist shields himself by disappearing; in the other, he pretends to show himself but hides behind his exhibitionism. Whereas Espacio Aglutinador situated itself in a marginal position and encouraged an aesthetic of the unpredictable, injecting chaos into the ritual order of the social sphere or the art world, the artists in the 1994 Biennial sought to rearticulate the relationship between art and the state. They wanted to create art that stood front and center, not off to the side. They had lost everything, but they would not give up; they wanted to play again. To paraphrase Heidegger,

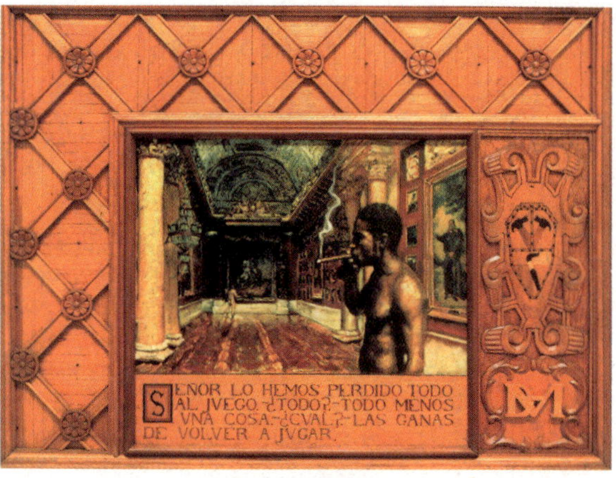

FIGURE 5

Los Carpinteros, *Marquilla Cigarrera Cubana
(Cuban Cigar Label)*, 1994, wood, oil on canvas

the important thing is not to get out of the game, but to get in—provided one does so in the appropriate manner.[8]

They did this by making art that was no less critical but that employed metaphor and double meanings, used rumor and the lexicon of the street, merged fiction and reality, in order to evade censorship and control. The Biennial artists redefined the strategies for a game with—and within—the institutional sphere. Extraofficial language had truly penetrated and deconstructed the official.

This method of playing with viewpoints, pretending to be on the inside instead of the outside, or vice versa, constitutes the essence of Manuel Piña's aesthetic. From the beginning of his career, he has been obsessed with spatial relations—not only the physical aspects but also and especially the ideological, conceptual, and ethical. Piña's art involves the spectator and calls into question points of view settled by morality, art, ideology, history, or politics, domains whose edges he twists until they touch.

The most important element in Piña's images is the edge, the limit. In his series *Aguas baldias (Water Wastelands)* (1992-94), he focuses on the Malecón, the wall and the waters that separate Cuba from the rest of the world. But for Manuel Piña the borders are, again, moveable; in one photograph a man rushes headlong into the waters.

As we shift our position, our perception of things is altered. Each point of view is connected with a point in space, with a profile of reality, with a version of the truth. This is the conclusion the artist reaches in this and other series, such as *Ave. 51* (1991), *De construcciones y utopias (Homenaje a Eduardo Muñoz)* (*[De]constructions and Utopias [Tribute to Eduardo Muñoz]*) (1995), and *Manipulaciones, verdades y otras ilusiones (Manipulations, Truths and Other Illusions)* (1995-2000).

Recently Manuel Piña has created billboards placed in the public space. Ironically, he has titled them *Trabajos domestico (Domestic Labors)* (1999-2000). These billboards are built on a principle as simple as shock therapy. In one, against a white background, a hand signals "stop." But this familiar symbol is accompanied by a text that leaves us speechless: "Stop! Why be such a fool. Why be such a shit-eater. Steal!" In another billboard, the hand holds a utensil for mashing food; the text repeats, "Crush. Crush. Crush. It's easy!"

Piña's intent is to shake people up in public by revealing what they practice in private. Of course, the artist has yet to find a gallery in Cuba willing to exhibit the billboards. These works seem condemned to circulate on the periphery: rumor is their subject and also, perhaps, their destiny. Piña reverses roles, urging his viewers *do* instead of *don't*—a strategy that in the end is much more powerful. But this time the game Piña is proposing is very serious, for it touches on highly delicate ethical matters in a world we could—with Tania Bruguera—describe as "postwar," a world that does not want to admit that the most basic values have collapsed. The artist makes clear that certain situations are indeed ethically questionable: such as buying stolen products on the black market, prostituting oneself in any way, or "crushing" one's peers in the competition of daily life. Almost no one escapes from such socially pervasive ethical lapses; yet people resist taking note of them. Piña explains, "The fact that I appropriate advertising language and that the works are supposed to be sited in public spaces has to do with the intention to place the viewer among everyone. There is no longer *I* and *the others*, but *we*. I provoke an awkward situation that can be the start of a reaction. It is simply a matter of changing points of view and questioning the absolutes."

At this point in the Cuban art game, there is probably not much interest in legitimizing its complicated rules or in disagreeing with the stubbornness of the other players. What is truly important is to recognize where we stand and then question that point of view, tossing the dice of reality in the air. The possibilities for error are infinite. So too is the desire to keep playing.

—

Eugenio Valdés Figueroa is an independent curator, lecturer, art critic, and art historian who lives in Havana.

1   "Although conceived on the basis of, and for, the art works, the event-program also involves notions of assistance or collaboration, through an alliance with the institutions." Alexis Somoza and Félix Suazo, from the exhibition catalogue for *El objeto escufturado*, Centro de Desarrollo de las Artes Visuales (Center for the Development of the Visual Arts), Havana, May 1990.

2   One year later—stimulated by the ideas proposed in *La casa nacional*—Dagoberto Rodriguez Sánchez and Alexandre Arrechea Zambrano (who later formed Los Carpinteros with Marco Castillo Valdes) presented *Para Usted (For You)* in the Partagás Cigar Factory (Havana, 1991).
In a 1998 interview, Los Carpinteros recounted to me the importance that this event had for the future trio: "In that show," explained Alexandre, "we wanted to offer as a work of art what we'd learned from the tobacco industry. Indeed, the model for the production of our art came from that sui generis industry: its union activity, the creation of a single object through the artisanship of various individuals, the finite nature of the product in the hands of the consumer, the provisional life of *el habano*...." Before an audience comprised essentially of tobacco rollers, they tried to create the flux and reflux of the codes and procedures in the production of art and in the artisanal manufacture of tobacco. They complemented all this with a performance in which they pretended to be professors of "tobaccology." The performance made clear that the artists wished to give back what they had extracted from the factory, through a detailed cultural, sociological, and historical investigation. Referring to *Para Usted*, Dagoberto insists that the connections established there between the artistic and extra-artistic were aimed not so much at a dissolution of those boundaries but rather at "the creation, in a metaphorical sense, of a circularity in the very meaning of tobacco production for the nation; of this, the tobacco worker had no immediate consciousness, at least during the act of production." (Author interview with Dagoberto Rodriguez Sánchez and Alexandre Arrechea Zambrano, Havana, 1998.)

3   Tania Bruguera, *Memoria de la postguerra* (editorial note), Havana, November 1993, 1.

4   Luis Camnitzer, "Memoria de la postguerra," *Art Nexus*, no. 15, Jan.-March 1995, 30.

5   Author interview with Sandra Ceballos. All of the remaining quotes in this essay are taken from interviews by the author between 1998 and 2000.

6   These exhibitions include *Daño (Harm)*, Glexis Novoa, 1994; *Viven del cariño (They Live on Love)*, Marta Maria Perez, 1995; *Chago-Eyaculaciones con antecedentes penales (Ejaculations with a Criminal Past)*, Chago Armada, 1995; *Work in Progress*, Luis Gómez, 1995; *Trofeos de guerra fría (Cold War Trophies)*, Ernesto Pujol and Manuel Alcaide, 1995; *Adentro es mio (What's Within Is Mine)*, Ezequiel Suárez, 1995; *Entre Miami y La Habana (Between Miami and Havana)*, Eduardo Aparicio, 1996; *Historias del Barrio (Stories from the Barrio)*,

Alberto Casado, 1996; *El increado* (*The Uncreated*), Ernesto Leal, 1996; *Naches* (*Nights*), Ibraham Miranda, 1996; *El debutante renuente* (*The Reluctant Beginner*), Jorge Luís Marrero, 1996; *Ojos desnudos* (*Naked Eyes*), Abigail González, 1998; and *Adorado Wolffi* (*Darling Wolffi*), Sandra Ceballos, 2000.

7   At the Fourth Biennial in 1991, the work of such important artists as Luís Gómez, Ibrahim Miranda Ramos, Belkis Ayón, and Kcho gave the lie to the generally accepted judgment that Cuban art was in an irreversible crisis. Kcho was not, in fact, a participant in the Biennial, but his solo exhibition *Paisaje Cubano* (*Cuban Landscape*) at Galería 23 y 12 took place at the same time. The success of this extraordinary show guaranteed the artist not only an invitation to the next Biennial but also an immediate and definitive place in international circles. Kcho's high acclaim in the established art world during those years was unique for a Cuban artist.

By using an ironic title, *Paisaje Cubano* (*Cuban Landscape*), a minimalist aesthetic, and recycled or discarded objects and materials, Kcho alluded to a fragile and precarious ideological universe. This heralded key themes in the development of his future work, which would deal with the issues of exile, insularity, the national identity, the temporary versus the eternal, and migration. One year later, Kcho had a solo exhibition in the Museo Nacional in Havana and immediately began to participate in important international events. among them the biennial art shows of Havana, São Paulo, Johannesburg, Istanbul, and Kwangju, South Korea; he also received the 1995 UNESCO Prize, among other awards.

8   I refer to Heidegger's well-known statement: "The point is not to exit the circle, but to enter it in the correct manner."

Wilfredo Prieto is a conceptual artist who does not predetermine the political implications of his work; rather, this is accomplished through his method of *object trouvé*—art created from unaltered objects not considered traditional art materials—within the Cuban context. In Cuba, the strategy of using provisional materials, and often the lack of having a studio, is understood as a consequence of the Cuban economic crisis after the collapse of the Soviet Union. Prieto has been one of the main followers of this provisional aesthetic in Cuba that had a resurgence in the early nineties in dialogue with other international art scenes, such as the activity in Mexico spearheaded by artist Gabriel Orozco. In *Miren el tamaño de este mango* (*Look at the size of this mango*), the artist confronts the alienation of the everyday perception of these two objects, a mango and a BlackBerry cell phone.

The artwork performs the kind of critical inquiry suggested by scholar Marshall Berman regarding the modernism of underdevelopment: "But what happened in areas outside the West, where, despite the pervasive pressures of the expanding world market, and despite the growth of a modern world culture that was unfolding along with it...modernization was not going on?"[1] A new relationship emerges between two seemingly disparate objects, and two apparent realities collide: the underdeveloped natural atmosphere—tropical and agrarian—and the developed technological world represented by a mobile phone. Their union is a metaphor that closely fits the uncertain Cuban reality of the post-economic crisis years in the 2000s, when in an effort to diversify the impoverished situation of its economy the government tentatively opened Cuba to the international market.

A.G.F.

1   Marshall Berman, *All That Is Solid Melts into Air: The Experience of Modernity* (New York: Penguin, 1982), 174.

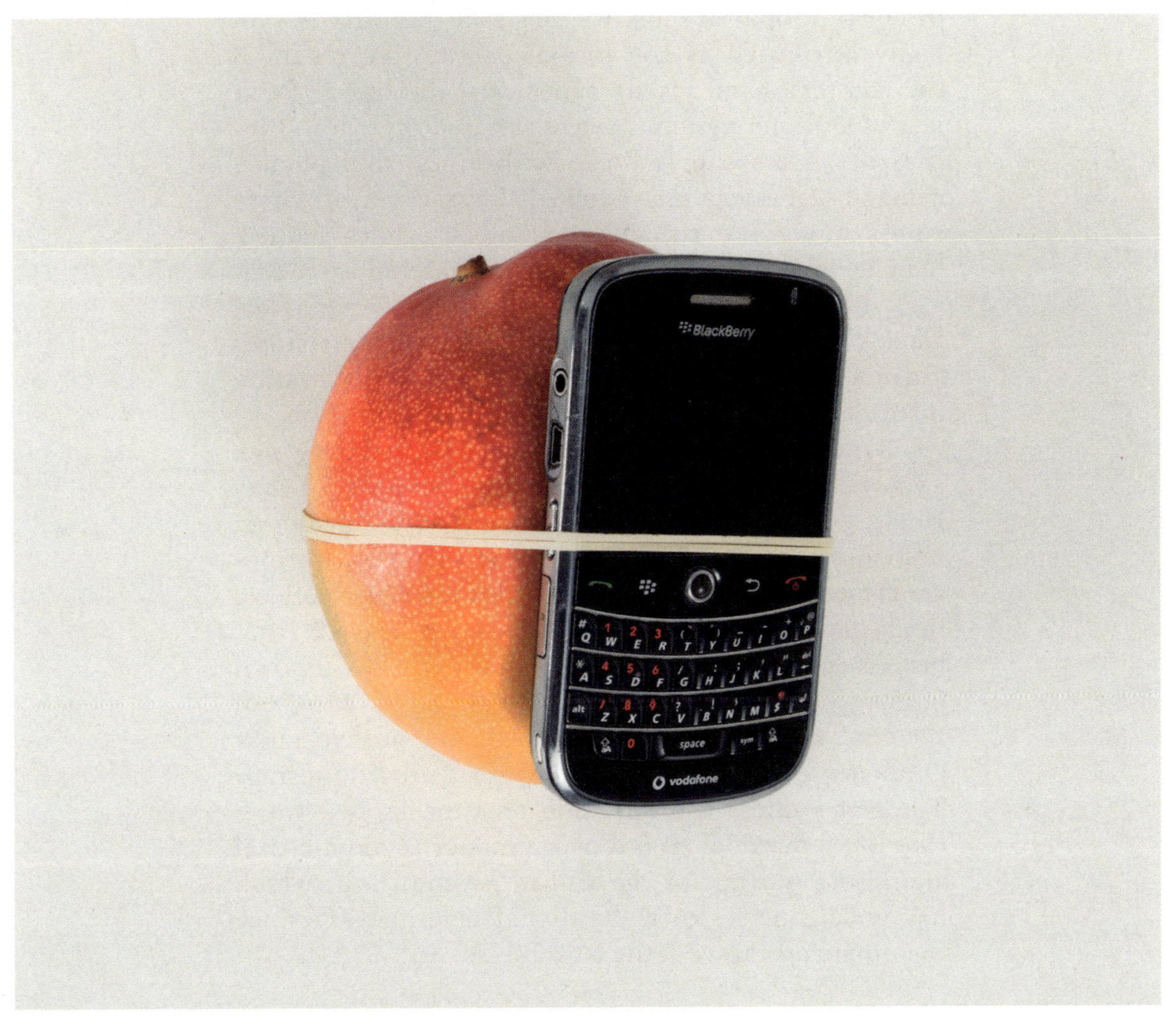

Miren el tamaño de este mango (*Look at the size of this mango*), 2011,
mango, BlackBerry, rubber band   cat. no. 68

In conventional art history, abstract painting is typically attributed as the formal or emotive result of the painter's hand via its appendage, the brush. Paint is a ubiquitous material selected based on color affinities at an art supply store with stock to replenish demand. American artist John Baldessari corrals these paints under the title "artist colors"—hues named, branded, and promoted for their destination on a canvas. "Landlord colors" are their antithesis—unnamed, generic remnants. In the case of Cuba, such art stores are nonexistent; most material comes from negotiation instead of preference.

Rarely does paint, as a raw material, have its own agency; however, in the *Degradation* series by Diana Fonseca Quiñones, paint has autonomy—each color an individual sample of history. These abstract paintings are created with found chips of paint the artist collects from different architectural façades in Havana that have turned to ruin. Each paint fragment has its own origin story. Collectively, they create an inventory of the city's architecture that likely did not survive, since Quiñones often sources them from demolition sites. The series offers a rumination on time in two ways: they are a material record over years of economic trial and also a portrait of the Cuban psyche itself, which has undergone its own durational deterioration since the utopic promises of the Revolution.

A.G.F., L.M.

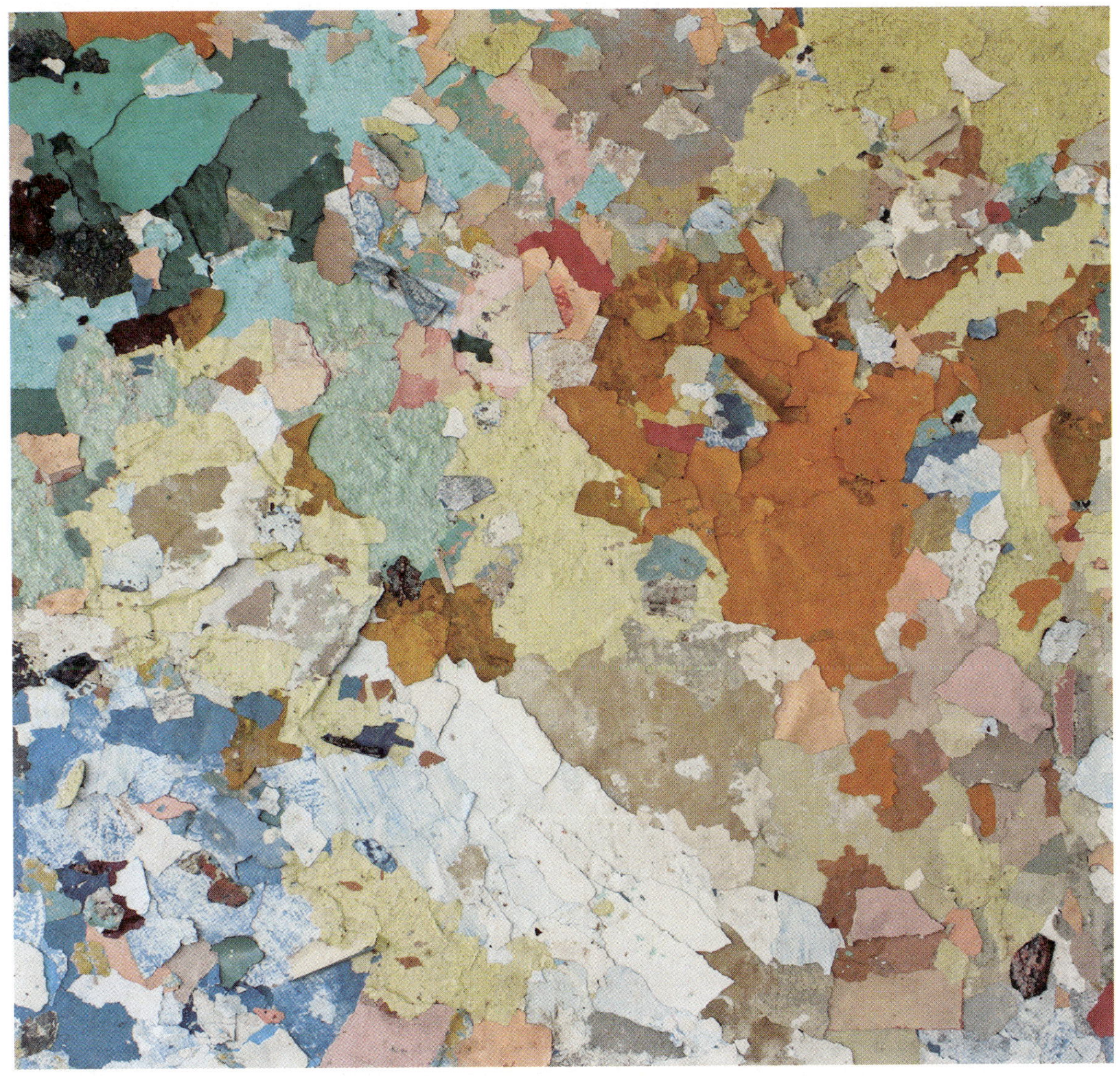

Untitled, from the *Degradation* series, 2017, paint extracted from exterior facades on wood   cat. no. 69

CHRIS SCHANCK

Designer Chris Schanck's work ranges from stand-alone sculptures to limited-edition furniture pieces, most often made with his signature process Alufoil. In this series of works, the artist forms a structural armature made of industrial materials that are then covered in aluminum foil and coated in resin. Impermeable to oxygen and water, aluminum foil became ubiquitous in America in the early twentieth century. The artist's idiosyncratic use of the domestic staple dates to his childhood encounters with the material. He recalled that as a child he would visit his father, who worked summers at a local aluminum factory, and that his mother utilized the household item as a last-minute solution to wrap Christmas gifts. "What was inside those boxes didn't matter; it was the vision of the reflective landscape that I've always remembered," he said. "The use of the material is in part a homage to the notions of the preservation of such memories of our familial experience."[1]

While his selection of the material originates in the personal, his studio production is influenced by sociopolitical interests, which recall the radical Italian avant-garde of the 1960s and 1970s, such as Riccardo Dalisi's collaborative experiments building papier-mâché chairs with the children of Naples. Schanck's practice makes visible the hands of the laborers who assist in the making process. He often employs residents from his surrounding neighborhood, which includes a large Bangladeshi population.

T.R.A.

1   Annie Block, "10 Questions With... Chris Schanck," *Interior Design*, February 20, 2018, https://www.interiordesign.net/articles/14533-10-questions-with-chris-schanck/.

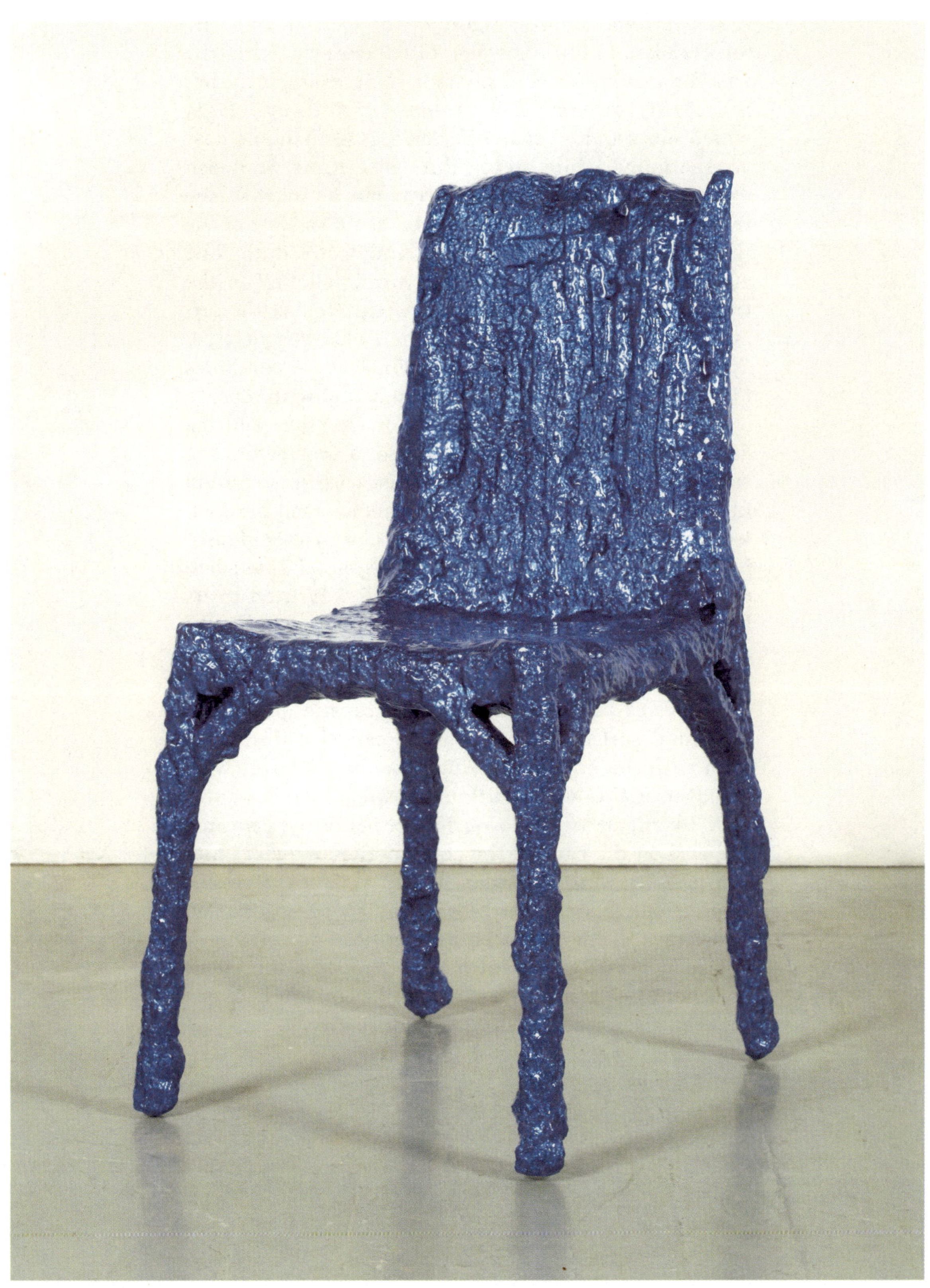

Untitled (Alufoil Chair), 2019, steel, polystyrene aluminum foil, resin   cat. no. 70

GILDA SNOWDEN

A stalwart and admired figure of the Detroit art scene for decades, Gilda Snowden often engaged with the city for inspiration and content. One example is her series *City Album: Department of Railways 1929*, which incorporated charcoal rubbings of manhole covers she found while biking through Detroit. Snowden described her work as autobiographical, in that she reaches back to her ancestors who came to Detroit via the Great Migration from the American South. She authored several series with the word "album" in the title, which collectively can be interpreted as the artist's poetic visual scrapbook. In the 1980s, she also created a series of *Constructions*, which were combines featuring found materials and often bound with rope.

Functioning almost like an oracle, the painting *Silent Preacher* was created in 1986, a year before the significant loss and gain for the artist with three family funerals—her mother, father, and uncle—and her own wedding. At the center of the work are two old-fashioned wooden mail slots with a small metal nameplate that reads "THE SILENT PREACHER." Written to its left is the word "tithe." Tithes are the one-tenth contribution of earnings given to the church, a lifetime of individual sacrifice for the benefit of a collective. The multilayered, three-dimensional encaustic piece has a textural surface into which she carved a tic-tac-toe form with three X's occupying some of the boxes with no adversarial O's. In addition, Snowden includes a tornado-like figure in the lower left corner of the painting, and also on the back of the construction, which is hidden from viewers. Snowden herself was not necessarily religious, but the work bears the coded negotiation of upheaval being mediated by sacrifice and ceremony. Snowden herself might also be regarded as the silent preacher who existed as a shaman-like conduit between the seen and unseen, reality and spirituality.

T.R.A., L.M.

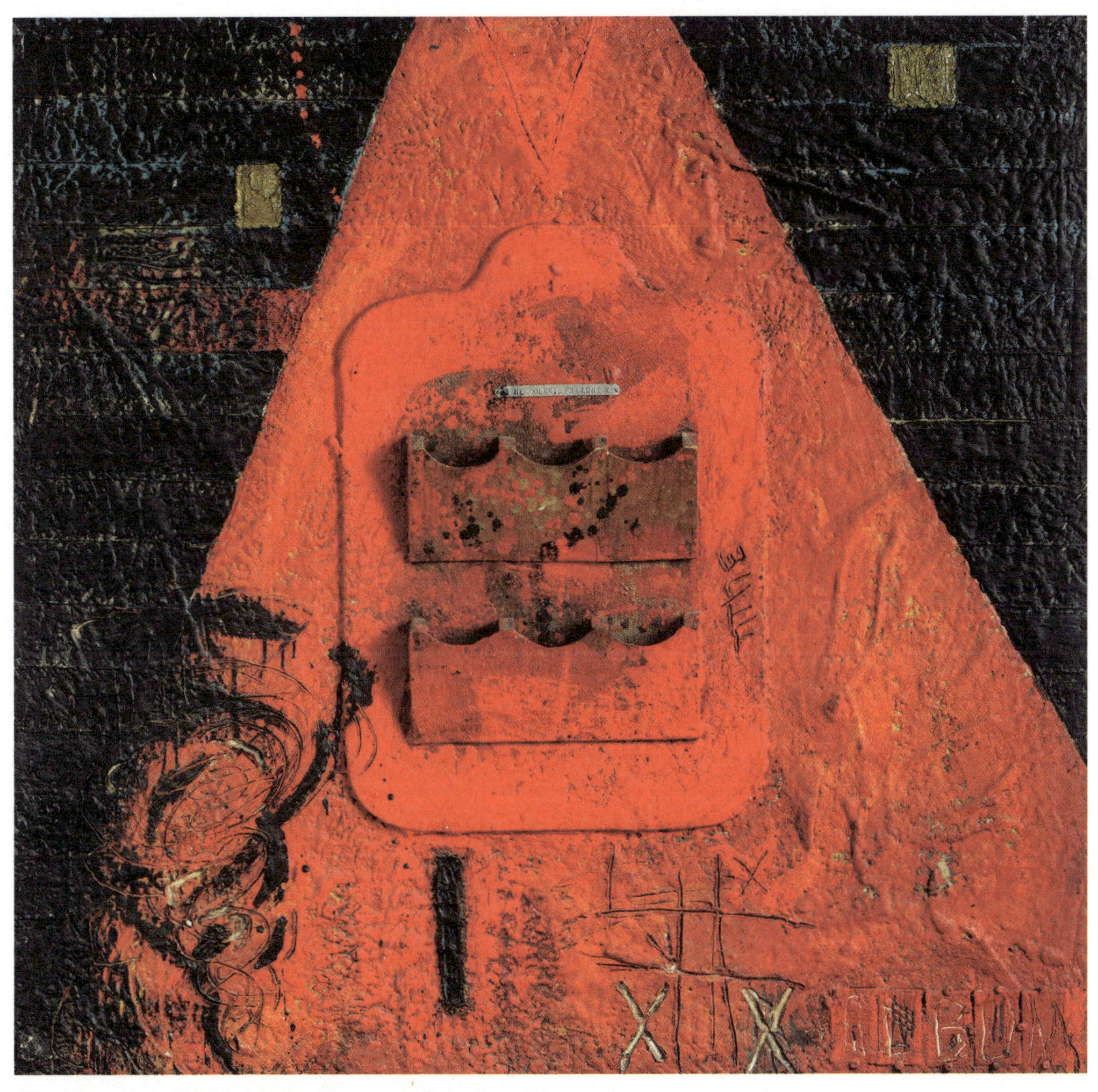

Silent Preacher, 1986, mixed media on wood   cat. no. 71

In 2012, artist Socratis Socratous started collecting bits and pieces of the National Garden in Athens without permission and bringing them to his studio. This accumulation of nonnative and indigenous organic materials from one of Greece's national landmarks was then molded in brass, cast in bronze, or plated in gold or silver. The artist transforms the humble leaves and branches into precious materials. Using sculptural techniques that resonate with traditional Greek cultural production, he stages new artificial landscapes that are site and context specific, sometimes installed as several discrete objects, or alternately as a single expansive installation.

The National Garden plays an important sociopolitical role in Greek history. It was first created as a royal garden by Queen Amelia, the spouse of Otto I, the first modern king of Greece—both German aristocrats. Later in the 1920s, the park opened to the public, adopted its current name, and claimed its place in Greek national identity. As critic Kostas Prapoglou notes, "Seamlessly blending actual reality with hyperreality through the appropriation of phytomorphology, Socratous underlines notions of socio-cultural re-molding, urbanization, industrial impairment and political disparities."[1] The artist's act of looting from the National Garden also parallels the fragmentation of the nation, particularly in the aftermath of the country's 2009 government-debt crisis and the subsequent precariousness induced by austere fiscal policies imposed by foreign entities as part of its bailout program. Scattered and entangled, the elements of the work communicate a post-catastrophe aesthetic that echoes this condition. The once-organic materials hold their shape and will never age, thereby forming a surrogate portrait of the Garden as a chronicle of history and ideology.

L.C., L.M.

1   Kostas Prapoglou, "Socratis Socratous," *The Seen*, June 30, 2016, http://theseenjournal.org/art-seen-international/socratis-socratous -point-centre-contemporary-art/.

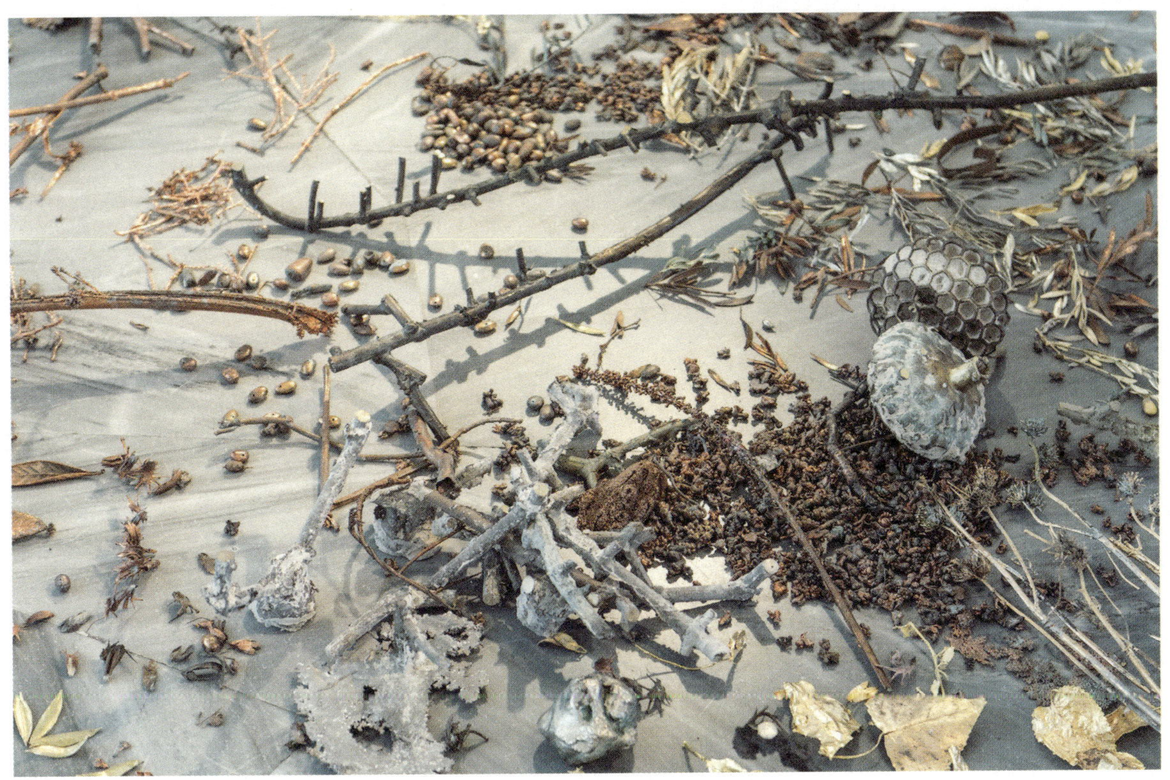

Stolen Goods (detail), 2009–15, gold, copper, bronze, silver   cat. no. 72

EZEQUIEL O. SUÁREZ

The work of Ezequiel O. Suárez defies easy classification as he moves through many domains, materials, and attitudes. During the 1990s, Suárez collaborated with artist Sandra Ceballos to create Aglutinador, one of the most significant alternative contemporary art spaces since the Cuban Revolution, a situation combining precariousness and mischief with the cultural vanguard. Several of Suárez's works explore the condition of being an artist in Cuba, as well as themes of voyage and emigration.

The graffiti-style wall text—*Si tú eres artista, vamos a sufrir (If you are an artist, we will suffer)*—is an aesthetic important to the artist and refers to the dichotomy between the new global trend of Cuban art as a luxury and the rest of the island's artists who lack economic and professional recognition. The title is a promise: if you are an artist, the rest of us suffer. The suitcase, which recalls the seminal Fluxus boxes of the 1960s, functions as a metaphor for the necessary space needed to create art. The suitcase is packed with small readymades, suited for the artist with no studio, who needs only the objects within reach to carry out his or her work. Suárez's practice is very influential within Cuba, particularly with artists of the current generation, as he reorients society's rubbish as objects of significance, rich with meaning.

A.G.F.

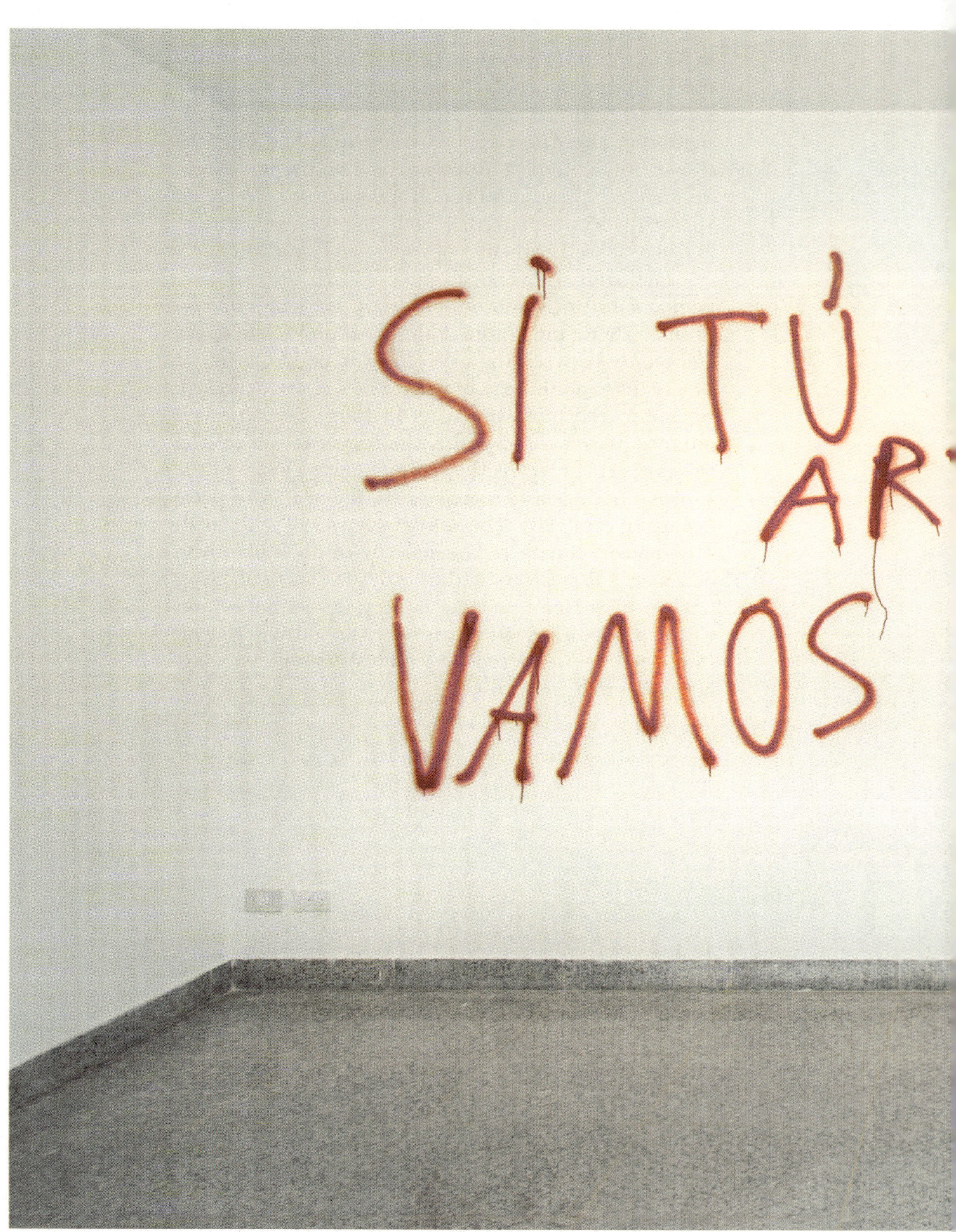

Ezequiel O. Suárez, *Si tú eres artista, vamos a sufrir* (*If you are an artist, we will suffer*), 2009–16, personal objects from the artist's collection, suitcase, graffiti   cat. no. 73

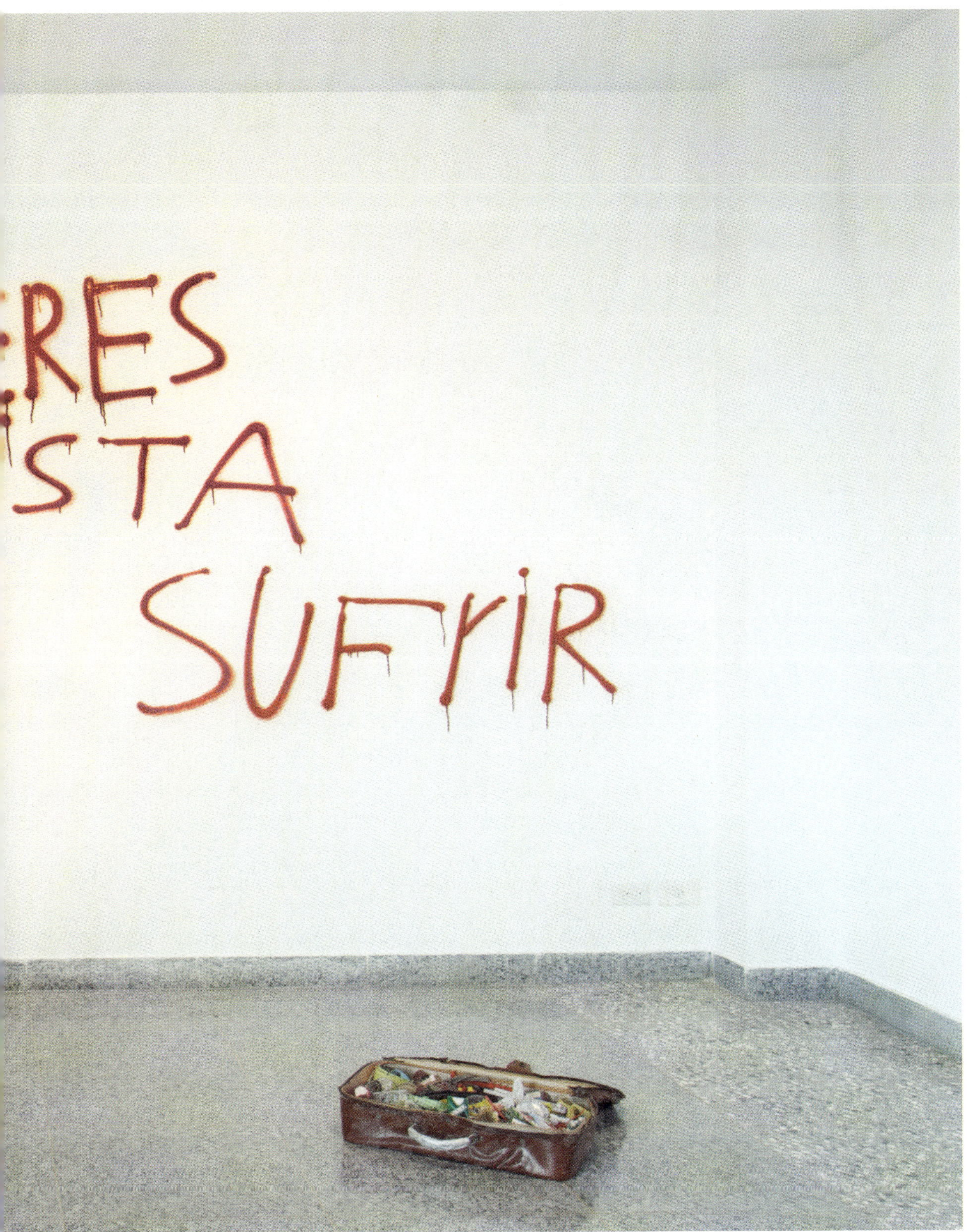
ERES
STA
SUFrIR

YORGOS TZIRTZILAKIS

PASA DYNAMIS ADYNAMIA*

When the use of crisis becomes the stage of existence: The particular character of contemporary art in Greece

Originally published by online journal South
As A State Of Mind, *2012.*

Could this be the time—*kairos*, or the right point in time, the "crucial moment" in the ancient Greek meaning of the word—to talk about contemporary "Greek art?" If so, what is it that gives us this opportunity today? What is it that makes it timely or untimely?[1] Finally, what is it that makes it a "special case?"

One almost self-evident answer to these questions is that "Greek art"—which we should call "contemporary art in Greece" if we were to observe the terms of post-national correctness—begins to acquire international interest today because Greece is in the throes of an extended crisis; that is, not because of a sudden attraction exerted by its social preoccupations, its aesthetic idiom or its territorial conceptual framework, however weak it may be, but because its geopolitical trace and its territorialization are shaken to the core.

One does not need to be particularly stochastic to suspect that a country's attraction is usually heightened at a weak moment, which it strives to conceal or repress in every possible way. As always, however, a repressed weakness always returns to exact its revenge. Indeed, I would add that it accrues interest until the day of its "bankruptcy," literal or symbolic.

The weak moment, however, denotes not only a country's "dark side" and "inferiority" but also the scandalous imaginings and translations that other societies and countries build for it through a peculiar correlation of knowledge and power. In a certain way these are constructs of the "other," charged with spectres and primordial fears and feeding on the colonial and the earlier past. Yet all this shapes the psychopathology and the behaviour of large sections of the population.

So what comes upon us from all sides is not just the crisis but also the use of the crisis,

229

which becomes the stage of existence. Its anthropological and social conditions are linked together in a single chain of meaning and tend to evolve into a stereotypical, normative discourse which is not of an economic nature. I have listed here some oft-cited anthropological conditions behind the "Greek crisis" to shed light on the pragmatic and ideological edges of the issue: inertia, delays, emotionalism, black economy, vagueness, procrastination, inefficiency, nihilism, sloth, apathy, rash impulsiveness, lack of competitiveness, irrationalism, waste, suspended modernisation, mystical relics, Oriental propensities, focus on the past, remnants of orthodox spirituality,[2] and so forth.

I should make it clear, lest I be misunderstood, that I am describing the phenomenon of constructing contemporary representations, which we all know and spontaneously recall as soon as we hear the word "Greece," and I certainly do not intend to justify it. This kind of list makes up the cultural anthropology of crisis and describes the mental behaviour of its victims, who are often described using medical terms. Indeed, the word crisis itself has, in addition to its ancient Greek origin, a prominent medical meaning as well. This is the critical moment, the threshold at which the patient "either dies or follows an entirely different course,"[3] and "the body gets healed after it has come out of the crisis." The *sêmata* that

preceded it are not recognised as warning signs until after the event. Of course, the question here remains which of these anthropological traits will be suspended or changed after the critical moment of the crisis and what will replace them. In other words, what shall we be like after the crisis? And what can we really talk about after the crisis?

For the moment, in any case, anyone who has these traits in an adequate combination is vulnerable to the disease of the crisis at any moment. The more easily perceptible among them—hence the most translatable—are also the most popular ones in a debate, lending themselves to long-winded media reports, stochastic or scientific interpretations, calculations and statistical analyses. As with every ailment, the suffocating spread of fear concerns not the symptoms themselves, but the ultimate end they may bring (bankruptcy, regressing into conditions similar to those in the Balkan states that emerged after the fall of Eastern European regimes, underdevelopment, poverty, the end of the welfare state, uncontrollable conflicts).

What does all this show? That the weak moment comes inescapably when a country's culture is literally different. This means the kind of vagueness and irresolution that flourishes at geographical and cultural borders and is seen as the scandalous relic of earlier processes—authentic and precious when promoted as a tourist attraction, a purulent abscess when it comes to implementing fiscal bail-outs. This is the very moment at which the country differs not in the established, stereotypical way but by following routes that deviate from an acceptable, generic, and dominant model.

Aristotle in *Metaphysics* links "impotentiality" with its opposite, "potentiality," the "non-being" with "being." This symmetrical interdependence gives a different meaning to our perception of "impotentiality" as well as of "non-being." The philosopher defines "impotentiality" as "a privation contrary to potentiality. Thus all potentiality is impotentiality of the same and with respect to the same." (pasa dynamis adynamia). [4] In other words, "potentiality" is always the relationship with its absence, i.e. with "impotentiality."

This is why what we see as impotentiality is also our truth, the ultimate social and cultural condition which may mean something. Strange as it may seem, therein lies its "innovation." Italian philosopher Giorgio Agamben starts from Aristotle's definition and focuses on the structure of "sovereignty," in which *adynamia* (translated as "impotentiality," "weakness," "inability") and inoperativity (*désoeuvrement*) are excluded in order to produce an opposition where potentiality is represented as something absolute. In this spirit he proposes the concept of the

"irreparable," which we can recontextualize and introduce here: "Irreparable means that these things are consigned without remedy; […] but also means that, in their being, thus they are absolutely exposed and absolutely abandoned."[5] Just like "the insalvable that renders the salvable possible, the irreparable allows the coming of the redemption."

"Impotentiality" and the "irreparable" function here as a metaphor, a "substitute of the signifier," since, in psychoanalytical terms, they denote one thing through another. This is why the crisis brings out a collective truth which reveals, in its own way, that "we have never been modern.... Modernity has never begun."[6] Therein lies the special character of contemporary art in Greece.

*	*Aristotle, Metaphysics, Theta, 1045 a, 31. Excerpt from a more extensive paper on "Crisis and Mourning in the Contemporary Greek Culture," on the occasion of the exhibition Ντέρτι Humanism, curated by Nadja Argyropoulou, Faggionato Fine Arts, London, July–August 2010.*

1	The *untimely* is a Nietzschean term for something that opposes the hypertrophy of the hegemonic historical knowledge and the constructed time we have got used to: Friedrich Nietzsche, *The Untimely Meditations 1873–1876*, trans. R.J. Hollingdale, Cambridge, 2nd edition, 1997. The ancient Greek meaning of kairos—what we call "opportunity" today—manifests itself as the ideal balancing of the parameters in a situation.

2	Stelios Ramfos attempted an anatomy of the roots of crisis by exploring a "modern-Greek anthropology" in Αδιανόητο τίποτα. Φιλοκαλικά ριζώματα του νεοελληνικού μηδενισμού, Athens, 2010. The "Philokalia" cited in the title refers to the anthology of ascetic texts by the "Neptic Fathers" of Oriental Christianity; it was printed in Venice in 1782 and, according to Ramfos, shaped the "empty self" of modern Greeks. Cf. the same author's Ο καημός του ενός. Κεφάλαια της ψυχικής ιστορίας των Ελλήνων, Athens, 2000, and Ni kolaos Loudovikos, "Από τον διευθυντικό ή συγκρουσιακό εκσυγχρονισμό στη διαλεκτική της πραγματι κής ιστορίας. Με αφορμή τον Καημό του ενός του Στέλιου Ράμφου", Indictos, 17, 2003, 116–131.

3	Michel Serres, *Le temps des crises* (2009), Greek ed. *Καιρός των κρίσεων*, trans. Laokratia Lakka, ed. Vangelis Bitsoris, Athens, 2011, 15–16.

4	Aristotle, "Metaphysics," 1046 e25-32, trans. W.S. Hett (Harvard Univ. Press, Cambridge, MA 1986).

5	Giorgio Agamben, *The Coming Community*, trans. Michael Hardt, Minnesota 1993, 39.

6	Bruno Latour, *We Have Never Been Modern* (1991), trans. Catherine Porter, Harvard University Press, 47.

The practice of Kostis Velonis traverses the boundaries of political paradigms in contemporary Athens,
where sentiments of anarchy are still ever present and
the aesthetics of political activism are part of everyday life set against the background of antiquity. His
sculptural works and installations are often predicated
on research and theoretical exploration of the ideologies of twentieth-century modernism within the
Greek context. For *Landlord Colors*, Velonis visited
Detroit and chose to create a work in the prominently
shared material of the city and his home of Athens:
concrete. In *Assembly of a Tenament* (a continuation
of his ongoing series *Life Without Tragedy*), a slice of
an amphitheater typically found in Athenian plazas is
recreated as a concrete sculptural maquette. An example of such a theater is found near the artist's studio in
Koumoundourou, where festivities are now the excep-
tion, and the space is most frequently used as makeshift housing by homeless refugees.

Herein, Velonis enacts the conversion he has
observed within Greek culture and how critique is performed within the discursive space of the art scene:
"Contemporary sculpture replaces the meaning that
theater had in ancient Athens, raising the question
about the practice of power through tragedy or com-
edy.... The same social practice of the theatrical performance is equal with the displayed character of
sculpture. The real importance of those changes in the
sculptural field opens the way to understand sculpture
as an architectural construction for the public forum
that confronts discussions and actions. Sculpture is
becoming the *estia koine* (common place) for politics,
not only in the institutional sense but politics in a
sense that there is a site for reflection and re-evalua-
tion of what a political society is."[1]

L.M.

1   Daphne Vitali, "Between Direct Democracy and Socialist Politics /
An Interview with Kostis Velonis," *ARTPULSE*, http://artpulsemagazine
.com/between-direct-democracy-and-socialist-politics-an-interview
-with-kostis-velonis.

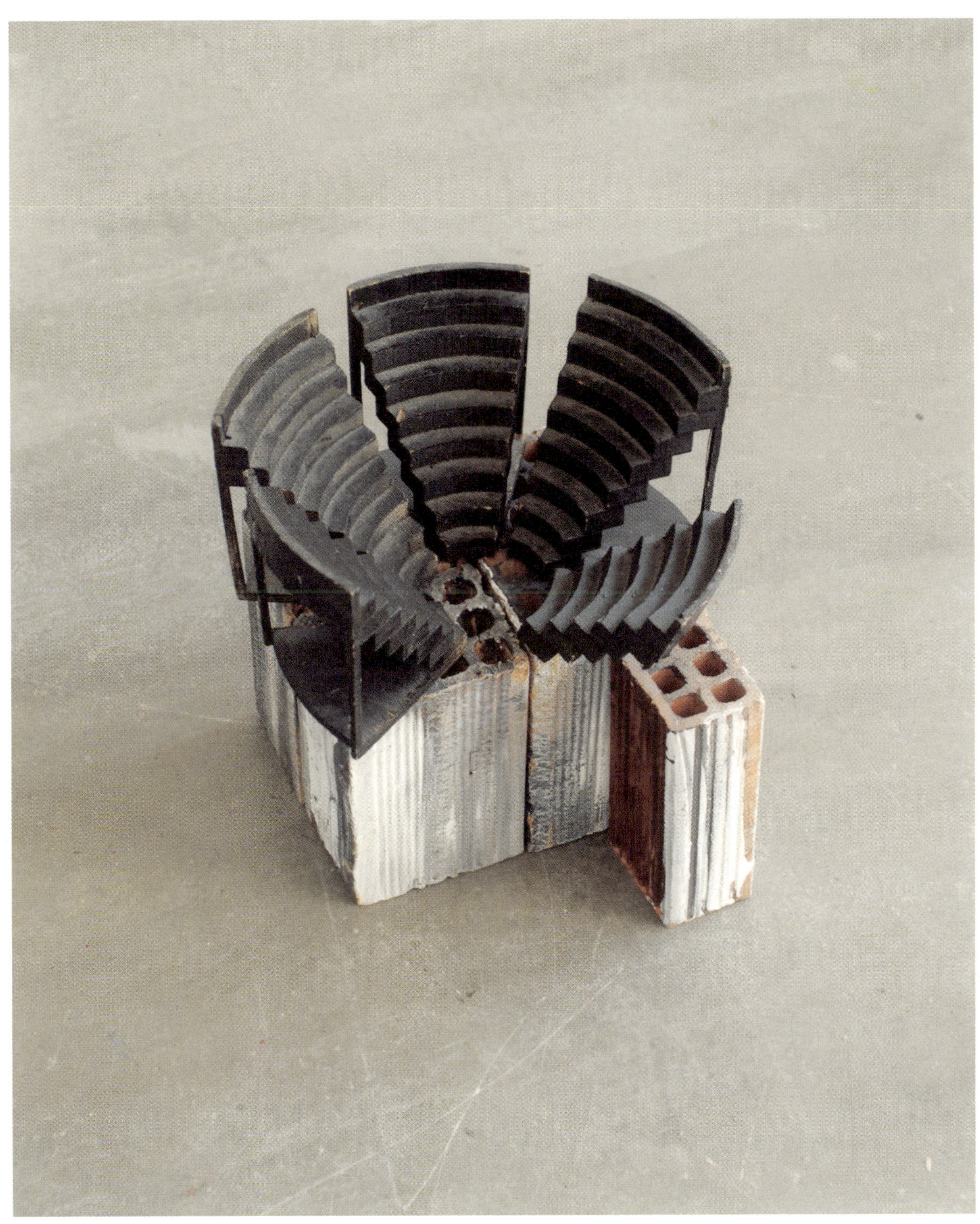

Life Without Tragedy, 2009, ceramic, wood, acrylic

IN CONVERSATION

For the occasion of Landlord Colors, *Vincenzo de Bellis, curator at the Walker Art Center, interviewed preeminent arte povera artist Michelangelo Pistoletto in Turin on December 28, 2018.*

Vincenzo de Bellis : Michelangelo, your work emerged in the early 1960s at a time of great social and political developments. In particular, there are two moments that I would like to discuss, which are very different and at the same time important for your work: the Venice Biennale of 1964, when American pop art "invaded" Europe, and 1967–68 that marks the true beginning of the *arte povera* movement. Only a three-year difference, but the two produced an incredible phenomenon of upheaval that happened all over the world.

Michelangelo Pistoletto : The 1964 Biennale represents a moment of great change for the art world. Clearly artists such as Jasper Johns and Robert Rauschenberg, the latter the winner of the Golden Lion prize at the Biennale, represented the forerunners of an important change, which led to what had not yet been defined as pop art. Through Rauschenberg's

award, the United States achieved the ultimate degree of artistic and cultural recognition at the time. For many, American pop was viewed as an invasion in the exhibition, but certainly not for me. I did not feel overwhelmed on that occasion, in fact, I thought the prize was deserved. I was part of that family, I knew and held in esteem those artists. I was living in Venice at Ileana Sonnabend's home, where Leo Castelli, the gallerist of those artists, was also a guest. In conjunction with the 1964 Biennial, I also had an exhibition of my mirror paintings in Venice, at the Lion Gallery. My work therefore began to be known in parallel with that of the pop artists.

At the same time, it was clear that there was an obvious political interest by the American government to bring out a vanguard movement coming from the United States. In fact, some additional works by Rauschenberg, featured in an external exhibition, were brought before the jury of the Biennale in the US pavilion to add weight to the works already exhibited. Their transport was aided by the American Navy.

But we have to say that certainly the awarding of the Golden Lion to Rauschenberg, and therefore the certificate of esteem of the Biennale jury, truly was due to the value of the works and not for political reasons. Rauschenberg admired Alberto Burri's work and, in 1964, he also bought one of my mirror paintings that he kept in the center of his home until the end. I am not saying this for personal pride, but because it explains how the knowledge and recognition were mutual. However, at that moment in Italy, it was as if everything was reversed, and only America and pop art existed. It was a sort of cultural somersault. But this also happened in the rest of Europe.

Meanwhile, my story was intertwined with that of the United States, and the artistic, socio-political consequences were felt later. In 1963, when I had an exhibition at Galleria Galatea, with whom I had had a contract since 1958, the Fiat magnate Gianni Agnelli came to visit. The gallerist received him, saying in reference to my mirror paintings, "Forgive me for this exhibition; unfortunately he is an artist under contract." I was astonished and immediately left for Paris where I met Ileana Sonnabend, who came to Turin after a week, bought the whole show, and took over my contract. Then Leo Castelli brought my work to America. In 1964 the Museum of Modern Art acquired one of my works, as did other US museums. In 1966 I held my first retrospective at the Walker Art Center in Minneapolis.

VDB : Let us move on to the following two years: 1967–68. These are years of great social change, capitalism had quickly upset society, and the so-called Years of Lead were going to start in Italy. Similar phenomena of unrest were happening all over the world, even if the artistic production of the Italian avant-garde remains one of the most widespread cultural documents of that time. I would like to discuss with you the context in which your work has been developed as one of the artists who started what would be called *arte povera*. How and how much has the social context of Turin, one of the centers that had more political, social, labor, and trade union turmoil than not only in Italy, but all of Europe, affected your work?

MP : Actually, I think that Turin was one of the many industrial centers that, on a global level, saw the social conflict growing between the two opposite poles of capitalism and communism. Clearly where there was more critical mass, there were many individuals who addressed these issues, and therefore the friction became more apparent. In Turin, Fiat represented the clash between capitalism and working class in an emblematic way.

VDB : How involved were you politically?

MP : I have been politically engaged exclusively in the search for balance. I did not know that many years later I would be dedicated to the symbol of balance, but I was already looking for proposals of change. I clarify: I never thought that the act of revolt was the purpose. I thought and I think that criticism, even the most pronounced criticism, has been and still is important but not as a finality. For me, the purpose must be a proposal of solution.

In 1968 I was invited to the Venice Biennale, along with Pino Pascali, and we were the only Italian artists. I decided on that occasion to present my Manifesto of Collaboration. It is written: "With this manifesto I invite people who wish to collaborate with me at the XXXIV Venice Biennale. By collaboration I mean not a competitive human relationship, but a sensitive and perceptive understanding. To give a part of myself to those who want to give up a part of themselves is the work that interests me." My proposal preceded the protest that took place at the opening of the exhibition. I did not go to Venice personally then. Instead, other artists, critics, and intellectuals went there to demonstrate, even violently. That idea of collaboration was not realized at the Biennale, but instead, a few months later, it took place in Amalfi.

VDB : I guess you refer to *Arte Povera Più Azioni Povere* (*Arte Povera More Poor Actions*)—an exhibition held at the Amalfi Arsenals in 1968—as one of the most important events that took place at the end of the 1960s, thanks to the interest and cultural activity of Marcello Rumma. Work, performances, and debates took place in three intense days at the beginning of October, and I think I can state that they helped develop the identity of an art destined to leave the canons and traditional territories in favor of a direct intervention in life and in society.

MP : Yes, exactly, Amalfi was an extraordinary moment.

VDB : I think I also can say that yours was a rather unusual presentation, at least the part of it with *L'uomo ammaestrato* (*The Trained Man*). Tell me about this moment of transition from an individual authority to collaboration as a process and attitude. All of the subsequent works, including the latest ones, derive from this. But, above all, it is the one that has generated and then regenerated your performative work, especially out of the designated places, using the road, the city.

MP : To talk about all this, I have to go back a few years because each step was preparatory and fundamental in the development of my artistic activity. In 1964, in Paris, Leo Castelli told me, "Listen, you have to come to the United States or there's nothing more I can do for you. You're doing very well, but either you join our family or it won't be possible to go on." In response, I returned to Italy and made the *Oggetti in meno* (*Minus Objects*) (fig. 1). I wanted to react to a powerful artistic-economic-political condition that forced it to be included in a hegemonic system or to be alone and excluded. I chose to be alone, because

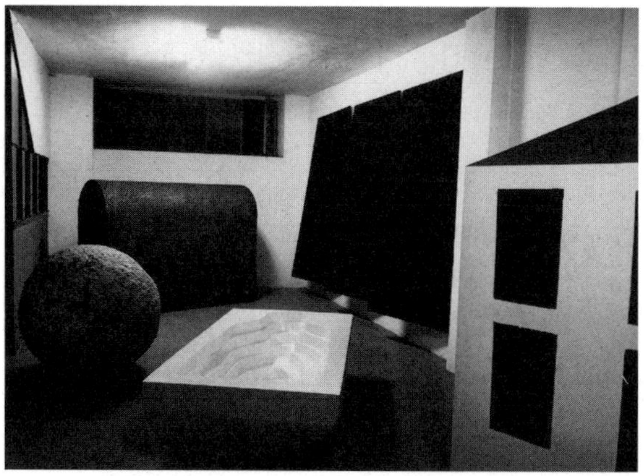

FIGURE 1

Michelangelo Pistoletto, *Oggetti in meno*
(*Minus Objects*), 1965–66, Pistoletto's studio,
Turin, 1966

I was strongly convinced that what I had developed was a work originated on a cultural territory that was not disinherited, but a profound legacy. At that time, I had my studio, a former printing shop in Via Reymond in Turin, which also served as a home. The *Minus Objects* were born through a process linked to spontaneity and contingency. These works were each different from the other and presented themselves as if they were a collective exhibition. I broke the dogma that every work of an artist had to be stylistically recognizable, like a standardized trademark. Those works have opened the path of *arte povera*. And besides, what I was developing was the idea of generating debate and cooperation with others.

In 1967 I carried out some collective actions: on March 6th, *La fine di Pistoletto* (*The End of Pistoletto*), at the Piper Club in Turin; on December 4th, on the occasion of the collective exhibition *Con-temp-l'azione*, held simultaneously in three galleries (Sperone, Stein, Il Punto), I participated by running through the street the *Sfera di Giornali* (*Sphere of newspapers*), one of the *Oggetti in meno*, involving the artists and the bystanders. In December, with a Manifesto, I announced the opening of my studio, which was a consistent way for me to proceed. I had opened the picture in the presence and with the participation of everyone; at that point the transition consisted of opening the physical space to participation.

Many artists of different languages came: poets, musicians, filmmakers, actors. The meetings were continuous, and from these originated collective actions, until the formation of the group Lo Zoo (The Zoo), by which the art was brought out to the streets. Between 1968 and 1970, we made shows and conceived as creative collaborators on public land. The first was, as you mentioned, *The Trained Man* (fig. 2), built on the square of Vernazza, a small town on the Ligurian Riviera. It was proposed for the second time in Amalfi, part of the *Arte Povera–Azioni Povere* exhibition. It is the story of an animal in human form that is "trained" to become a civilized man; of course, civilization was perceived in a totally ironic sense.

VDB : Let us move forward a few years to 1976. This marks a fundamental moment because in that year you realize a further gap in your way of thinking about exhibitions and works. I refer to *One Hundred Exhibitions in October ....*

MP : I made *Le Stanze* (*The Rooms*), twelve consecutive shows, one every month, for the duration of one year from September 1975 to September 1976, at the Galleria Stein in Turin. Following this I undertook at the Persano Gallery the work *Cento mostre nel mese di ottobre*, (*One Hundred Exhibitions in the Month of October*). The hundred exhibitions are a concentration, and at the same time an extension of times and places. When I think about doing an exhibition, I plan it. In one month, I worked out a hundred projects, which were printed in November in a small yellow square book. The book is a sort of tentative exhibitions and works,

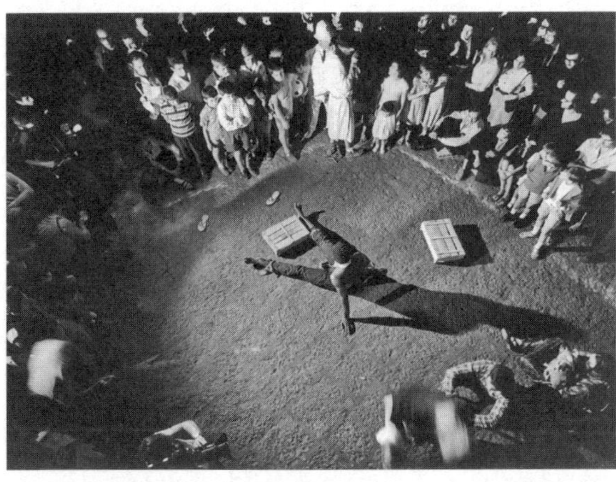

FIGURE 2

Michelangelo Pistoletto, *L'uomo ammaestrato* (*The Trained Man*), 1968, action by Lo Zoo (The Zoo), streets of Amalfi, October 4, 1968

many of which will be realized later. These include the video *Chi sei tu?* (*Who Are You?*) 1976; *Mobili capovolti* (*Overturned Furniture*),1976; *Lo zoccolo* (*The Hoof*), 1979; *Segno Arte* (*Art Sign*), since 1993; and *Spazio libero* (*Free Space*), 1999.

VDB : Then in 2013 you created fifteen new works, described in *One Hundred Exhibitions in October*, which you showed in two solo exhibitions held simultaneously at the two venues of the Galleria Continua in San Gimignano and Boissy-le-Châtel. Among these is *Metamorfosi* (*Metamorphosis*), 1976/2019 (p. 197), that you also present here at the Cranbrook Art Museum for Detroit. Do you believe that this work has a conceptual core, or is its meaning completely malleable to the exhibition context?

MP : One of the hundred projects described the realization of a wire mesh that crossed a space. On one side, leaning against the net, was a pile of colored rags, and on the other side a pile of white rags. This is a reference to the works carried out starting from the *Venere degli Stracci* (*Venus of the Rags*). This work clearly compared the one color with the multiplicity, evident in the differences of the colors. In 2013, on the invitation of the GALLERIA CONTINUA, I rethought the project I had already made at Fuoriuso in Pescara in 1995. Instead of the wire mesh, I used the mirror. That is how *Metamorfosi*, with the white rags reflected in the mirror, originated. The viewer, turning around the work, sees the white transformed into a heap of color and vice versa.

VDB : With another leap of about fifteen years we come to the foundation

241

of Cittadellarte, from which a series of works and more recent operations are connected, always in the idea of collaboration and interaction....

MP : Cittadellarte was born in 1991, at the same time as my professorship at the Vienna Academy. In 1989 I had exhibited the *Minus Objects* at the Vienna Secession. The director of the Secession at that time told me that he would be part of the board of directors of the Vienna Academy the following year, where he would ask me to go and teach. So, it was. At first, I refused because I did not want to be a professor. Then he told me that his idea was to completely change and renew the approach to art in that academy, which was the only one in the world to have stayed in the same building for 400 years. He told me that if I accepted, I would have carte blanche. Then I understood that this was a perfect place to research and experiment with young people. I worked there until 2000.

Also, in 1991 I was by chance on a trip to Biella, where a gallery owner had organized an exhibition of mine and invited me to see the show. I went, and to his question about what was in my head for the future, I replied that I was looking for a space to create a place of activity that would link the arts with life and civil society. Looking out of the window I saw a large vacant factory and said a space like that would be perfect. He replied that it was for sale, and half an hour later I had paid a deposit for the purchase of that building, which became Cittadellarte.

With Cittadellarte I was able to realize an activity that, by gathering all the experiences made in previous years, became a transformation laboratory for the company. I created a place where, in addition to the languages of art, the various sectors of social life—from economics to politics, from science to religion, from technology to agriculture, from training to communication, from design to behavior—were connected.

VDB : Do you think that the *Terzo Paradiso* (*Third Paradise*) would have been born without Cittadellarte?

MP : I have to think about it because it is a question for which I am not prepared. But I think so. In the end I think so. It would have been born, but without the possibility of immediate realization. Instead, with Cittadellarte I had this chance.

VDB : Let us linger on *Third Paradise*. Everything started in 2003 with another Manifesto ...

MP : The *Third Paradise* is the fusion between the first and the second paradise. The first is the natural one in which human beings were totally integrated into nature. The second paradise is the artificial one that generates, in parallel with the beneficial effects, irreversible processes of degradation and consumption of the natural world. The *Third Paradise* is the third phase of humanity, which is realized in the balanced connection between artifice and nature. *Third Paradise* means the passage to an unprecedented stage of planetary civilization, which is indispensable for assuring the human species of its own survival. For this purpose, we must first reform the ethical principles and behaviors that guide our common life. The symbol of the *Third Paradise*, the reconfiguration of the mathematical sign of the infinite, is composed of three consecutive circles. The two outer circles represent all the differences and the antinomies, including nature and artifice. The central one is the interpenetration between opposing circles and represents the generative womb of the new humanity. The symbol of the *Third Paradise* is a drawing, a flag, but it is also a sort of star that shows us the way.

Recently a decisive passage took place for the evolution of the *Third Paradise*, linked to a very precise moment. If you remember, in 2012 it was rumored that, according to a prophecy of the Mayan, the end of the world would have happened on December 21st of that year. At Cittadellarte we decided to take that date to celebrate the rebirth of the world. December 21st also corresponds to the winter solstice, the shortest day of the year, from which the new season starts. We have therefore decided to turn December 21st into the Rebirth-Day.

On December 21, 2012, the world day of rebirth was held simultaneously in different parts of the world, the Third Paradise Day. The documentation of this event was presented in

the context of my personal exhibition *Année un–Le paradis sur terre* (*Year One–Paradise on Earth*) held from April to September 2013 at the Louvre Museum in Paris.

Since then it has become an annual recurrence, thus giving rise to a large number of events and a dense network of relationships, from which come the Third Paradise Embassies, extending gradually into different parts of the world. Everyone can participate by sharing the project, whose essential points are Equilibrium, Connection, Cooperation, and Sustainability, as described in my 2017 Manifesto "Ominiteism and Demopraxia."

VDB : Cuba is an important site in the *Third Paradise* and also a fundamental presence in the *Landlord Colors* exhibition. Can you talk about your interest in Cuba and why it has such importance in your artistic practice?

MP : Fate, which is a great ally of mine, gave birth to a Rebirth Third Paradise Embassy in Cuba in 2013. This came after an intense work of "artivation" realized with the fishermen and their boats, the day of December 16, 2014, a great *Third Paradise* on the sea of Havana (fig. 3). The next day, US President Barack Obama telephoned President of Cuba Raúl Castro to propose reopening diplomatic relations between the two countries. The symbol of encounter and balance immediately became reality. On November 23, 2015, I met President Raúl Castro, who was in

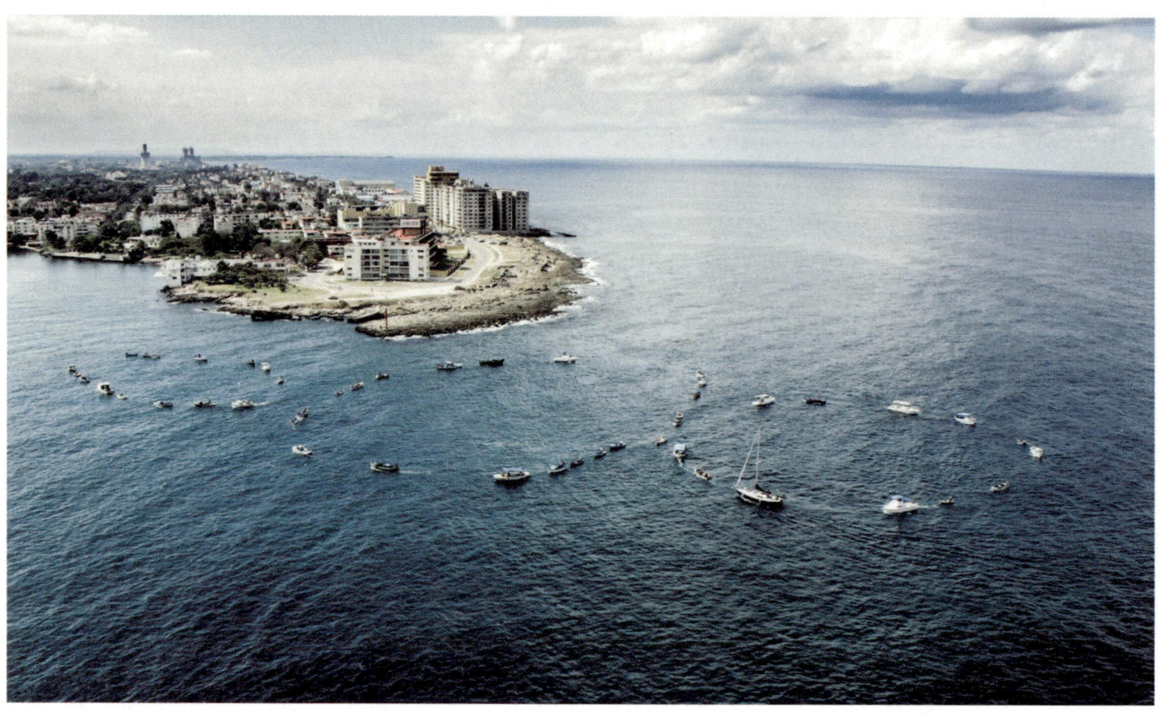

FIGURE 3

Michelangelo Pistoletto / GALLERIA CONTINUA in collaboration with KCHO and Laura
Salas Redondo, *Terzo Paradiso: Cuba, Havana - December 16, 2014*, in the sea of Havana, December
16, 2014, the day before the conversation between Barack Obama and Raúl Castro

perfect agreement with the meaning of the *Third Paradise*. The next day we started the first Rebirth Third Paradise Forum in Havana, which was prepared through a whole year of intense activity.

In November 2018, the fourth Forum was held, by this time totally directed to the development of the "demopractical method" dedicated to the realization of democracy. Other Rebirth Forums are taking place gradually in different parts of the world from Rome to Bali, from Melbourne to Tirana, and beyond. But Cuba is the country in which we started to build the "demopractic path" through direct experience. Cuba was our first laboratory; we found fertile ground, starting with the fact that there are no political parties—hence the possibility of experimenting with a post-ideological culture that leads to achieving democracy "demopractically." In Cuba we have no direct involvement in official politics, but we have full freedom of action.

In continuation of this investigation and ethos, Michelangelo Pistoletto will present a site-specific incarnation of the Third Paradise *and activate a Rebirth Forum in Detroit during summer 2019. See section:* Landlord Colors: Material Detroit *(p. 249).*

Beyond its vital role in the history of Eastern abstraction, the work by painter Yun Hyong-Keun can be understood as emotive documentation of the various wars and conflicts in which Korea engaged during the twentieth century, resurrecting a sense of oppression into the present. In Susan Sontag's *Regarding the Pain of Others*, on confronting photographs of war, she reports on the perspective of a survivor in Sarajevo: "[People turn on] their evening news and say 'Oh, how horrible,' and then look for another program. It's normal. It's human. Wherever people feel safe … they will be indifferent."[1] Whereas graphic depictions of war come with detail specificity—time period, location, adversaries—Yun accesses the sentiments of trauma through abstraction, transporting the viewer into the universality of the human condition.

Yun was imprisoned three times for political activism in Korea and was even threatened with execution as a student in the early 1950s. In his seminal works from the 1970s after decades of conflict, Yun began to divide the pictorial space of the canvas with dark bars of paint on raw linen. When experienced in person, the paintings elicit an imposed reverence from the body and the psyche, like the tentative approach towards an unmarked doorway or an escape through the night woods. The tension between dark and light is felt inherently, a place where the imagination expands when confronted with the vulnerability of the unknown. In addition to drawing from his own experiences, the artist furiously painted in the aftermath of the Gwangju massacre in 1980, in which approximately 600 protesters were killed in a confrontation with police. In these paintings, the pillars started to fall down on top of each other. Yun cited heaven and earth as a crucial metaphor in his thinking; however, stark polarities of real consequence are also derived from his work—north and south, freedom and incarceration, life and death.

L.M.

1   Susan Sontag, *Regarding the Pain of Others* (New York: Picador, 2003), 78.

Umber-Blue, 1978, oil on linen   cat. no. 75

LANDLORD COLORS: MATERIAL DETROIT

From its inception, *Landlord Colors: On Art, Economy, and Materiality* was designed to extend throughout the city that serves as its conceptual spine. *Landlord Colors: Material Detroit* is a performance and public art series that complements the exhibition and publication. One can regard *Material Detroit* as the outgoing, extroverted sibling born of this research, where ideas leap off the pedestal or page and become voices, movements, and experiences.

The task of rooting the project in the city became a collaborative effort between three Detroit curators and institutions, cross-pollinating their missions and expertise: Taylor Renee Aldridge (Co-Founder of ARTS.BLACK), Laura Mott (Senior Curator at Cranbrook Art Museum), and Ryan Myers-Johnson (Executive Director and Curator at Sidewalk Detroit). *Material Detroit* is a continuation of Cranbrook Art Museum's Detroit-based initiatives that began with *Nick Cave: Here Hear* (2015) and The Cause Collective's *In Search of Truth: The Truth Booth* (2016). ARTS.BLACK is a journal of art criticism from Black perspectives predicated on the belief that art criticism should be an accessible dialogue—a tool by which to question, celebrate, and talk back to the global world of contemporary art. Sidewalk Detroit investigates creative solutions to public space challenges and spatial equity through the lens of arts and culture, commissioning artists to create socially relevant, place-based work across the built environment.

From conception to engagement on the ground, the curators devised the program to connect art to vortexes of history and contemporary life across Detroit. The series expands like an energy grid throughout the city with site-specific artworks,

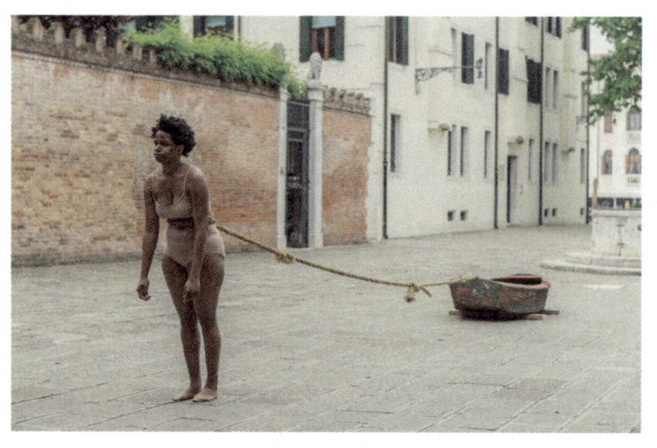

FIGURE 1

Susana Pilar, *Dibujo Intercontinental*, performance at the Venice Biennale, 2017, video still

performances, and conversations anchored with community partners. Some of the projects have lifespans well before and after the project. For instance, Dabls' MBAD African Bead Museum has been a cultural nexus since the late 1990s and an exhibition by Detroit artist Elizabeth Youngblood within the Bead Museum's gallery space serves as a momentary companion to this creative pillar. Likewise, *Material Detroit* hosts the first months of Anders Ruhwald's ongoing project *Unit 1: 3583 Dubois* that occupies an entire apartment in Detroit's Eastern Market neighborhood. Ruhwald investigates themes of transformation and memory in this installation of black ceramic, charred wood, molten glass, and perceptual environments.

Also consumed with notions of fire and resurrection, Sterling Toles will enact a performance of *Resurgent Cinerbus*, a sound work that sources news coverage from the 1967 Detroit Rebellion in tandem with narration of his father's personal history. Havana-based, Afro-Cuban artist Susana Pilar likewise draws upon a true story from the Detroit Rebellion; through a collaboration with local musicians, she honors the music of The Dramatics whose founding member Cleveland Larry Reed survived the police siege on The Algiers Motel. Big Red Wall Dance Company, led by choreographer Erika Stowall, will present an original place-based movement work in Detroit's 250-acre Eliza Howell Park, exploring the Black female body's relationship to Detroit green-space and issues of security and safety in public space. The work will feature live accompaniment and selections from guest choreographers based in Detroit. Fringe Society (Ash Arder and Levon Kafafian) will debut a new site-specific outdoor installation and movement work at Sidewalk Festival. Utilizing a colorful alley as its platform, the work will examine fiber, materiality, and the urban built environment as it relates to identity, economic security, and the pursuit of Utopia.

Detroit artists Jennifer Harge and Billy Mark each undertake long durational performances paired with a sculptural installation. Invested in ritual and monastic practice, Mark creates a hoodie with twenty-five-foot arms attached to three flag poles near his home in Northeast Detroit. Each morning for forty days, he raises the hands of the sweatshirt at dawn and lowers them at dusk. Harge's project *Fly|Drown* at the Detroit Artist Market recreates African-American interior domestic space through vernacular objects. One month of performance and public salons will serve as platforms for Black womxn to explore their sovereignty in this context.

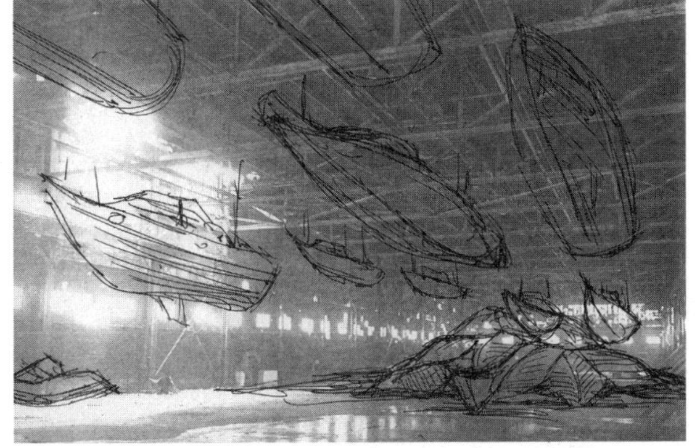

FIGURE 2

Scott Hocking, *Bone Black*, installation proposal sketch, 2019, ink on paper

Scott Hocking's monumental installation near the Detroit riverfront utilizes a collection of the metaphorical bones of Detroit's once prosperous economy—the many boats abandoned throughout the city. Theatrically presented as a fleet, Hocking applies "Bone Black" paint to the boats,

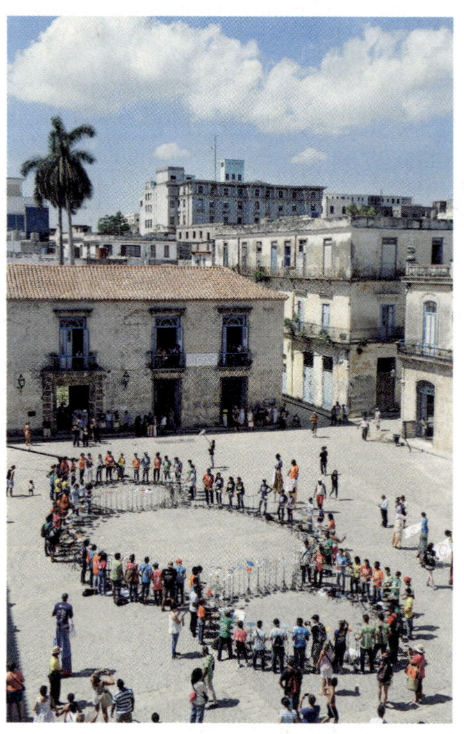

FIGURE 3

Michelangelo Pistoletto,
Terzo Paradiso (Third Paradise), 2003–
2013, 346 cymbals, lids

an industrial pigment produced from animal bones that has been produced in Detroit since the nineteenth century. Seminal artist Michelangelo Pistoletto explores the cyclical nature of life through his philosophically expansive manifesto, installation series, and discursive forum titled *Il Terzo Paradiso* (*The Third Paradise*). Pistoletto has enacted the *Third Paradise* symbol in various performance and installation-based forms throughout the world. It consists of the reconfiguration of the mathematical infinity sign into three connected circles that represent nature and artifice being mediated by a generative new humanity. For Detroit, *Third Paradise* will be created through an epic performance of Detroit choir members alongside the choir of Christ Church Cranbrook orchestrated in the shape of the symbol.

Landlord Colors: Material Detroit performance and public art series is archived on the museum's website.

WORKS IN THE EXHIBITION

ANDREAS ANGELIDAKIS
(b. 1968)

1   *Building an electronic ruin*, 2011
Single-channel video
Duration 5' 03"
Courtesy The Breeder

GIOVANNI ANSELMO
(b. 1934)

2   *Direzione (Direction)*, 1967–70
Schist, magnetic compass, glass
6.25 × 70.25 × 27.5 in.
(15.9 × 178.435 × 69.8 cm)
Collection Walker Art
Center, Minneapolis
The Frederick R. Weisman
Collection of Art and the T.B.
Walker Acquisition Fund, 1996

BELKIS AYÓN
(b. 1967; d. 1999)

3   *Ya estamos aquí (We are already here)*, 1991
Collagraph, 6 pieces
86.25 × 72.45 in. (219 × 184 cm)
Collection of Carole and
Alex Rosenberg and courtesy
the Belkis Ayón Estate

CAY BAHNMILLER
(b. 1955; d. 2007)

4   *Der Imker*, 1993–96
Mixed media construction
on wood
28 × 30 × 9.25 in.
(71.1 × 76.2 × 23.5 cm)
Detroit Institute of Arts,
Founders Society Purchase,
Lila Silverman Tribute
Fund, with funds from the
Friends of Modern Art, 1996.30

KEVIN BEASLEY
(b. 1985)

5   *Untitled (chest pack)*, 2014
Urethane foam, resin, long
sleeve shirt, battery charger
13.5 × 30 × 12 in.
(34.3 × 76.2 × 30.5 cm)
Collection of Martin and
Rebecca Eisenberg

6   *Untitled (street shirt one)*, 2014
Resin, long sleeve shirt, spit
1 × 30 × 33 in.
(2.5 × 76.2 × 83.8 cm)
Courtesy Casey Kaplan
Gallery

7   *Untitled (street shirt two)*, 2014
Resin, t-shirt, pillow cover,
altered glove
1 × 28 × 27 in.
(2.5 × 71.1 × 68.6 cm)
Courtesy Casey Kaplan
Gallery

TANIA BRUGUERA
(b. 1968)

8   *El peso de la culpa
(The burden of guilt)*, 1999
Photograph, performance
documentation
Dimensions variable
Courtesy the artist

9   *Manifesto on Artist's Rights*, 2012
Offset print on paper
Dimensions variable
Courtesy the artist

JAMES LEE BYARS
(b. 1932; d. 1997)

10   *The Philosophical Nail*, 1986
Gilded iron
10.75 × 1.25 × 1.25 in. (27.3 ×
3.2 × 3.2 cm)
Collection Walker Art
Center, Minneapolis
Gift of the Judith Rothschild
Foundation, 1999

PIER PAOLO CALZOLARI
(b. 1943)

11   *Non (studio per grande opera
"Non")*, 1969–70
Virginia tobacco leaves, blue
fluorescent tubes, transformer
11.75 × 32.5 × 2.75 in.
(30 × 83 × 7 cm)
Private collection, courtesy
Marianne Boesky Gallery,
New York and Aspen

YOAN CAPOTE
(b. 1977)

12   *Island (see-escape)*, 2010
Oil, nails, fish hooks on
jute on panel
106 × 315 × 4 in. (269.24 ×
800.1 × 10.16 cm)
Collection Pérez Art
Museum Miami, museum
purchase with funds
provided by Jorge M. Pérez

ELIZABET CERVIÑO
(b. 1986)

13   *Breeze Testimony - Crags*, 2015
Iron oxide on linen
118 × 78.7 in. (300 × 200 cm)
Courtesy GALLERIA
CONTINUA

WORKS IN THE EXHIBITION

OLAYAMI DABLS
(b. 1948)

14 *Iron Teaching Rocks Table Manners*, 2006, from the series *Iron Teaching Rocks How To Rust*, 2000–Present
Rocks, iron, acrylic and oil paint, wood, table, chairs, plates
160 × 160 × 21 in.
(406.4 × 406.4 × 53.34 cm)
Courtesy the artist

DORA ECONOMOU
(b. 1974)

15 *THE HORROR, THE HORROR*, 2018
Pumice stone, paint
Variable dimensions
Courtesy the artist
and RIBOT Gallery, Milan

ELEMENTARY SCHOOL CHILDREN

16 *Chair*, 2019
Cardboard, paper, glue, wood
41 × 20 × 14 in. (104.14 × 50.8 × 35.56 cm)
Designed and made by fifth graders from Pontiac Public Schools, Michigan, based on instructions by Riccardo Dalisi (b. 1931) for the *Throne* series, 1973

LUCIO FONTANA
(b. 1899; d. 1968)

17 *Concetto Spaziale, New York 7*, 1962
Brass
35.43 × 25.5 in. (90 × 65 cm)
Maxine and Stuart Frankel Foundation for Art, Bloomfield Hills, Michigan

BRENDA GOODMAN
(b. 1943)

18 *Self Portrait, No 1*, 1977
Canvas, feathers, wood, wire
64.25 × 18.75 in.
(163.2 × 47.6 cm)
Detroit Institute of Arts, Founders Society Purchase, James Pearson Duffy Fund, 78.35

19 *Self Portrait, No 3*, 1977
Canvas, feathers, wood, wire
65 × 14.75 in. (163.2 × 47.6 × 44.5 cm)
The Gayle and Andrew Camden Collection

20 *Self Portrait, No 4*, 1977
Canvas, feathers, wood, wire
65 × 16 in. (163.2 × 47.6 cm)
Courtesy the artist and Sikkema Jenkins & Co.

TYREE GUYTON
(b. 1955)

21 *Caged Brain*, 1990
Mixed media
16 × 14 × 10.5 in.
(40.6 × 35.6 × 26.7 cm)
Detroit Institute of Arts, Founders Society Purchase, Twentieth Century Painting and Sculpture Fund and Dr. and Mrs. George Kamperman Fund, 1991.177

HA CHONG-HYUN
(b. 1935)

22 *Untitled 72-(A)-1*, 1972
Barbed wire on panel
47 × 94.5 in. (120 × 240 cm)
Courtesy the artist and Kukje Gallery

23 *Conjunction 79-9*, 1979
Oil on hemp cloth
43.3 × 15 in. (110 × 40 cm)
Courtesy the artist and Kukje Gallery

CAROLE HARRIS
(b. 1943)

24 *In A Silent Way*, 2017
Fiber, rust
42 × 49 in. (106.68 × 124.46 cm)
Courtesy the artist

MATTHEW ANGELO HARRISON
(b. 1989)

25 *Dark Povera: Manufactured Primitives*, 2019
Steel, aluminum, electronic components, clay, resin
Dimensions variable
Courtesy the artist and Jessica Silverman Gallery

PATRICK HILL
(b. 1972)

26 *Untitled (What We Do Is Secret)*, 2009
Wood, glass, aluminum, marble, steel, concrete, dye, ink, epoxy
50 × 42 × 42 in. (127 × 106.7 × 106.7 cm)
Courtesy the artist

SCOTT HOCKING
(b. 1975)

27 *Bone Black*
Bone black pigment, photograph, various objects
Dimensions variable
Courtesy the artist and David Klein Gallery

JANNIS KOUNELLIS
(b. 1936; d. 2017)

28 *Untitled*, 1968
Jute bags, coals
86.625 in. diameter (220 cm)
The Rachofsky Collection

KWON YOUNG-WOO
(b. 1926; d. 2013)

29 *Untitled*, 1976
Korean paper
63.7 × 51 in. (162 × 130 cm)
Courtesy the artist's estate and
Kukje Gallery

MARIA LAI
(b. 1919; d. 2013)

30 *Book*, 1984
Fabric, thread
7.5 × 5.5 × 1.25 in.
(19.1 × 14 × 3.2 cm)
Samuel Zell Revocable
Trust Collection

ADDIE LANGFORD
(b. 1974)

31 *Verso Phthalo Series:
BR Blue / #1 / LU*, 2018
Acrylic on industrial
composite hide, verso
79 × 54.5 in. (200.6 × 138.4 cm)
Courtesy the artist and
Hill Gallery

LEE UFAN
(b. 1936)

32 *Relatum*, 1971/2011
Rubber, stones
11 × 65 × 73 in.
(27.9 × 165.1 × 185.4 cm)
Solomon R. Guggenheim
Museum, New York,
Gift of the artist, 2011
2011.6

JULIO LLÓPIZ-CASAL
(b. 1984)

33 *Archivo I*, 2014
Paper label, magnetized
floppy disk
5.25 × 5.25 in. (13.34 × 13.34 cm)
Courtesy the artist

34 *Archivo II*, 2014
Paper label, magnetized
floppy disk
5.25 × 5.25 in. (13.34 ×
13.34 cm)
Courtesy the artist

KYLIE LOCKWOOD
(b. 1983)

35 *Porcelain Legs in the
Posture of David*, 2016
Pigmented porcelain, unfired
clay, nail polish, plastic bag
27 × 25 × 17.5 in. (68.6 ×
63.5 × 44.5 cm)
Courtesy the artist and
Simone DeSousa Gallery

ANDREAS LOLIS
(b. 1970)

36 *Untitled*, 2012
Marble
56.3 × 16.95 × 8.6 in.
(143 × 43.05 × 21.844 cm)
Michael J. Frishberg Collection

37 *Untitled*, 2014
Marble
45.3 × 31.5 × 5.125 in.
(115.06 × 80 × 13 cm)
Alistair Economakis
Collection

38 *Untitled*, 2012
Marble
12.6 × 17.75 × 15 in.
(32 × 45.09 × 38.1 cm)
Alistair Economakis
Collection

39 *Untitled*, 2012
Marble
17.3 × 23.25 × 3.15 in.
(43.942 × 59.06 × 8 cm)
Alistair Economakis
Collection

40 *Untitled*, 2013
Marble
23.65 × 4.75 × 2.75 in.
(60.07 × 12.07 × 6.985 cm)
Alistair Economakis
Collection

ALVIN LOVING
(b. 1935; d. 2005)

41 *Untitled*, 1973
Acrylic on canvas
105 × 88 in. (266.7 ×
223.52 cm)
Collection Akron Art
Museum, Purchased with
funds from Mr. and Mrs.
Lawrence Mohr and the
Museum Acquisition Fund.
1975.10

MICHAEL LUCHS
(b. 1938)

42 *Untitled*, 1976
Synthetic fiber, paint,
cardboard
36 × 43 in. (91.4 ×
109.2 × 10.2 cm)
Wayne State University
Collection

TIFF MASSEY
(b. 1982)

43 *White Out (Black)*, 2018
Cotton fiber
36 × 24 in. (91.44 × 60.96 cm)
Courtesy the artist

44 *White Out (Red)*, 2018
Cotton fiber
36 × 24 in. (91.44 × 60.96 cm)
Courtesy the artist

45 *White Out (Green)*, 2018
Cotton fiber
36 × 24 in. (91.44 × 60.96 cm)
McArthur Binion Collection

CHARLES McGEE
(b. 1924)

46 *Urban Extract I*, 1979
Mixed media, wood, plaster
48 × 32 in. (122 × 81.2 cm)
Susan Tait Collection

WORKS IN THE EXHIBITION

ALLIE McGHEE
(b. 1941)

47   *The Ku Klux Klown*, 1969
Mixed media, banana
16 × 20 in. (40.64 × 50.8 cm)
Courtesy the artist

48   *Rainy Night*, 2018
Mixed media, paper,
binding clip
34 × 35 × 4 in.
(88.9 × 86.4 × 10 cm)
Courtesy the artist

MARIO MERZ
(b. 1925; d. 2003)

49   *Igloo*, 1971
Steel tubes, neon tubing, wire
mesh, transformer, C-clamps
39.375 × 78.75 × 78.75 in.
(100 × 200 × 200 cm)
Collection Walker Art
Center, Minneapolis
T.B. Walker Acquisition
Fund, 2001

MARISA MERZ
(b. 1926)

50   *Living Sculpture*, 1966
Wood, aluminum
31.5 × 19.75 × 19.75 in.
(80 × 50.16 × 50.16 cm)
The Rachofsky Collection

JASON MURPHY
(b. 1976)

51   *Superman II*, 2019
Concrete, rebar, Oatey's,
clamps, paint
144 × 54 × 24 in. (365 ×
137 × 61 cm)
Courtesy the artist

GORDON NEWTON
(b. 1948; d. 2019)

52   *Diamond Follow*, 1975
Canvas, paint, polymer resin
and synthetic fabric on wood
112 × 59 × 39 in.
(284.5 × 149.9 × 100.3 cm)
Wayne State University
Collection

REYNIER LEYVA NOVO
(b. 1983)

53   *Untitled (Immigrants)*, 2019
Clothing
192 × 192 in. (488 × 488 cm)
Courtesy GALLERIA
CONTINUA

GIULIO PAOLINI
(b. 1940)

54   *L' altra figura* (*The Other
Figure*), 1984
Plaster, two plinths
Installation dimensions
variable; sculptures:
24.75 × 16.5 × 12.12 in.
(62.9 × 41.9 × 30.8 cm)
The Rachofsky Collection

PANOS PAPADOPOULOS
(b. 1975)

55   *Temple of Hephaestus*,
2013–14
Oil and marker on canvas
84.64 × 57 in. (215 × 145 cm)
Steven and Lizzie Blatt
Collection

PARK HYUN-KI
(b. 1942; d. 2000)

56   *Untitled*, 1984
Video installation, single-
channel video, color, silent;
monitor, stone, steel
26.375 × 94.375 × 23.5 in.
(66.993 × 239.713 × 59.69 cm)
The Rachofsky Collection

PARK SEO-BO
(b. 1931)

57   *Écriture No. 65-75*, 1975
Oil and pencil on canvas
51 × 76.8 in. (130 × 195 cm)
Courtesy the artist and
Kukje Gallery

ZOË PAUL
(b. 1987)

58   *Untitled*, 2017
Wool, thread, refrigerator grill
48.75 × 29 × 2.375 in.
(124 × 74 × 6 cm)
Collection of Charlotte and
Herbert S. Wagner III

59   *Untitled*, 2018
Wool, thread, metal grill
39.375 × 39.375 × 6 in.
(100 × 100 × 15 cm)
Collection of Charlotte and
Herbert S. Wagner III

60   *Untitled*, 2018
Wool, thread, metal grill
39.375 × 39.375 × 6 in.
(100 × 100 × 15 cm)
Collection of Kate and
Gerald Chertavian

61   *Untitled*, 2018
Wool, thread, metal grill
39.375 × 39.375 × 6 in.
(100 × 100 × 15 cm)
Collection of Kate and
Gerald Chertavian

62   *Untitled*, 2019
Site-specific wall painting
Acrylic paint
Approximately 396 × 144 in.
(1005.84 × 365.76 cm)
Courtesy the artist

MICHELANGELO PISTOLETTO
(b. 1933)

63 *Metamorfosi*, 1976/2019
Mirror, rags
Dimensions variable
Courtesy GALLERIA
CONTINUA

EDUARDO PONJUÁN
(b. 1956)

64 *Monument to
Columbus I*, 1997
Book, lamp, alabaster, kaolin
stones, carborundum)
11.811 × 9.06 × 5.905 in.
(30 × 23 × 15 cm)
Courtesy El Apartamento

65 *Explanation of the Mirage*,
from the series *New
Universal Geography*, 1997
Book, TV remote control,
carborundum, rear view
mirrors, kaolin stones, chain
12 × 10 × 4.33 in.
(30.5 × 25.5 × 11 cm)
Courtesy El Apartamento

66 *Iconoclast in Abyssinia*,
from the series *New
Universal Geography*, 1997
Book, action figure, compass,
metal, leather
12.59 × 8.66 × 3.93 in.
(32 × 22 × 10 cm)
Courtesy El Apartamento

67 *Aroma of Pinar I*, 1999
Book, jute, shark´s teeth,
magnifying glass,
a-trainers, kaolin stones,
spoons, forks
13.35 × 8.8 × 4.8 in.
(34 × 22.5 × 12.5 cm)
Courtesy El Apartamento

WILFREDO PRIETO
(b. 1978)

68 *Miren el tamaño de este
mango* (*Look at the size of
this mango*), 2011
Mango, BlackBerry,
rubber band
Variable dimensions
Courtesy NoguerasBlanchard
Gallery

DIANA FONSECA QUIÑONES
(b. 1978)

69 *Untitled*, from *Degradation*
series, 2017
Paint extracted from exterior
facades on wood
47.244 × 47.244 in. (120 ×
120 cm)
Courtesy El Apartamento

CHRIS SCHANCK
(b. 1975)

70 *Untitled (Alufoil Chair)*, 2019
Steel, polystyrene,
aluminum foil, resin
35 × 21 × 18 in. (88.9 ×
53.3 × 45.7 cm)
Courtesy the artist and
Friedman Benda Gallery

GILDA SNOWDEN
(b. 1954; d. 2014)

71 *Silent Preacher*, 1986
Mixed media on wood
48 × 48 × 2 in. (121.92 ×
121.92 × 5 cm)
Wayne State University
Collection

SOCRATIS SOCRATOUS
(b. 1971)

72 *Stolen Goods*, 2009–15
Gold, copper, bronze, silver
Dimesions variable
Courtesy The Breeder

EZEQUIEL O. SUÁREZ
(b. 1967)

73 *Si tú eres artista, vamos
a sufrir*, 2009–16
Personal objects from
the artist's collection,
suitcase, graffiti
Variable dimensions
Courtesy El Apartamento

KOSTIS VELONIS
(b. 1968)

74 *Assembly of a Tenement*, 2019
Concrete, wood
78.7 × 84.2 in. (200 × 214 cm)
Courtesy the artist. Assistance
by Eli Gold and Leda
Lycourioti

YUN HYONG-KEUN
(b. 1928, d. 2007)

75 *Umber-Blue*, 1978
Oil on linen
51.125 × 72.875 in.
(130 × 185 cm)
Courtesy Blum & Poe

CONTRIBUTORS

TAYLOR RENEE ALDRIDGE is a Detroit-based writer and independent curator. In 2015, she co-founded ARTS.BLACK, a journal of art criticism from black perspectives. Taylor has worked for the Detroit Institute of Arts, the N'Namdi Center for Contemporary Art, the Ethelbert Cooper Gallery of African & African American Art, and The National Museum of American History (Smithsonian Institution) as a Goldman Sachs Junior Fellow. She received her ALM in Museum Studies from Harvard University.

ANDREW BLAUVELT is the Director of Cranbrook Art Museum and Curator-at-Large for the Museum of Arts and Design, New York. Prior to joining Cranbrook in 2015, Blauvelt served in various curatorial, design, and administrative positions at the Walker Art Center in Minneapolis for seventeen years. Blauvelt received an MFA in Design from Cranbrook Academy of Art.

LAURIE CHEVROT is a Curatorial Intern at Cranbrook Art Museum and cultural producer in Detroit. She has held various positions internationally at the French Institute of South Africa in Johannesburg, the Contemporary Art Biennale of Lyon, and MoCADA in Brooklyn, among others. She received her MA in Administration of Cultural Institutions from the Institute of Bordeaux.

VINCENZO DE BELLIS is Curator and Associate Director of Programs, Visual Arts at the Walker Art Center. Prior to joining the Walker in 2016, de Bellis was Director and Curator of Peep-Hole Art Center in Milan, which he co-founded in 2009. He has also served as Artistic Director of Miart, International Fair of Modern and Contemporary Art, Milan since 2012. Previously, de Bellis held curatorial roles at Museion, Bolzano and GAMeC, Bergamo. De Bellis received his MA in Curatorial Studies from the Center for Curatorial Studies, Bard College.

ABEL GONZÁLEZ FERNÁNDEZ is a writer and independent curator from Havana, Cuba. He has curated exhibitions at the Reinbeckhallen Foundation in Berlin, Spiral Garden in Tokyo, and the Wilfredo Lam Contemporary Art Center in Havana, among others. He is a columnist for the Cuban contemporary art magazine *El Estornudo*. He received a BA in Literature from the University of Havana.

REBECCA K. MAZZEI is an independent curator, writer, and co-owner of Trinosophes, a contemporary art space and café operating in Detroit since 2013. She was previously Deputy Director at the Museum of Contemporary Art Detroit where she curated multiple onsite exhibitions in addition to the Detroit Pavilion at the 2012 Shanghai Biennale. She holds an MA in Modern Art History, Theory and Criticism from the School of the Art Institute of Chicago.

LAURA MOTT is the Senior Curator of Contemporary Art and Design at Cranbrook Art Museum. Prior to joining the museum in 2013, she held various curatorial and lecturer positions in the United States and Europe, including at the University of Gothenburg in Sweden, Gothenburg Konsthall, IASPIS in Stockholm, Mission 17 in San Francisco, and the Whitney Museum of American Art in New York. In 2016, she was the recipient of a Warhol Curatorial Fellowship. Mott received her MA in Curatorial Studies from the Center for Curatorial Studies, Bard College.

IAN GABRIEL WILSON is the Jeanne and Ralph Graham Collections Fellow at Cranbrook Art Museum. He has held positions at the journal *ARTMargins* and at the Sullivan Galleries of the School of the Art Institute of Chicago. In 2015 he was awarded a Graduate Curatorial Fellowship by the Institute for Curatorial Research and Practice. He received dual MA degrees in Modern Art History, Theory & Criticism and Arts Administration & Policy from the School of the Art Institute of Chicago.

LENDERS TO THE EXHIBITION

Akron Art Museum
El Apartamento
McArthur Binion
Steven and Lizzie Blatt
The Breeder
Gayle and Andrew Camden
Casey Kaplan Gallery
Elizabet Cerviño
Kate and Gerald Chertavian
Dabls' MBAD African
    Bead Museum
David Klein Gallery
Detroit Institute of Arts
Alistair Economakis
Dora Economou
Martin and Rebecca Eisenberg
Michael J. Frishberg
GALLERIA CONTINUA
Brenda Goodman
Ha Chong-Hyun
Carole Harris
Matthew Angelo Harrison
Hill Gallery
Patrick Hill
Scott Hocking
Jessica Silverman Gallery
Kukje Gallery
Estate of Kwon Young-Woo
Addie Langford
Julio Llópiz-Casal
Kylie Lockwood
Marianne Boesky Gallery
Tiff Massey
Maxine and Stuart Frankel
    Foundation for Art
Allie McGhee
Jason Murphy
NoguerasBlanchard Gallery
Park Seo-Bo
Zoë Paul
Pérez Art Museum Miami
The Rachofsky Collection
Carole and Alex Rosenberg

Samuel Zell Revocable
    Trust Collection
Chris Schanck
Sikkema Jenkins & Co.
Simone DeSousa Gallery
Solomon R. Guggenheim Museum
Susan Tait
Kostis Velonis
Charlotte and Herbert S. Wagner III
Walker Art Center
Wayne State University

REPRODUCTION CREDITS

TEXTS

65–69: Courtesy the author

99–102: Courtesy the author. From *Detroit Free Press*, December 2 © 1979 Gannett-Community Publishing. All rights reserved. Used by permission and protected by the Copyright Laws of the United States. The printing, copying, redistribution, or retransmission of this content without express written permission is prohibited

121–26: Courtesy the author

139–45: Courtesy Yongwoo Lee and Kukje Gallery. Translated by Ines Min

191–92: Courtesy the author and Kukje Gallery. Translated by Hajin Jun, courtesy Blum & Poe, Los Angeles/New York/Tokyo

201–13: Courtesy the author and *ART CUBA* edited by Holly Block. Copyright © 2001 Holly Block. Used by permission of Harry N. Abrams, Inc., New York. All rights reserved. Translated by Marguerite Feitlowitz

229–32: Courtesy the author

237–45: Translated by Michele Alonzo

IMAGES

25: © 2019 Olayami Dabls. Photo: PD Rearick

29: Courtesy the artist and Martos Gallery, New York

30: © Scott Hocking 2019. Courtesy the artist and David Klein Gallery, Detroit

33: Courtesy Fondazione Merz, Turin. Photo: Renato Rinaldi, Milano

36: Courtesy the artist and Kukje Gallery. Hirshhorn Museum and Sculpture Garden Collection

37: Courtesy the artist and Kukje Gallery

38: © Yoan Capote. Courtesy the artist and Jack Shainman Gallery, New York

40: © The Estate of Ana Mendieta Collection, LLC. Courtesy Galerie Lelong & Co.

42: Artwork © Kara Walker, courtesy Sikkema Jenkins & Co., New York. Photo: Fanis Vlastaras & Rebecca Constantopoulou

47: Courtesy the artist and Jessica Silverman Gallery. Photo: Corine Vermeulen

53: © Andreas Angelidakis, Courtesy The Breeder, Athens

55: Collection Walker Art Center, Minneapolis. The Frederick R. Weisman Collection of Art and the T.B. Walker Acquisition Fund, 1996

57: Courtesy the Belkis Ayón Estate, Havana, Cuba. Photo: José A. Figueroa

59: Courtesy the Detroit Institute of Arts, Founders Society Purchase, Lila Silverman Tribute Fund, with funds from the Friends of Modern Art, 1996.30

61: © Kevin Beasley, Courtesy Casey Kaplan Gallery. Photo: Jean Vong

63: © 2019 Tania Bruguera / Artists Rights Society (ARS), New York. Courtesy Estudio Bruguera

71: Collection Walker Art Center, Minneapolis. Gift of the Judith Rothschild Foundation, 1999

73: © 2019 Pier Paolo Calzolari / Artists Rights Society (ARS), New York. Courtesy Archivio Fotografico Calzolari, and Marianne Boesky Gallery (New York – Aspen). Photo: Michele Alberto Sereni

76–77: © Yoan Capote. Courtesy the artist and Jack Shainman Gallery, New York

79: Courtesy the artist and GALLERIA CONTINUA, San Gimignano / Beijing / Les Moulins / Habana. Photo: Michel Pou

81: © 2019 Olayami Dabls

83: Courtesy Collection Frac Centre-Val de Loire. Photo: François Lauginie

90–91: Courtesy the artist and RIBOT Gallery, Milan

93: © 2019 Artists Rights Society (ARS), New York / SIAE, Rome

95: © Brenda Goodman, courtesy the artist and Sikkema Jenkins & Co., New York. Image courtesy Detroit Institute of Arts, Founders Society Purchase, James Pearson Duffy Fund, 78.35

97: Courtesy the artist and Martos Gallery, New York. Image courtesy Detroit Institute of Arts, Founders Society Purchase, Twentieth Century Painting and Sculpture Fund and Dr. and Mrs. George Kamperman Fund, 1991.177

106–7: Courtesy the artist and Kukje Gallery

109: © 2019 Carole Harris. Photo: Eric Law

111: Courtesy the artist and Jessica Silverman Gallery. Photo: PD Rearick

113: Courtesy the artist

115: Courtesy Burton Historical Collection, Detroit Public Library

118–19: © 2019 Artists Rights Society (ARS), New York / SIAE, Rome. Courtesy The Rachofsky Collection. Photo: Kevin Todora

129: Courtesy the artist and Kukje Gallery

131: Courtesy Archivio Maria Lai and Marianne Boesky Gallery, New York and Aspen. Photo: Object Studies

134–35: Courtesy the artist and Hill Gallery

137: © 2019 Artists Rights Society (ARS), New York / ADAGP, Paris. Photo: David Heald © The Solomon R. Guggenheim Foundation, New York

147: © 2019 Julio Llópiz-Casal

149: © 2019 Kylie Lockwood. Courtesy the artist and Simone DeSousa Gallery

151: © Andreas Lolis, Courtesy The Breeder, Athens. Photo: Blaise Adilon

153: Courtesy the Estate of Al Loving and Garth Greenan Gallery, New York. Image courtesy Collection of the Akron Art Museum, Purchased with funds from Mr. and Mrs. Lawrence Mohr and the Museum Acquisition Fund. 1975.10

155: Courtesy the artist and Simone DeSousa Gallery. Photo: Alex Mandrilla, courtesy Eastern Michigan University Galleries program

157: Courtesy the artist and Library Street Collective

159: Courtesy the artist and Detroit Institute of Arts, Gift of Gilbert and Lila Silverman, 1983.33

165: © 2019 Allie McGhee. Collection of the Detroit Receiving Hospital

166: © 2019 Carole Harris. Photo: Eric Law

167: Courtesy the Gilda Snowden Estate, LLC., donated to the permanent collection of Wayne State University, dedicated in memory of Dr. John Thomas Snowden. Image courtesy the Wayne State University Art Collection

171: © Allie McGhee. Photo: PD Rearick

173: Collection Walker Art Center, Minneapolis. T.B. Walker Acquisition Fund, 2001. © 2019 Artists Rights Society (ARS), New York / SIAE, Rome

175: Courtesy The Rachofsky Collection and Fondazione Merz, Turin. Photo: Kevin Todora

177: © 2019 Jason Murphy. Photo: Jesse Wakeman

179: Photo: Corine Vermeulen for the exhibition *Considering Detroit*, MOCAD, 2008, courtesy Eastern Michigan University Galleries

181: Courtesy the artist. Photo: Andrew Miller

183: © Giulio Paolini. Courtesy The Rachofsky Collection. Photo: Kevin Todora

185: © 2019 Panos Papadopoulos

187: © The Estate of Park Hyun-Ki. Courtesy the Estate, Gallery Hyundai, and The Rachofsky Collection. Photo: Kevin Todora

189: Courtesy the artist and Kukje Gallery

195: Courtesy the artist

197: Courtesy GALLERIA CONTINUA, San Gimignano / Beijing / Les Moulins / Habana. Photo: Alicia Luxem

199: Courtesy El Apartamento. Photo: Pedro Abascal

209: Photo: Carlos Garaicoa

210: Collection of the Morris and Helen Belkin Art Gallery, Vancouver

215: Courtesy NoguerasBlanchard, Barcelona/Madrid. Photo: Roberto Ruiz

217: Courtesy El Apartamento. Photo: Alain Cabrera

219: Courtesy the artist and Friedman Benda Gallery

221: Donated by the Gilda Snowden Estate, LLC., to the permanent collection of Wayne State University. Photo: Tim Thayer, courtesy the Wayne State University Art Collection

BOARD OF GOVERNORS
CRANBROOK ACADEMY OF ART
AND ART MUSEUM
2018–2019

Jennifer Gilbert (Chair)
Bharat C. Gandhi (Vice Chair)
David Jaffe (Treasurer)

Jim Berline
Lynda Charfoos
JJ Curis
Peggy Daitch
Gretchen Davidson
Antoine Dubeauclard
Frank M. Edwards
Marilyn Finkel
Maxine Frankel
Tanya Heidelberg-Yopp
Jennifer Hermelin
Roslyn Jacobson
Eric Charles Jirgens
Helen Davis Johnson
Mariana Keros
Timothy W. Mast
Phillip Morici
Jo Obasuyi
Peter E. Robinson
Pamela Rodgers
Allan Rothfeder
Harrell Scarcello
Catherine Schwartz
Janice Steinhardt
Karen P. Swanson
Musa Tariq
Nancy Tellem
Robert T. Wilson

LIFE GOVERNORS
Maggie Allesee
Mary Lou Brous
Warren Coville
Denise Anton David
Henry M. Hogan, Jr.
James A. Kelly
David Klein
Bonnie Larson
Arthur C. Liebler
Beverly Moore
Sally Parsons
JoAnne Petersen
Horace Rodgers
Catherine Simmons Rosenthal
Susan Sosnick
Robert S. Swanson
Gary L. Wasserman
Evie Wheat
Lillian Zonars

MUSEUM COMMITTEE
CRANBROOK ART MUSEUM
2018–2019

STAFF
CRANBROOK ART MUSEUM
2018–2019

ADMINISTRATION
Andrew Blauvelt, Director
Kim Larsen, Program
Administrator

**COLLECTIONS AND
REGISTRATION**
Jon Geiger, Head Preparator and
Exhibition Coordinator
Corey Gross, Registrar
Wade Tullier, Associate Preparator

COMMUNICATIONS
Julie Fracker, Director of
Communications
Bianca Ibarlucea, Communications
Designer and Website Editor

CURATORIAL
Isabella Achenbach, Curatorial
Affairs Manager
Laura Mott, Senior Curator of
Contemporary Art and Design
Ian Gabriel Wilson, Jeanne
and Ralph Graham
Collections Fellow

**EDUCATION AND
PUBLIC PROGRAMS**
Kelsey Cumbow, Visitor Services
Supervisor
Lindsey Dezman, Museum
Educator and Art Lab
Coordinator
Sarah Doty, Associate Curator
of Education
Judy Dyki, Director of Academic
Programs and Library,
Cranbrook Academy of Art
and Art Museum
Kelly Lyons, Curator of Education

**MEMBERSHIP AND
DEVELOPMENT**
Kelly Lewis-Gump, Director of
Annual Giving and Membership
Autumn Parrott, Senior Director
of Development
Michael J. Stachowiak, Director
of Grant Development
& Administration, Cranbrook
Educational Community
Debra Watson, Development
Coordinator
Alexis Weisbrod, Assistant
Director for Donor Relations

COLOPHON

Published on the occasion of the exhibition *Landlord Colors: On Art, Economy, and Materiality*, curated by Laura Mott, Senior Curator of Contemporary Art and Design, and organized by Cranbrook Art Museum.

Cranbrook Art Museum
Bloomfield Hills, Michigan
June 22 – October 6, 2019

Landlord Colors: Material Detroit is a series of public art installations, performances, and conversations in the city of Detroit held in conjunction with the exhibition and curated and presented by Taylor Renee Aldridge, ARTS. BLACK; Laura Mott, Cranbrook Art Museum; and Ryan Myers-Johnson, Sidewalk Detroit.

Landlord Colors: On Art, Economy, and Materiality and *Landlord Colors: Material Detroit* are generously supported by the Andy Warhol Foundation for the Visual Arts, the Maxine and Stuart Frankel Foundation, the John S. and James L. Knight Foundation, the National Endowment for the Arts, and donors to the Detroit Initiatives Fund for Cranbrook. Curatorial research and travel was supported by the Andy Warhol Foundation for the Visual Arts.

The Andy Warhol Foundation
for the Visual Arts

Maxine & Stuart Frankel
Foundation

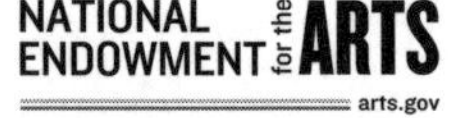

First edition © 2019
Cranbrook Art Museum
All rights reserved under pan-American copyright conventions. No part of this publication may be reproduced or utilized in any form or by any means without permission in writing from the publisher. Inquiries should be addressed to: Publications Director, Cranbrook Art Museum, 39221 Woodward Avenue, P.O. Box 801, Bloomfield Hills, MI, 48303.

Every reasonable attempt has been made to identify owners of copyright. Errors or omissions will be corrected in subsequent editions.

Available through D.A.P./ Distributed Art Publishers, 75 Broad Street, Suite 630, New York, NY 10004. www.artbook.com

ISBN 978-0-9891864-9-0

Designer:
Chad Kloepfer

Editors:
Andrew Blauvelt, Judy Dyki, Laura Mott, and Ian Gabriel Wilson

Publications Manager:
Isabella Achenbach

Image Production:
Randal Stegmeyer

Proofreaders:
Sarah Doty and Susan Larsen

Typeset in Trump Mediaeval designed by Georg Trump, Union designed by Radim Pesko, FF Elementa designed by Mindaugas Strockis, and printed on 90gsm Munken Print White and bound in JHT Series 3 JHT – 1106; JHT Series 1 JHT – 4703; JHT series 2 JHT – 3009; and JHT Series 2 JHT – 5412.

Printed and bound in Singapore by Pristone Pte Ltd.